Introduction

The Samoa Islands constitute a homogeneous nation politically divided. On both sides of the 171st meridian which divides the US territory of American Samoa from the Independent State of Samoa (previously known as the Independent State of Western Samoa), people speak the same language, practise the same customs and pass on the same traditions. But the atmospheres and characters of each country is quite distinct.

Independent Samoa is Polynesia at its purest and most traditional. No other place in the Pacific has so well maintained its identity in the face of so many outside influences. Composed mainly of two bulky volcanic islands which slope gently from sparkling beaches to nondescript summits, it is larger and younger than American Samoa.

Though the mountains appear less dramatic than those of its neighbour, parts of the northern slopes of the largest island, Savai'i, are covered in lava from volcanic eruptions that destroyed property and buried villages early this century.

Api_____, is the capital. Many South Pacific travellers believe it to be the most enchanting of all tropical ports. Nevertheless, the rambling island bears scars from foreign occupation and the subsequent courting of outside support by warring chiefs. As a result, Independent Samoa seems more reluctant than other Pacific nations to open up to foreign interests.

Contentment on the island appears to reign supreme. The people have resisted the economic temptation of increased industrialisation and turn a healthy and happy face upon the rest of the world. Friendly and welcoming, they enchant every outsider and most visitors imagine they have stumbled upon a long-sought idyll. The English poet Rupert Brooke observed that Samoa and Samoans are:

the loveliest people in the world, moving and dancing like gods and goddesses, very quietly and mysteriously, and utterly content. It is sheer beauty, so pure that it's difficult to breathe it in.

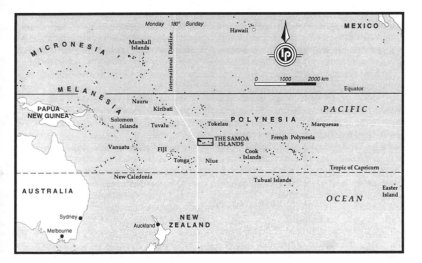

Scottish writer Robert Louis Stevenson, one of Samoa's most famous residents, concurred.

They are easy, merry, and leisure-loving...Song is almost ceaseless.

It's a proud country, and a clean one, with hardly a space in any village not deliberately decorated with shells, white coral rock, black pebbles or flowers. There is no filth and, while few are wealthy, there is no poverty. Every village has a *malae* (green) where people gather every day, when chores are finished, to play *kirikiti* (Samoan cricket) or volleyball. They sing and play music all week then go to church on Sunday and sing some more.

All is well in an island paradise it would seem. But beware of the hidden reef just below the surface. The social system of Independent Samoa produces as much pressure and mental agony as it does well-being. Beneath the lightheartedness a strict and demanding code of behaviour is upheld with expectations that can stifle individuality, ingenuity and creativity and produce as much insecurity and psychosis as materialism does. Add to this the rapid modernisation in the Pacific and you have a potentially explosive mix. Some people learn to deal with this situation but others, especially young men, feel that they can't measure up to the society's expectations and become violent or suicidal.

Despite the paradoxes, it is a rare traveller who doesn't like Samoa. There is plenty to see and do and although it is possible to visit most of the high points in a week, to really appreciate the country will take longer. Slide down a waterfall into a tropical pool, climb over lava to a gaping volcanic crater, hike to an ancient jungle-covered pyramid or just stroll down a country road on a Sunday morning and watch the smoke from countless cooking fires wafting up through the trees. But take your time.

Just 100km to the east of Independent Samoa lie the equally fascinating and dramatically beautiful islands of American Samoa, a US territory since the turn of the century. These spectacular islands consist of four incredibly rugged volcanic peaks – dragon-like Tutuila (the main island) and the three small but wildly steep islands of the Manu'a group.

Because of the ruggedness of the terrain the islands have retained some areas of native forest and the US Government has set aside more than 4000 hectares of land and offshore waters on Tutuila and the remote Manu'a Islands as national park (the land is leased from the traditional owners who are still able to live on and cultivate their land). The park offers good hiking and bird watching possibilities as well as some of the best snorkelling on either of the Samoas.

Off the eastern end of Tutuila is tiny Aunu'u Island with its traditional village, its fiery red quicksand lakes, its beautiful crater and wild, rolling surf. In the farthest reaches of the territory are remote Swains Island, actually one of the Tokelau Islands, and Rose Atoll, a US wildlife refuge. About 95% of American Samoa's population of 58,000 lives on Tutuila, mostly around Pago Pago (pronounced 'pango pango') Harbor and on the Tafuna plain to the south-west of the harbour. On a sunny day or a fine evening, the view down onto Pago Pago Harbor from the surrounding mountains is breathtaking. In Pago (as the locals say) you'll come face to face with the Pacific, American style. Fast food (though McDonald's got to Independent Samoa first), fast cars, cable TV and American football all feature prominently against the fading Polynesian scene.

Most American Samoans have been to the mainland (which includes Hawaii, as far as they're concerned) and most of the younger ones seem to have liked what they saw there. American Samoa is heavily subsidised by the US government. About one third of the workforce is employed by the government, either federal or territorial. The remainder, including many Independent Samoans, Tongans, Koreans and Chinese are involved in the tuna-fishing industry or in retail and service jobs.

For the visitor, American Samoa provides

In the Name of Clarity

When the Independent State of Western Samoa passed a law in August 1997 to drop the word 'Western' from the country's title, the world didn't really notice. Few people outside the Samoas had every really understood anyway that there were two separate political entities which laid claim to the name Samoa and, as Prime Minister Tofilau Eti Alesana pointed out to the parliament, his country had been called Samoa at the United Nations since 1976. Therefore, he argued, to avoid confusion, it was time to make the name official.

But on Tutuila and Manu'a Islands, there was great confusion. In fact, for many of Prime Minister Alesana's brothers in the United States territory of American Samoa, this decision was more than a name game. This was cultural genocide and worthy of a vicious war of words.

Were they not as much Samoan as those who lived on Upolu? One district governor in American Samoa, who is closely related to the head of state of the neighbouring country, was quoted as saying that the move made those residing in the US territory feel as if they were only half-Samoans, not full-blooded at all.

To emphasise their displeasure, representatives in the territory's House of Representatives then threatened to fight back with legislation which would deny access to anyone who tried to enter American Samoa using passports and official documents bearing the words Government of Samoa.

Shortly afterwards the Senate and House of Representatives approved a bill which, if ratified, will deny ownership of land on American Samoa's main islands to Samoans from outside the territory who are not 50% Samoan.

Moderates argue that the introduction of this law has nothing to do with the controversy over which islands have the right to call themselves Samoa. Others, however, continue to call names across the water. ■

Wendy Owen

a unique cultural study and a distinct counterpoint to the sublime appeal of its historical 'other half' – Independent Samoa. It is still trying to decide whether it is Samoan or American as the social structure changes. People are abandoning their traditional foods for imported tinned and frozen foods; traditional *aiga* structures are breaking down; the environment is being sacrificed to American 'throwaway' technology and foreign values and influences are beginning to control the islands' cultural destiny. It's not surprising that many are tempted by the 'American dream' in place of the strict demands of *fa'a Samoa* – the Samoan way. Fortunately, a few enlightened American Samoans seem to believe that a more positive balance can be struck and there are laws in place aimed at limiting outside influence. Americans cannot immigrate at will from the USA; non-Samoans may not own land and foreign

companies and franchises may not compete with private Samoan businesses. Thanks to these regulations, American Samoa has not suffered from the exclusive condominium developments, high-rise cities and large-scale ruination that Hawaii has experienced.

American Samoa has been much less successful than Independent Samoa at attracting tourists. Over the past couple of decades these have mostly been limited to airline passengers on obligatory stopovers, business travellers and yachties stocking up on cheap groceries. Few of Tutuila's visitors see any more than the congested stretch of highway between the airport and the Rainmaker Hotel. But travellers who make the effort to get to the remote Manu'a Islands or off the beaten track on Tutuila will be rewarded by typical, open-hearted Samoan hospitality and some of the most fabulous scenery in the Pacific.

Facts about the Region

HISTORY

Samoa is a divided nation; the histories of the Independent State of Samoa (previously the Independent State of Western Samoa) and American Samoa were the same until the islands were divided up by Europeans at the beginning of the 20th century. There was no need to distinguish between the Samoas until this contact with European powers caused them to head in different directions.

Prehistory

The Samoan people are Polynesians. The area called Polynesia, meaning 'many islands', forms a triangle with points at Hawaii, Easter Island (off the west coast of South America) and New Zealand and also includes outlying islands scattered through Fiji and the East Indies.

Polynesian peoples are presumed to have entered the Pacific from the west – the East Indies, the Malay Peninsula or the Philippines. Because lapita (decorated pottery), similar to that found in the Bismarck Archipelago and New Caledonia, has also been found in the Samoas and Tonga (made from about 1500 BC to the time of Christ), and because no use of pottery was evident there at the time of European contact in the 17th century, it seems likely that those islands were the first Polynesian areas settled. It is thought that the people stopped using pottery because the local clay was unsuitable and

alternatives such as coconut shells and sea-shells were readily available.

The theory proposed by the unconventional Norwegian anthropologist Thor Heyerdahl, that the Polynesians migrated not from Asia but from the Americas, is based primarily on the presence of the *'umala* (sweet potato) in the Pacific and South America, but not in Asia. Interestingly, the Mormons, ubiquitous throughout the Pacific, also tell a tale of colonisation of the islands by South American mainlanders. Members of the scientific community, however, question this theory.

Some anthropologists believe that the Samoas were initially settled by Fijians or Tongans or that the first Samoans were conquered early on by chiefs and warriors from those countries. Samoan legends, which have Fijian kings and princesses as their heroes, seem to support this view. In 950 AD warriors from Tonga established rule on Savai'i, the nearest island to Tonga, then moved on to Upolu, where they were opposed by Malietoa Savea, the chief of the Samoas, whose title was derived from the words *malie toa*, meaning 'brave warriors'. A treaty of peace between the two countries was drawn up and the Samoans were left by Tongans to pursue their own course.

The earliest known evidence of human occupation in the islands is the site of a lapita village, partially submerged in the lagoon at

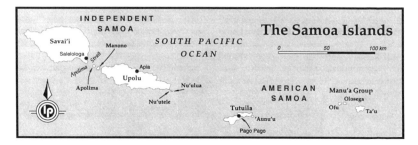

Mulifanua on the island of Upolu. Carbon tests have tentatively dated the site at 1000 BC. Undecorated pottery, known as Polynesian plainware, of a comparable age has been found at Aoa on the island of Tutuila and at To'ga on the island of Ofu.

At numerous other sites on Upolu, Savai'i and Tutuila (and to a lesser extent on Manono and Ta'u), archaeologists have discovered some odd platforms which have stone protrusions radiating from their bases which have been dubbed 'star mounds'. Information gathered from oral traditions and archeological studies suggests that these structures were used in the ancient sport of pigeon-snaring (see the star mound aside in the Tutuila Island chapter).

On Savai'i, near the village of Palauli, is the pyramid of Pulemelei, the largest ancient structure in the Pacific, and there seems to be no tradition or speculation surrounding it. Evidence suggests that in ancient times many more Samoan settlements were located inland in the valleys and on hillsides and that the increase in coastal settlement was due to European influence and trade.

European Contact

Although whalers, pirates and escaped convicts had landed in the islands earlier, the first European on record to approach the Samoan islands was Dutchman Jacob Roggeveen. He sighted the Manu'a Islands in 1722 while searching for the *terra australis incognita*, the great unknown southern continent. He gave Dutch names to the islands and then sailed on without landing.

In May 1768 the French explorer Captain Louis-Antoine de Bougainville passed through Samoan waters and, upon seeing the islanders travelling about in ocean-going canoes, christened the archipelago Les Îles des Navigateurs (the Navigator Islands). He bartered with the inhabitants of the Manu'a Islands and merely sighted the more westerly islands.

Next came Bougainville's compatriot Jean-Francçois de Galaup, Comte de La Pérouse, who landed at Fagasa on the north coast of Tutuila in 1787. The Samoans went

about helping themselves to the intriguing bits of iron found aboard his ships *La Boussole* and *Astrolabe* and the French sailors made examples of a few by punishing them. Word evidently spread westward because the following day, while the sailors were collecting water at Aasu, the locals attacked, killing 12 crewmen, including Commander Viscount de Langle. La Pérouse estimated that at least 39 Samoans also died during the encounter. The bay of Aasu was named Massacre Bay and the Europeans departed posthaste.

In 1791, the British ship HMS *Pandora*, under the command of Captain Edward Edwards, called in while in search of the Bounty mutineers, who had set their Captain William Bligh and 18 crewmen adrift in Tonga two years earlier. The ship was attacked off the coast of Tutuila and as a result many Samoans were killed.

These two events dramatically introduced the Samoans to the power of European weaponry; and gave the Samoans a reputation in foreign circles for being a hostile people.

The European traders, who had by this time begun plying the Pacific trade routes carrying whale products, sandalwood and bêche-de-mer (a species of sea-slug) to China in exchange for silk, tea and porcelain, steered clear of the Samoas until the early 1800s. By the 1820s quite a few Europeans had settled in the islands, most of them escaped convicts and retired whalers – welcomed by the unsuspecting islanders because they knew the strange ways of the *palagi* (Europeans) and were willing to share their technological expertise. Of course the palagi also brought with them diseases to which the islanders had no immunity.

The Missionaries

Some of the itinerants who found themselves in the Samoas during the early 19th century – and several Christian converts from other parts of Polynesia – had introduced a form of Christianity known as the Sailors' *Lotu* (Church). Given the similarity of the Christian creation beliefs to Samoan legend regarding a prophecy by Nafanua, the war goddess, that a new religion would take root in the islands, the Samoans were quite well prepared to accept the message of the missionaries who arrived to convert them. The wondrous possessions of the palagi were also used as evidence that the white man's god was more generous than the gods of the island peoples.

Peter Turner, a Wesleyan Methodist missionary based in Tonga, visited the Samoas briefly in 1828 and passed his message along to many Samoans, but he never established a mission there. In 1830, missionaries John Williams and Charles Barff of the London Missionary Society arrived on Savai'i and AW Murray came to Tutuila in 1836. Shortly after, others carried their message to Manu'a.

The *lotu Pope* (Pope's church) was brought to Falealupo on Savai'i in 1845 by French Catholic missionaries – who established a Marist mission – from Wallis and Futuna. This paved the way for the European rivalry between Catholics and Protestants which extended throughout the Pacific islands.

It didn't take long for the Christian gospel to be accepted wholesale by the Samoans and it has remained an integral part of island life to the present day. So much so, in fact, that the Samoas, along with Tonga and some neighbouring islands, have come to be called the 'bible belt of the Pacific'.

The *lotu Mamona* (Mormon church), a latecomer, was introduced by two missionaries sent by an imperialistic white politician in Hawaii named Walter M Gibson, who believed that he could use religion to help annexe the Samoan islands to the Kingdom of Hawaii. By 1888 the missionaries had settled in with Samoan wives and had established an official mission in Pago Pago. Shortly afterwards another mission was established in what is now Independent Samoa.

European Control

In 1838 the British Captain Bethune, of HMS *Conway*, set up a code of commercial regulations that dealt with customs and ports in the Samoas. The following year the

Americans sent a scientific expedition under the command of Charles Wilkes, who was charged with surveying lands and observing the natural element among the more obscure islands of the South Pacific. Wilkes made a trading treaty of sorts with the chiefs of the islands and thereby established another nation's interest in the Samoas.

The first British consul to the Samoas was G Pritchard, formerly of the London Missionary Society, who was appointed in 1847. At the time, word of Pago Pago's harbour was spreading throughout the European powers and it was becoming one of the prime whaling ports in the Pacific.

Between 1850 and 1880 many European settlers arrived in the islands, especially on Upolu, primarily for the purpose of trade. They established a society in Apia and a minimal code of laws in to govern their affairs, all with the consent of Upolu chiefs, who maintained sovereignty in their own villages.

One extremely important arrival in Apia was that of August Unshelm, a representative of German trade tycoon Johann Cesar Godeffroy who was interested in trading in Polynesia. By 1861 his firm had established stations in Fiji and Tonga. When Unshelm died, Theodor Weber took over the firm and spread the Godeffroy empire to thousands of islands around the southern, central and western Pacific. He purchased 300sq km of land on Upolu and set the stage to realise his dream of raising the German flag over the Samoas. His plans were interrupted, however, by the bankruptcy of Godeffroy and the outbreak of the Franco-Prussian War, and the colonisation scheme was put to rest for a while. Still, quite a few German colonists remained in the Samoas and the entrepreneurial void was immediately filled by a trading company with the long-winded name of Deutsche Handels und Plantagen Gesellschaft der Sudsee Inseln zu Hamburg (DHPG).

Squabbling Powers

There were (and still are) four 'paramount' families – equivalent to royal dynasties – in what is now Independent Samoa: the Malietoa, Tupua Tamasese, Mata'afa and Tu'imaleali'ifano. During the 1870s the Samoans became involved in a civil dispute between two kings, one in the east and one in the west, contending for supreme power. Samoans sold their lands to the Europeans to acquire armaments to settle the matter.

In the meantime, Britain and the USA were struggling to attain some sort of peace in the islands. In 1872 the USA had been offered exclusive rights to a naval base in Pago Pago Harbor by the high chief of Tutuila, in exchange for the protection and backing of the US government. The following year Colonel AB Steinberger, serving as an official agent of the US government, drafted a constitution and bill of rights for the Samoas and set up a government whereby the squabbling kings would serve alternate four-year terms. Steinberger ultimately became Premier of Samoa. He severed ties with the US government and began negotiations with the Germans regarding taxes, German land claims and administration of German financial interests in the Samoas.

The British and American consuls were unhappy that Steinberger had usurped power and arranged to have him deported to Fiji. As soon as he was gone the Samoan self-government scheme collapsed, leaving a number of factions seeking political advantage. A delegation of Samoans sought protection from the British in Fiji and the Americans in Washington but both refused. Because the USA had ignored the invitation to set up a naval base on Tutuila, the Samoans made both Germany and Britain the same offer.

By the late 1880s warships of all three powers had been sent to Apia Harbour and the affair had heated up sufficiently to inspire tension all around. As one Samoan author put it, they were 'like three large dogs snarling over a very small bone'.

As if nature were reprimanding the three bickering countries, on 16 March 1889, Apia Harbour was hit by one of history's worst typhoons. The Germans lost three warships – *Olga*, *Adler* and *Eber*. The Americans also lost three – *Vandalia*, *Trenton* and *Nipsic*.

The British warship *Calliope* battled her way out of the harbour in time to escape destruction. There were 92 Germans and 54 American crew members killed in the storm.

All three powers mellowed a bit after the disaster and made a real effort to settle the issue by drawing up the Berlin Treaty of 1889. This stipulated that an independent Samoa would be established under the rule of a foreign-appointed Samoan king and that the consuls of Britain, Germany and the USA would be given considerable advisory powers on the island of Upolu.

After the Berlin Treaty the Malietoa king was given the official vote of confidence, but his hold on power was tenuous. In the years that followed the Mata'afa king continually challenged the Malietoas' right to power. He wrote a lengthy epistle to Germany, Britain and the USA pleading for fairness for his country. Part of it reads as follows:

I rejoice, and my people are glad, at the prospect of a new and stable government for Samoa. If the Great Powers will send good men to take charge of the government, and not those who care only for the money they will receive, Samoa will become peaceful, happy, and prosperous.

The Samoan factions continued their struggle and the Western powers again began to quarrel. At last the foreign rulers realised that they were going nowhere in their attempts to settle the dispute. The Berlin Treaty was declared void, and on 2 December 1899 the Tripartite Treaty was drawn up, giving control of western Samoa to the Germans and that of eastern Samoa to the Americans. Britain stepped out of the picture altogether in exchange for renunciation of all German claims to Tonga, the Solomon Islands and Niue.

The Germans placed Mata'afa in the puppet position of paramount chief of their territory, abolishing the kingship altogether lest the Samoans be allowed too much power over the new German colony. One of the objectives of the Mau Movement (see the History section in the Facts about Independent Samoa chapter) would be to increase

German and, later, New Zealand respect for the nation's highest ranking native son, but until his death Mata'afa remained only a figure head.

From this point, the histories of the Samoas diverged. The period from 1900 to the present appears in the introductory History sections for each area.

GEOGRAPHY & GEOLOGY

The Samoas are made up of mostly high but well-eroded volcanic islands that lie more or less in the heart of the South Pacific, 3700km south-west of Hawaii. To the south lies Tonga, to the east the northern Cook Islands and to the north the Tokelau Islands.

Independent Samoa, with a total land area of 2934sq km, consists primarily of the two large islands of Savai'i, with 1700sq km, and Upolu, with 1115sq km. Both are of volcanic origin and are much higher and newer than the islands of American Samoa. The Samoas' highest peak, Mt Silisili in Savai'i, rises to 1858m.

Independent Samoa's other two inhabited islands, Manono and Apolima, lie in the 18km-wide strait separating Upolu and Savai'i. A few other rocky islets and outcrops are found to the south-east of Upolu.

American Samoa, which occupies the territory east of the 171st meridian, is comprised of seven islands and a few rocky outcrops. Its land area is 197sq km, 145 of which belong to the main island of Tutuila.

Tutuila is a narrow, dragon-shaped island 30km long and up to 6km wide, consisting of a sharp, winding ridge and plunging valleys. The island is nearly bisected by Pago Pago Harbor, a deep indentation in its south coast. The only significant level area of Tutuila is the plain lying west of the harbour area between Pago Pago International Airport and the village of Leone.

Aunu'u Island is a small volcanic crater off the south-east coast of Tutuila. The Manu'a group, about 100km east, consists of the three main islands of Ta'u, Ofu and Olosega, with 39, six and five sq km, respectively. All are wildly steep and beautiful examples of volcanic remnants.

One hundred kilometres east of Manu'a is tiny Rose Atoll which comprises the two sandy islets of Rose and Sand. Access is restricted by and to the US Fish & Wildlife Service because the islets serve as nesting grounds for numerous sea birds. Swains Island, 350km north of Tutuila, is a small, privately owned atoll which is geologically part of the Tokelau group of islands.

Darwin's theory about the life of a Pacific island can be roughly traced by travelling west to east through the Samoan islands. Savai'i, a very young island, remains volcanically active and has erupted during this century. It contains large areas of lava flow and occasional tremors are still felt there. Just to the east, Upolu appears to be extinct at the moment but its subtle peaks and ridges illustrate that it is still a fairly new island.

Tutuila and the Manu'a group, on the other hand, are wildly eroded and many of the volcanic craters they once contained are broken and submerged in the sea. Peaks and ridges are sharp and dramatic, having undergone aeons of weathering. There is, however, a still active submarine volcano lying south of the islands of Ofu and Olosega.

Rose Atoll, the easternmost island of the Samoas, has no peak of any kind. In fact, the volcano that caused it is not visible above the surface of the sea; the island is merely the result of coral polyps that have colonised its remains.

CLIMATE

Because both Samoas lie near the equator, between latitudes 13° and 16° south, the conditions are hot and humid most of the year. There is a distinct wet season (summer) between November and April and a dry season (winter) from May to October. The average annual temperature is 26.5°C in coastal areas, with a decrease in temperature as the land rises inland. There is more cloud and relative humidity inland than on the coast. The shores of Independent Samoa and the Manu'a Islands which face the wind get about 5000mm of precipitation each year,

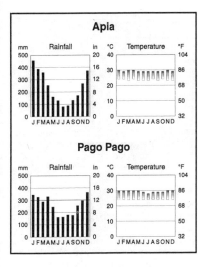

Apia

Rainfall | Temperature

Pago Pago

Rainfall | Temperature

but Independent Samoa's capital, Apia, receives only about 2900mm.

The driest and most comfortable period to visit the Samoas is between May and October but even during the rainy season most precipitation occurs at night and the main discomfort will be caused by the leth-argy–inspiring heat and humidity. The exception is the harbour area of Tutuila, American Samoa, where the famous Rain-maker Mountain (known as Mt Pioa by some local residents) ensures that the region receives over 5000mm of precipitation annu-ally. To best enjoy Pago Pago visit between June and September when chances of fine weather are a bit better. December and January are normally the wettest months.

The average temperatures range from 21°C to 32°C. Year-round humidity averages about 80% but the uncomfortable effects of this are tempered considerably by the south-easterly trade winds which blow from April to October and intermittently at other times.

Tropical Cyclones

The Samoas lie squarely within the South Pacific's notorious cyclone, or hurricane, belt and have experienced quite a few dev-astating blows over the years. Cyclones orig-inate from low-pressure centres near the equator and travel to higher latitudes, accel-erating along a curving path. The season for tropical storms and cyclones is between November and April.

In 1987, Cyclone Tusi caused extensive damage to property, vegetation and wildlife on the island of Ta'u in American Samoa. Cyclones seem to occur, on average, every 10 to 15 years but in the early 1990s the Samoas were devastated by two of the strongest and most destructive storms on record. Cyclone Ofa struck in February 1990, bringing winds of up to 250kmh, killing 16 people and levelling much of the island of Savai'i.

Then on 6 December 1991, just 22 months later, the clean-up was interrupted by Cyclone Val, widely reported to be the 'planet's worst storm in living memory'. Val pummelled the islands for five days with winds up to 260km/h and waves of up to 25m in height. Although the storm destroyed nearly three times as much as its predecessor, the death toll was exactly the same. Again, Savai'i was hardest hit. Total damage was estimated at US$380 million.

ECOLOGY & ENVIRONMENT

Though the rainforests of Samoa have sus-tained a culture for 3000 years, today's pressures of population and the push for Western-style development threaten their existence.

Visitors to Samoa can help conservation efforts by learning about Samoan culture, visiting and staying in villages that have pledged their willingness to protect the envi-ronment as well as participating in various 'eco-friendly' activities that villages are operating themselves in an effort to sustain their resources.

Independent Samoa

Of all the environmental challenges facing Samoa, deforestation is one of the most serious. In Independent Samoa, forest accounts for less than 37% of land area, The current rate of forest depletion is estimated to be about 3000 hectares per year – 80% due to agriculture and other activities; 20% the result of logging. The protection of Samoa's forests is crucial for the conservation of water and soil resources as well as to ensure the survival of unique island ecosystems.

In 1993 the South Pacific Regional Environment Programme (SPREP), funded by the United Nations Development Programme, put together a detailed national environment and development management strategy (NEMS) to pave the way towards sustainable development in Independent Samoa. Since then, several key areas in Upolu and Savai'i have been declared conservation areas and a growing number of villages are committing themselves to protecting their forests and marine resources and moving towards sustainable development. Travellers can assist greatly by supporting these villages and visiting declared conservation areas (see National Parks in the Flora & Fauna section).

Samoan marine resources are also under serious pressure. Over-fishing combined with modern, non-selective fishing techniques has resulted in a decline in fish stocks. Coastal habitats have been damaged by the illegal use of dynamite and poisons to catch fish as well as by an increase in siltation and pollution. Coral has been seriously reduced by outbreaks of crown-of-thorns starfish (which may be the result of unnaturally high volumes of nutrients feeding the young starfish) and cyclone damage.

Mangrove swamps and wetland areas, which provide vital feeding and breeding grounds for fish, are under continuing pressure from land reclaimation and agricultural development. Vaiusu Bay, the largest mangrove swamp in eastern Polynesia, was used for many years as Apia's rubbish dump. The mangroves here are still being reclaimed and leachate from the disused dump remains a threat to the marine environment.

Waste disposal in general is a growing problem, with an accumulation of plastics, metals, chemical and industrial waste becoming a threat to both the natural environment and public health. An inadequate sewage system (in Samoa private homes are served by systems ranging from septic tanks to toilets on drains or over the sea) has resulted in the contamination of groundwater and lagoons.

A national waste management strategy has been initiated. Conservation groups are working hard to make people aware of environmental issues and are strongly encouraging local village projects such as the building of composting toilets. Recycling is being encouraged and several small-scale operations are operating successfully.

Other issues facing Independent Samoa include the lack of town planning in Apia (which has resulted in traffic congestion, overcrowding, poor segregation of industry and dwellings and some very ugly buildings) and increasing pressure on limited urban facilities as more people move to the capital from rural areas.

The South Pacific Regional Environment Programme continues to tackle the environmental issues facing Samoa as do other locally based groups such as the Fa'asao Savai'i Society and the O le Siosiomaga Society. Eco-Tour Samoa, which runs environmentally friendly tours around Upolu, supports villagers in their efforts to conserve and protect their environment. Village 2000 is an initiative of Eco-Tour and local villages to create two truly sustainable villages –

Crown-of-thorns starfish

Ulutogia in the Aleipata Islands area of Upolu and Faleu on Manono Island – by the year 2000

American Samoa

The biggest issues affecting the environment in American Samoa are a population growth rate of 3.7% per year (which means a doubling in less than 20 years), the increased preference of a growing population for Western goods and equipment, increased generation of waste, greater demand for treated water and the development of land for homes and other uses.

The main source of industrial waste in American Samoa is the tuna canneries which operate inside Pago Pago Harbor. For many years cannery waste was discharged directly into the harbour in front of the canneries and sludge was disposed of in pits on the island. Since the US Environmental Protection Agency has brought in strict waste disposal requirements, the canneries have installed a pipeline to the outer harbour and now transport the majority of the waste to an ocean dump site 9km from the harbour. Cannery smells continue to be a problem but an upgraded filtering system has improved things somewhat.

In 1991 a government study found the fish in the inner harbour of Pago Pago to be contaminated with heavy metals and organochlorine compounds. The sources of the contamination appeared to be related to past military practices for disposal of waste. Ship repair and power generation industries had also contributed. The government is carrying out further studies to determine the extent of fish contamination and the sources of pollutants.

Solid waste collection on Tutuila is inadequate. After heavy rain Pago Pago Harbor is ringed with floating rubbish carried out by streams. The only recycling programme deals with aluminum cans as these bring a profit. Unfortunately, any profit from recycling other materials are cancelled out by shipping costs. Recent initiatives, including the Paradise 2000 Programme which aims to make American Samoa the cleanest islands

by the year 2000, are, however, expected to improve waste management.

Increased land clearing for development and agriculture are causing erosion and a degrading of water quality. By the early 1990s there was only 28% of native rainforest still remaining on Tutuila Island. The Natural Resources Conservation Service encourages landowners to practice contour hedgerows, mulching, critical area planting and terracing. Key areas of remaining rainforest have been protected with the establishment of the National Park of American Samoa.

Many coastal mangrove swamps, inland freshwater marshes, numerous streams and some cultivated taro fields have been lost to development. Between 1960 and 1990, 4.6% of the wetlands of American Samoa were lost each year. The Department of Commerce is running a village-based programme to pass on the functional values of wetlands and their economic and cultural significance.

FLORA & FAUNA

On all the islands, most of the upland areas which haven't been altered by agriculture or logging are covered in lush forests. Rainforest of broadleaf evergreens, vines, ferns and mosses predominate. On the heights of Savai'i, Upolu, Ofu, Olosega and Ta'u one finds more temperate forest vegetation, featuring tree ferns, grasses, wild coleus and epiphytic plants, ie. mosses, or plants that grow on another plant but is not parasitic on it. Particularly on cloudy days, these forested heights take on an otherworldly aspect.

The magnificent banyan tree dominates the landscape of the higher areas of these islands, especially on Savai'i and Upolu. Other parts of the Samoas are characterised by scrublands, marshes, pandanus forests and mangrove swamps.

The rainforests of Samoa are a natural apothecary, containing some 75 plant species which are used by traditional healers to treat up to 200 different types of disease. To date, six new pharmacologically active compounds have been isolated from Samoan medicinal plants. The compound prostratin, derived from *Homalanthus nutans* (*Mamala* in Samoan), has been found to prevent reproduction of the HIV-virus in human cells. Samoan healers use the compound to treat viral diseases. See Traditional Medicine later in this chapter.

Because the Samoas are relatively remote islands, few animal species have managed to colonise them. Apart from two species of flying fox, now protected throughout the islands after being hunted close to extinction (see the aside on flying foxes in the Tutuila Island chapter), the small, sheath-tailed bat and the Polynesian rat, mammals are limited to the marine varieties. Whales, dolphins and porpoises migrate north and south through the Samoas, depending on the season. Most common are the pilot whales which are frequently seen in the open seas around the islands.

Skinks *(pili)* and geckos *(mo'o)* can be seen everywhere. The harmless Pacific boa *(gata)* is found only on Ta'u Island and the green turtle and the endangered hawksbill turtle are rare visitors. The hawksbill breeds on the Aleipata Islands and occasionally on remote beaches on Savai'i, Tutuila and the Manu'a Islands. The green turtle nests on Rose Atoll; the black sea turtle is an infrequent visitor and the leatherback, loggerhead, and olive ridley turtles may also visit American Samoa. Incidentally, the Samoan word for sea turtles is *laumei*.

Marine toads were introduced from Hawaii in an attempt to control insects but seem to have had little effect.

Birds are now less plentiful in the Samoas than they once were because most were considered to be very good eating. The greatest variety can be found in American Samoa, where 59 species have been recorded. There are numerous sea birds such as petrels, white-tailed tropicbirds, boobies, black noddies, curlews, frigate birds and terns. Other species include the nearly flightless banded rails which are in danger from cats and other introduced predators; the barn owl, seen occasionally in the Manu'a Islands and the beautiful blue-crowned lory, which Samoans call the *sega* or parrot. While

walking in the forests, listen for the haunting calls of native doves and pigeons, found throughout the islands.

The beaches and reefs all over the Samoas are home to brilliant tropical fish and numerous species of shellfish, starfish and crustaceans. So far almost 900 species of fish and nearly 200 species of coral have been documented. There are also several shark species but fortunately they don't present much of a problem for divers because they're generally small and remain outside the reefs and lagoons.

National Parks
As yet there are only two fully fledged national parks in the Samoas. On the southern shore of the island of Upolu in Independent Samoa is O Le Pupu-Pu'e National Park, which contains a cross section of island environments from the coastline up to the misty heights around the spine of the island. Development in the park is limited but there are a couple of walking tracks and basic camp sites as well as Independent Samoa's best opportunities to observe native forest and bird life (see Around the Island in the Upolu chapter for more details).

American Samoa's contribution to nature conservation is the 4000-hectare National Park of American Samoa which consists of three areas: a large chunk of the upland forest and wild coastline and offshore waters of northern Tutuila Island; the magnificent stretch of beach and coral along the southern shore of Ofu; and the offshore waters, rugged cliffs and rainforested volcanic highlands of southern Ta'u Island. Combined, these areas encompass the largest tracts of wilderness in the Samoas, with most of the island environments represented.

The National Park of American Samoa also contains the greatest collection of indigenous plant and animal species in the Samoas. At the time of writing, the park maintained just one major walking trail – the track leading to the top of Mt Alava on Tutuila. Ambitous plans for the park include extending the trail down to the village of Vatia on the north coast of Tutuila, replacing the defunct cable car that once ran across Pago Pago Harbor to Mt Alava, and establishing hiking trails, basic camp sites and a rainforest canopy walkway in the Ta'u section of the park.

For park information, contact the National Park Visitor Information Centre (☎ 684-633 7082; fax 684-633 7084; NPSA-Administration@nps.gov), Pago Plaza, Pago Pago, American Samoa 96799-5137.

Other protected areas in American Samoa are Fagatele Bay National Marine Sanctuary on Tutuila Island and Rose Atoll, which is a wildlife refuge for nesting sea turtles and seabirds.

In Independent Samoa, an increasing number of villages are establishing their own conservation areas. To date, protected areas include: Palolo Deep Marine Reserve, Mt Vaea Scenic Reserve, Aleipata Islands Marine Reserve, Uafato Rainforest Conservation Area, Sataoa/Sa'anapu Wetlands Conservation Area, Manono Island Marine Reserves, Tafua Peninsula Rainforest Preserve, Falealupo Rainforest Reserve, and the Aopo/Letui/Sasina Conservation Area.

ECONOMY

See separate entries in Facts about Independent Samoa and Facts about American Samoa chapters.

POPULATION & PEOPLE

The indigenous people of both Samoas are large and robust folk of Polynesian origin. According to 1996 estimates, the population of Independent Samoa was 161,298, the majority Polynesian. Upolu is home to more than 115,000 and of these some 35,000 live in urban Apia. Savai'i has fewer than 50,000 residents and Manono and Apolima combined are home to less than 2000. About 40% of the population is under the age of 15 and the annual population growth rate is just over 2%. There is a high rate of emigration to New Zealand, Australia and the USA. However, that may well change as those countries revise their immigration policies and crack down more heavily on illegal immigrants and those who overstay their visas.

Independent Samoa has a substantial Chinese Samoan community which is centred in Apia. Most of the Europeans and Asians residing in the country are involved in UN development projects, business investment or volunteer aid organisations, such as the Peace Corps or VSO.

The population of American Samoa is around 58,000, with 95% concentrated on the main island of Tutuila and the remaining 5% living on the Manu'a islands. Tutuila has an annual growth rate of 3.7%, one of the highest in the world. There is no longer free migration between Independent and American Samoa but a large percentage of American Samoa's population is comprised of Independent Samoan citizens residing legally in the territory. A lot of American Samoa's drudgery work – especially that associated with the tuna canneries – is done by Independent Samoans and Tongans.

In addition, there are some 1500 foreigners residing in American Samoa, most of whom are Koreans or Chinese involved in the tuna industry. About one third of this number are North Americans, Australians or Europeans, most of whom hold teaching, health care or government jobs.

As their new name so clearly implies, Independent Samoans are citizens of an independent country, while the American Samoans are nationals of the USA. The latter may not vote in presidential elections until they opt to become US citizens, which they are free to do at any time. US citizens residing in American Samoa, however, must vote absentee. There are more than 100,000 ethnic Samoans from both sides of the border living in New Zealand, Australia and the USA (especially Hawaii). Many were born outside the Samoas.

ARTS
Dance & Fiafia

Originally, the *fiafia* was a village play or musical presentation in which participants would dress in a variety of costumes and accept money or other donations. These days the term 'fiafia night' refers to a lavish presentation of Samoan dancing and singing

And God Created Samoa

Samoans accept the scientific theory that Polynesians originally migrated to the islands from South-east Asia by way of Indonesia. However, they believe this applies to Maoris, Hawaiians, Tongans, Rarotongans, Easter Islanders and Tahitians but not to themselves. Their land is the 'cradle of Polynesia.'

Samoa, they say, was created by the god Tagaloa and their story is remarkably similar to the account given in the Bible in the Book of Genesis.

Before the earth, sky, plants or people existed, Tagaloa lived in the expanse of empty space. He created a rock, commanding it to split into clay, coral, cliffs and stones. As the rock broke apart, the earth, sea and sky came into being. From a bit of the rock emerged a spring of fresh water.

Next, Tagaloa created man and woman, whom he named Fatu and 'Ele'ele ('heart' and 'earth'). He sent them to the region of fresh water and commanded them to people the area. The sky, which was called Tu'ite'elagi, he ordered to prop itself up above the earth. Using starch and *teve*, a bitter-root plant and the only vegetation then available, he made a post for it to rest upon.

The god then created Po and Ao ('night' and 'day'), which bore the 'eyes of the sky' – the sun and the moon. At the same time Tagaloa made the nine regions of heaven, inhabited by various gods.

In the meantime, Fatu and 'Ele'ele were adding men and women to the area of fresh water. Tagaloa, reckoning that all these earthlings needed some form of government, sent Manu'a, another son of Po and Ao, to be the chief of the people.

From that time on, Samoan *tupu* (kings), were called *Tu'i Manu'a tele ma Samoa atoa*, or 'king of Manu'a and all of Samoa'.

Next, the countries were divided into islands or groups of islands. The world now consisted of Manu'a, Fiji, Tonga and Savai'i. Tagaloa then went to Manu'a and noticed that a void existed between it and Savai'i. Up popped Upolu and then Tutuila.

Tagaloa's final command, before he returned to the expanse, was: 'Always respect Manu'a; anyone who fails to do so will be overtaken by catastrophe, but men are free to do as they please in their own lands.' Thus, Manu'a became the spiritual centre of the Samoan islands and, to some extent, of all Polynesia. ■

---

staged at the larger hotels, usually accompanied by a huge buffet dinner. For more information on fiafia, see the Entertainment section in the Facts for the Visitor chapter.

Most of the dancing, including the *sa sa*, is performed by groups to the rhythm of a beating wooden mallet. The popular *siva* is a slow and fluid dance performed by one or two women acting out with their hands impromptu stories and expressions.

Traditionally, the final dance of the evening was called the *taualuga*, which is also the word for the finishing touch on the roof of a *fale*. It was normally a siva danced by the *taupou* (ceremonial virgin), dressed only in *siapo* (artistically decorated bark cloth, made from the mulberry tree), her body oiled seductively. It goes without saying that the missionaries quickly put an end to such a 'disgusting' practice.

Today, the dance usually performed as the grand finale is the dramatic fire knife dance,

the favourite of most visitors. Dancers gyrate, leap and spin while juggling flaming torches in time to a rapid and primaeval drum beat.

Music

Like most people, Samoans love music but it seems that the percentage of musically talented people in the Samoas is higher than in most other countries. The ability to harmonise and play musical instruments seems to be almost a birthright of the Polynesian islanders. One need only attend a choir practice or church service to hear the magnificent blend of voices raised in apparently heartfelt devotion.

Traditional music is quite beautiful and is normally sung in Samoan. Songs are written to tell stories or commemorate events, most of which are sad and stirring. Love songs are the most popular, followed by patriotic songs extolling the virtues of the Samoas. Others tell depressing or joyous tales of traditional life in the country.

Another highly respected institution is the brass band and musical competitions between villages are common. The most prominent brass band in the Samoas is the Police Band of Independent Samoa which marches from the police station in Apia every weekday at 7.45 am and performs as the flag is raised in front of the government offices.

Literature

The oral tradition of recounting myths, legends, histories and fables is still very much alive in Samoa. *Tala o le Vavau – The Myths, Legends and Customs of Old Samoa*, adapted from the collections of C Steubel, A Kramer and Brother Herman, and illustrated by Iosua Toafa, brings together some interesting material. Another good source of Samoan legends is *Fagogo: Fables from Samoa in Samoan and English* by Richard Moyle. *The Stone Maiden and other Samoan Fables*, retold by Daniel Pouesi and Michael Igoe, and illustrated by Michael Evanston, is a slim, well-produced collection of the some of the most famous legends.

Albert Wendt is Independent Samoa's most renowned scholar and author. His novels, *Leaves of the Banyan Tree, Flying Fox in a Freedom Tree, Pouliuli, Birth and Death of the Miracle Man, Inside Us the Dead, Shaman of Visions* and *Sons for the Return Home*, all deal with a serious and controversial social issue facing Samoa: how to accommodate the encroachment of Western technology and ideals while maintaining to some degree the values of fa'a Samoa and its related social structures.

Wendt realises that the issue is not unique to Samoa, however, and so, apparently, does the literary community. One reviewer has described Wendt's Samoa as a microcosm of the modern world. Wendt's growing list of novels and volumes of poetry, which tend to reflect this theme above all others, has been highly acclaimed by critics. In 1980, *Leaves of the Banyan Tree*, his third novel, won the New Zealand Wattie Book of the Year Award.

Samoan performance poet and writer Sia Figiel uses traditional storytelling forms in her work. Her powerful first novel, *Where We Once Belonged*, tells the story of a young woman growing up and searching for identity in a traditional village in Samoa. Published in 1996, the novel deromanticises Western perceptions of Pacific Islands women and tackles issues such as suicide, violence, incest and child abuse. Figiel has also published a volume of short stories called *The Girl in the Moon Circle*.

Another recommended novel is *Alms for Oblivion* by Fata Sano Malifa (published in 1993) which follows the wild wanderings of Niko who travels to New Zealand, America and finally back to Samoa in search of justification for his existence.

Architecture

The most prevalent manifestation of traditional – and practical – Samoan architecture is the *fale*. A fale is a Samoan home or meeting house but the word is also used to connote a business, a European-style dwelling or even a bus shelter, due to the lack of words for such things in the Samoan language.

The fale is an oval structure without walls. The thatched coconut-frond roof is supported by wooden poles and the floor consists of a platform of coral rock or pebbles which is covered with woven pandanus mats. The entire building is constructed without nails, the rafters and joints being tied with strong coconut fibres

Fale - a traditional Samoan house

called *'ofa*. Blinds made of woven coconut leaves are lowered to keep out wind and rain.

Fales are normally sparsely furnished but they nearly always contain a clothes chest and a store of sleeping and sitting mats. Lately, however, 'palagi' furniture, kitchen appliances, TVs and video machines have become more and more common. There is often a smaller kitchen fale, used for meal preparation, near the main home.

Traditional fales are found throughout Independent Samoa though many are now constructed with concrete slab floors, metal poles and tin roofs. Western-style square homes with walls, windows and doors, though uncomfortable and impractical given the climate of the Samoas, are becoming more common and in American Samoa have usurped the traditional fale completely. They are considered a symbol of wealth and status and offer a measure of privacy previously impossible to find.

Every village has one prominently elevated fale, the *fale talimalo*, in which the village council meets. It is the responsibility of the village women's committee to keep it clean and brightly decorated. The women skewer hibiscus, frangipani and ginger flowers on little pales to decorate the surrounding grounds. They hang strings of these flowers all through the building. Coconut fronds are plaited around all the posts in preparation for a council meeting.

The committee is also responsible for making inspections of village homes. They ensure that homes are clean and in order and that kitchens and toilets measure up to village health standards. Those families whose homes are deemed below standard must pay a fine. The government of Independent Samoa holds an annual competition and awards a prize to the village judged to be the most orderly and well cared for.

Siapo

The bark cloth known as *siapo*, or *tapa*, made from the inner bark of the paper mulberry tree *(u'a)*, provides a medium for some of the loveliest artwork in the Samoas. Originally used as clothing and coverings (don't

miss the exquisite siapo wallpaper in the former home of Robert Louis Stevenson in Apia), siapo is still used in customary exchanges.

A good place to see siapo production is in the village of Palauli on the island of Savai'i. Craft stores in Apia and Pago Pago sell siapo and a good selection can be seen at Apia's Arts and Crafts Fair, held in March, and the Teuila Festival, held in September.

In the first stage of siapo production, the mature trees are cut near their base, normally measuring only 3cm or so in diameter, and the bark is stripped away. The bast, or inner bark, is then peeled away from the rough outer bark. Next, the bast is soaked in water and scraped with three types of seashells in succession. After being beaten with a wooden mallet until it resembles a thin sheet of cloth, the bast is then stretched and dried.

Finally, the cloth is placed over a wooden board which has been carved with a traditional design and rubbed with a ruddy vegetable dye called *o'a*. The imprinted design is then handpainted with a mixture of o'a, which has an adhesive base, and rich earthy reds and browns derived from candlenuts and mangrove bark.

Fine Mats

Woven from pandanus fibres split into widths of just a couple of millimetres, fine mats (*ie toga*) take months of painstaking work and, when finished, have the look and feel of fine linen or silk. Never really used as mats, ie toga, along with other woven mats, siapo and oils, make up 'the gifts of the women' that must be exchanged at every formal Samoan ceremony. Agricultural products comprise 'the gifts of the men'.

Once upon a time, fine mats were made only by the daughters of high chiefs and consequently were believed to have sacred powers. Many individual mats have gained great historical significance as records of important alliances and exchanges.

Good examples of some very fine and quite old ie toga can be seen at the Robert Louis Stevenson Museum in Apia.

Samoan artwork by Rudi Steffaney, influenced by traditional *siapo* designs

SOCIETY & CONDUCT

More than any other Polynesian people, Samoans are tradition-oriented and follow closely the social hierarchies, customs and courtesies established long before the arrival of Europeans. Many visitors sense, correctly, that below the surface lies a complex code of traditional ethics and behaviour and, feeling awkwardly ignorant, may often become frustrated in their dealings with the locals.

At times, sensitive visitors to the Samoas are overwhelmed by the aura of mystery that surrounds the outwardly friendly and responsive Samoan people. The fa'a Samoa (Samoan way) is closely guarded and preserved, especially in remote villages where European influences are minimal, but visitors should not become discouraged. The people are understanding and most will be willing to answer questions regarding their customs. What most people won't readily divulge is their personal feelings about the system and the effects it has on their lives.

Traditional Culture

The *fa'amatai* (matai system of government) is practised throughout the islands of the Samoas and has its roots in ancient Polynesian culture. Each village *(nu'u)* comprises a group of *aiga* (extended families) which include as many relatives as can be claimed. The larger an aiga, the more powerful it can become and to be part of a powerful aiga is the goal of nearly every tradition-minded Samoan.

The aiga is headed by a chief, called a *matai*, who represents the family on the *fono* (village council). Matais, who can be male or female, are normally elected by all adult members of the aiga, but most candidates hold titles of some description and many inherit office automatically. The position of matai may, however, be granted to a non-family member whose relatives the family would like to bring into its sphere of influence.

Although matais hold title to all assets of the aiga they represent, many matais in smaller villages live remarkably austere lives. The matais are responsible for law enforcement and punishment of infractions that may occur in their village. Social protocol is taken extremely seriously and crimes such as manslaughter, adultery, violence, insubordination and even defiant cheekiness are punishable by all sorts of unpleasant rulings.

The most serious crimes require the offender to endure the humiliating but face-saving ritual of *fa'asifoga* (often just *ifoga*), the begging of forgiveness of the offended party. The guilty person and his or her matai, covered in fine mats, must carry gifts and food to the victims' fale and kneel before the door awaiting an invitation to enter. This must be done day after day until the wronged party feels that the offence has been atoned for by the humility of its perpetrator. It is interesting that in the Catholic church the penitent sinner appears before the priest and begs forgiveness in much the same way, thus making peace with God.

The fono consists of the matais of all the aiga associated with the village. The highest chief of the village, or *ali'i*, sits at the head of the fono. In addition, each village has one *pulenu'u* (a combination of mayor and police chief), and one or more *tulafale* (talking chiefs). The pulenu'u is elected every three years and acts as an intermediary between the village and the national (or territorial, in the case of American Samoa) government. The tulafale is an orator who liaises between the ali'i and outside entities, carries out ceremonial duties and engages in ritual debates.

The symbol of the tulafale's office is the *fue* (fly whisk), a 4kg mop of sennit that represents wisdom and must be carried when the tulafale speaks in an official capacity. He also carries a *to'oto'o*, a staff representing chiefly authority. Both items are handed down from father to son.

Meetings are held in a *fale talimalo*, a traditional open hut with a roof supported by posts, and all participants in the meetings are seated according to rank, the ali'i at one end and the chief of next highest rank at the other.

When a chief dies, villages effectively close down; at such times travellers are unwelcome. The sea around the village is also closed during the period of mourning and no fishing or swimming is permitted. In extreme cases, villagers cut off their hair, pigs are slaughtered, boats are smashed, and village treasures are destroyed to illustrate the villagers' grief at the loss of their leader.

Members of a village are divided into four categories. The society of untitled men, the *aumaga*, are responsible for growing the village food. Traditionally they were also the warriors of the village. The *aualuma* is the society of unmarried, widowed or separated women. They are responsible for providing hospitality and producing *toga* (women's wealth) in the form of fine mats, siapo and oils. Women who have married into the village, the wives of matais and the pulenu'u, are called *faletua ma tausi*. Their role revolves around serving their husband and his family. Children belong to the group called *tamaiti*. Close social interaction is generally restricted to members of one's own group.

In theory, all wealth and property in the Samoas are owned communally by the aigas; European concepts of property and wealth are not relevant to many traditional Samoans and regarded with varying degrees of suspicion. Although materialism is rapidly encroaching on Samoa, visitors who are able to reconcile themselves to existence in a communal situation may be happier there. However, recent changes are having profound effects upon the young, affecting their aiga, villages and roles in society. But in the villages, traditional standards remain.

Despite this communal attitude within the aiga, competition between the aiga themselves is enthusiastically accepted and the best matai is the one who can bring home the most bacon for the clan. A matai who fails in this calling may be stripped of his or her title, lands and esteem.

Perhaps the most important aspect of traditional Samoan life is the respect, even veneration, shown for those perceived to be higher than oneself. Children show respect for their parents, women for their husbands, aiga for their matai, and matais and tulafale for the ali'i. Teachers, doctors, politicians, ministers and priests are also held in great esteem.

Accepted Behaviour

As a foreigner, you will also be considered worthy of respect as long as you behave appropriately as far as the locals are concerned. This can be frustrating at times. Samoans will often keep themselves at arm's length in order to avoid the possibility of making you unhappy. They will often answer your questions with the response they suppose you'd like to hear rather than with the truth, which they believe may upset you. Usually they will not show emotion in your presence, even though they will openly weep at weddings and funerals and laugh, sing and dance on festive occasions – times that they perceive to be appropriate for such behaviour. The better you become acquainted with the people, of course, the more relaxed they will become.

It is perfectly normal in the Samoas for members of the same sex to hold hands and display friendship in public, but open displays of affection between men and women, married or not, will be met with disapproval. Samoan men are required to obtain the approval of a woman's brothers before showing admiring interest in her and, regardless of what Margaret Mead wrote on the issue, the Samoas are not playgrounds of free love.

While sexual indiscretions are not taken quite as seriously as they would be in many parts of the Christian world, young women are expected to protect their bodies from the advances of young suitors. It is also interesting to note that, particularly in Independent Samoa, people see marriageable foreigners as tickets out of the Samoas as much as foreigners see marriageable Samoans as

tickets in. Marriage to a Samoan – or any Polynesian – may provide you not only with a spouse but also with the responsibility to provide for his or her aiga. Family members may be happy to see one of their aiga joining up with someone whom they perceive to be rich. Those who cannot be dissuaded from such a marriage should at least be prepared! Keep in mind also that a local marriage does not always guarantee a foreigner the right to remain in paradise (although Americans in American Samoa will probably encounter few problems).

Another concept that causes breakdowns in communications between Samoans and foreigners is *musu*, which may be roughly translated as 'moodiness'. An otherwise pleasant and vivacious person may inexplicably become quiet and sullen. If this happens, don't worry – you haven't committed some unforgivable faux pas, so don't react with apologies or questions. Your friend is just experiencing musu and will usually get over it soon.

Dos & Don'ts

Although many visitors to the Samoas wish to see traditional villages, such visits can be extremely disruptive in a traditional society. This is not to say that visitors are not welcome. They are welcome, and to a degree unmatched in any Western country you'd care to name. A few guidelines, however, will go a long way towards keeping things on an even keel.

Certain rules of etiquette have their origins in ancient Samoa, while others are the direct result of Christianity. While special allowances are made for visitors, especially in American Samoa where many of the locals ignore established traditions, those who learn and respect traditions will endear themselves to the people and will be more readily accepted in rural areas.

Although guidelines are quoted in most tourist publications in the islands, some are repeated here for the benefit of intending visitors who may want to prepare themselves.

- It's best not to arrive in a village on a Sunday. The presence of a foreigner unknown to the village will interrupt the smooth customary flow of religious and family activities and, on occasion, village elders have been known to become visibly upset.
- Don't swim near a village or perform any manual labour on a Sunday. Excessive noise on the Sabbath is also deemed sacrilegious so uninhibited raging on Sundays should be confined to hotel rooms or remote beaches and mountainsides.
- If you're staying with a village family, politely refuse invitations to stay with other village families, since this will bring shame upon your hosts. Be prepared to repay your hosts with some token of your esteem, such as cash, 'store-bought' foods or small gifts representative of your home country; anything that is difficult to obtain in a village will usually be graciously received. Gifts should more or less reflect the value of the services the visitor has received from his or her hosts. If you've taken photos of the family you should send them later; such photos may well become family heirlooms.
- There are no real beggars in Samoa so avoid indiscriminately distributing gifts. This applies especially to children who have taken to begging foreigners for sweets, pens and money (thanks, no doubt, to earlier visitors who believed their largess constituted a good deed). Not only can it lead them to believe something can be had for nothing, it also sends misleading signals regarding foreign cultures in general. It can also be a real nuisance (and embarrassment) for the children's parents, relatives and village, as well as for travellers who follow.
- Although fashion and dress are becoming increasingly liberal (and Western) among Samoan youth on both sides of the border, many middle-aged and older people are still quite sensitive to it. Therefore, visitors would still do well to be particularly mindful of their appearance, especially in villages and remote areas. Throughout the Samoas, women are best advised to wear knee-length skirts or *lavalavas* (sarongs) and should avoid wearing shorts or bathing gear away from the beach no matter what the temperature. Men would do best to wear knee-length, baggy shorts (or lavalavas) and should always wear shirts while walking in the streets.
- Shoes should be removed when entering a fale. When invited into a fale, sit cross-legged or cover your legs. Never enter during prayers or meetings and don't make noise or commotion in the area while prayers are being said. If you inadvertently enter a village during *sa* (see under Religion later in this chapter), sit down and wait quietly until the all clear is sounded.
- Try not to address people while standing or strolling through a village. Don't eat while walking through a village or town and don't pass a meeting of chiefs while carrying a load on your shoulders or with an open umbrella.

- If you'd like to swim at a village beach, climb a mountain, take photos or merely have a look around, be sure to ask permission beforehand of the pulenu'u in the appropriate village. (Also see under Dangers & Annoyances in the Facts for the Visitor chapter)
- When walking in front of someone, lower your head and say '*tulou*' or 'excuse me'.
- Most importantly, avoid becoming visibly frustrated or angry when things don't happen as they would at home. Things rarely go to plan in the Samoas and inflexibility on your part will make for a miserable visit.

Sa

Sa, which means 'sacred', is the nightly vespers or devotional and it is taken very seriously in the Samoas. Sometime between 6 and 7 pm, or thereabouts, a village gong (most often made of an empty propane tank) sounds, signifying that the village should prepare for sa. All activity comes to an abrupt halt and motor and pedestrian traffic stops. When the second gong is sounded, sa has begun.

This time is used for devotionals and prayers in individual family homes and should not be interrupted under any circumstances. Samoan villagers who ignore the regulations of sa will incur fines and the ridicule of neighbours.

When a third gong is sounded, usually after about 10 or 15 minutes, sa is over and activities may be resumed. If you're caught out in a village during sa, stop what you're doing, sit down and quietly wait for the third gong to sound. These rules do not apply in Apia or the Pago Pago Harbor area.

Traditional Burials

Samoan burials are of interest to visitors. Chiefs get large, multi-tiered tombs – the more tiers, the higher the chief buried there. Family graves are rarely in a formal cemetery. Instead, people are buried in a place of honour in the front yard and their graves covered with an elaborate monument, which is usually well-cared for as a mark of respect. This explains the revered nature of traditionally-held aiga lands and the Samoans' reluctance to part with them.

Traditional Medicine

Traditional Samoan medical knowledge has been handed down through the generations for 200 years and nearly every Samoan family will have some knowledge of traditional folk remedies. As a profession, however, traditional healing is now a dying art and more and more people are looking to Western medicine.

Traditional healers are typically women who learn their methods from a long apprenticeship. Normally, a girl begins her training in early childhood when she assists her mother or a close female relative in her craft. The apprentice must learn to recognise several hundred species of rainforest plants, each with its own medicinal value. Modern healers are taught to take notes and to keep a close and accurate record of each patient's symptoms, their diagnosis, treatment and response.

Many healers specialise in particular diseases and become known for this expertise. As a general rule, there are four types of Samoan healers: the *fa'atosaga* or midwives; those who practise *fofo* or massage; the *fofogau* or orthopaedists (normally men capable of setting broken bones); and the *taulasea*, herbalists who utilise the diversity of Samoan rainforest flora in their treatment of disease. Other related types of healers include those who effect love potions or banish troublesome *aitu* (spirits).

A typical taulasea can diagnose and treat over 200 different diseases, many of which have no Western equivalent, with a combination of 120 or more rainforest plants. Such complaints can range from stomach upset to tension to personal hostility. Whenever an illness is diagnosed, the healer must visit the forest (or send her apprentice to do so) to collect the required combination of herbal remedies. Most of the treatments are applied externally with the aid of an oil base, although some are burned and inhaled while others are taken internally with water.

The Fa'afafine

Travellers to Samoa may be struck by the public presence of Samoan men with effeminate qualities. By traditional definition, a *fa'afafine* is a male who opts to dress and behave as a female, for whatever reason. The word translated means simply 'like a woman'. Some of the fa'afafine dress as women, but many do not. Unlike their counterparts in many other cultures, the fa'afafine are very much an integral part of the fabric of Samoan society. There is a saying in Samoa that translates as: 'everyone is important within their family' and the fa'afafine are no exception. In fact, the fa'afafine are considered to be extremely valuable to their families since they often do the work of both women and men.

In the public sphere, particularly in Apia and Pago Pago, many fa'afafine can be found working in shops, hotels, banks and offices where their skills have become important to the smooth running of businesses. It is often said in Samoa that if you want something done well, ask the fa'afafine to organise it. A number of the well educated fa'afafine are involved in the arts; they include dancers, playwrights, producers and directors of drama and organisers of the various fa'afafine contests that are held annually in both Samoas. Usually staged towards the end of the year, the contests are elaborate affairs where the fa'afafine dance, sing, play musical instruments and strut around on stage in lavish finery. One of Apia's most well known fa'afafines, Cindy, performs in her own show every Thursday evening at Magrey Ta's Beer Garden on Beach Road.

Dress

Western dress is becoming more common among the younger people of both Samoas, but many Samoans (and visitors) wear a *lavalava*, a wraparound piece of brightly coloured fabric decorated with floral or geometric designs. Many women wear a *puletasi*, a long skirt worn under a matching tunic.

The Samoan equivalent of the business suit is the *ie faitaga*, an undecorated lavalava of suit-coat material worn with a plain European-style white shirt. This outfit is nearly always accompanied by a briefcase and a rotund physique denoting high social status.

Tattooing

The *pe'a* (Samoan tattoo) is not merely a drunken sailor's whim or a mark of the individuality of its wearer but a centuries-old tradition that identifies the tattooed person as a proud and courageous Samoan.

Although the missionaries considered tattoos to be evil, pagan, personal adornments and though they consequently tried to discourage the perpetuation of the practice, the Samoans weren't interested in giving it up. While many young men have opted not to undergo the painful procedure, growing numbers, especially in Independent Samoa, are choosing to be tattooed as a mark of manhood and Samoan identity.

When a baby girl is born in Samoa her grandmother will begin weaving a fine mat to be given as her dowry when she marries. When a baby boy is born his grandmother will start collecting the dye for his tattoo. The soot from burnt candlenuts will be carefully gathered over many days, stored in a plugged coconut shell and presented to the grandson when he reaches puberty.

Tattoos normally cover the man's body from the waist to the knees with such artistic density that they resemble a pair of trousers. On occasion, women also elect to be tattooed, but their designs cover only the thighs.

The women's tattoos are to be shown in public only on community occasions, such as the when *kava* is mixed for a ceremony. Most traditional Samoans believe that male tattoos should also be kept hidden and considered only as a personal mark of courage and accomplishment. Although boys as young as nine have received tattoos, most people agree that it's better to wait until the mid-teens, so the design will not be distorted by growth.

There is a great deal of protocol behind the tattooing process. The skills and tools of the *tufuga*, the tattoo artist, are traditionally passed from father to son and it may be years before an apprentice is allowed to take

charge of the tattoo comb. Meanwhile his main task will be to stretch the skin so that the dye-filled lines of the tattoo remain straight.

The man receiving the tattoo lies on the floor while the tufuga works through the painful process of incising the intricate design on him with sharpened sharks' teeth or boars' tusks. The man being tattooed must not be left alone in case the *aitus*, or spirits, take him away (not surprising really). A special language is used when addressing the tufuga and he is assigned an off-limits, sacred fale for use as a resting place. Once begun, the tattoo should be completed or the young man will bring shame upon himself and his aiga. In most cases the entire procedure will take a month to complete.

'Ava Ceremony

'Ava, sometimes known as kava, is a drink derived from the ground root of the pepper plant *Piper methysticum* and the active ingredients include 12 or 14 chemicals of an alkaloidal nature. It is both an anaesthetic and an analgesic, high in fibre, low in calories, and serves as a mild tranquilliser, an antibacterial and antifungal agent, a pain killer, a diuretic and appetite suppressant. It is legal in North America and Europe and Samoans habitually send packages of it to family members overseas.

Visitors who try 'ava will often report that it tastes like dishwater – it certainly looks like well-used dishwater. Nevertheless, it

Traditional wooden Ava bowl

does grow on you and many foreigners actually come to enjoy it.

The 'ava ceremony is a ritual in the Samoas. Every meeting of matai and all government gatherings are preceded by an 'ava ceremony. Originally, the village taupou, a ceremonial virgin who was often the daughter of an ali'i, was responsible for serving the drink but now the job is often performed by a tulafale (a talking chief).

The ground root is mixed with water in a carved multi-legged bowl. Men seat themselves in an oval with the bowl, called a *tanoa*, at one end. When the 'ava is ready, the tulafale calls out the names of the participants in order of rank. He then dips the drink into half a coconut shell with a wad of coconut sennit and passes it to the recipient, who drips a few drops on the ground and says '*manuia lava*', the Samoan equivalent of 'cheers', before drinking it. Visitors who find the taste objectionable can merely pour the remainder onto the ground without causing offence.

A good place to observe 'ava drinking without participating is the Maketi Fou (New Market) in Apia, Independent Samoa. 'Ava ceremonies sometimes take place next to the Jean P Haydon Museum in Pago Pago, American Samoa.

RELIGION

The Christian missionaries did their job thoroughly, succeeding in turning both Samoas into overwhelmingly Christian entities. The official motto of Independent Samoa is *Fa'avae i le Atua Samoa*, meaning 'Samoa is founded on God'. American Samoa's motto is *Samoa, ia muamua le Atua*–'Samoa, let God be first'. There seems to be a consensus between the two about what is important, anyway.

It is significant that some of the early 19th century adventurers who found their way to the Samoa islands brought with them a form of Christianity that, on a limited scale, was to catch on. In addition, converted islanders from other Pacific countries arrived from time to time and spread the message they had accepted from the palagi.

Perhaps the most important factor leading to wholesale acceptance of the new religion in the islands, however, was a legendary prophecy made by the war goddess, Nafanua, that a new religion would arrive from the sky and be embraced by the people, bringing peace and prosperity to the land. The Samoan word 'palagi', which is used to identify all Caucasian peoples, means 'those who break the sky'.

In 1830 the Reverend John Williams of the London Missionary Society landed in western Savai'i in his crude ship the *Messenger of Peace*, which had been hastily constructed in Rarotonga. Given the turbulent situation in Savai'i at the time of his arrival, any suggestion of peace would have been appropriate. When the internal war ended, Williams was successful in converting the chief of the winning side, Malietoa Vainu'upo, to Christianity. The chief accepted eight teachers assigned by Williams, and matais and villagers joined the new church en masse. The Christian message spread quickly around the islands.

In nearby Tahiti and the Cook Islands, conversion to Christianity involved the tearing down of Polynesian idols and temples. The Samoans, having none of these things, were required to go through a different ritual. All Samoans had a personal *aitu* – a fish, bird or other animal that was sacred to them. To prove the sincerity of their conversions, the Samoans were required to eat their aitu, which the missionaries regarded as symbols of paganism. Aitu are still going strong in Samoa, but these days the word refers to any mischievous or wandering spirit.

The Wesleyan Methodists came to the Samoas under the direction of Peter Turner. Many Samoans who had connections with Tonga awaited the formation of a Wesleyan mission in Samoa similar to that on the nearby archipelago. Turner had originally visited the Samoas in 1828 but hadn't established a mission because of an informal agreement with the London Missionary Society that the Samoas would be left to them in exchange for the Wesleyans' free reign in Tonga and Fiji. Although Turner found many Samoans awaiting his message in the mid to late 1830s, the Wesleyan Church chose to honour the agreement and withdrew Turner.

The Catholics arrived on the scene in 1845, a little late to take part in the fury of conversion and dispute that had characterised the previous decade, but they still managed to win quite a few adherents. In the latter part of the century came the Mormons, who continue to entice the islanders away from other sects with opulence, emigration and educational opportunities, and a tale that all Polynesians are descended from the lost tribes of Israel.

These days, half of all Samoans belong to the Congregational Church, derived from the London Missionary Society. About one quarter are Catholics, 12% are Methodists and most of the remainder are Mormons.

The pastor's house is normally the largest in every village and, in most cases, it is provided by the villagers themselves. Samoans contribute what some people consider to be an exorbitant amount of money towards the upkeep of exisiting churches and the constant building of new ones.

The Mormons have a large and striking temple on the outskirts of Apia surrounded by an extensive educational compound.

The Baha'is, although not particularly well represented in the Samoas, have a beautiful temple (one of only seven in the world) in the highlands of Upolu.

LANGUAGE

The main language spoken in both Samoas is Samoan, although nearly everyone in American Samoa and the majority of people in Independent Samoa speak English as a second language. Except in remote villages on Savai'i, those who don't speak the indigenous language should have few problems communicating with Samoans.

Samoan is a Polynesian language similar to Maori, Tongan, Hawaiian and Tahitian. All of these belong to the Austronesian or Malayo-European family of languages (which includes Malay, Malagasy and Melanesian dialects), and many words are strikingly similar to Malay, suggesting Polynesian migrations to the islands from South-East Asia. It is likely that Samoan is the earliest of all the Polynesian languages.

Pronunciation

Samoan uses only 14 letters – five vowels and nine consonants. The five vowels may be long or short, depending on whether or not they are stressed, but the actual difference in sound between them is very slight to the untrained ear. A long vowel is conventionally indicated by a superscribed bar and is pronounced the same, only lengthened. Stress is normally placed on the next to last syllable. A glottal stop (represented by an apostrophe) is the sound you hear between the vowels in the expression 'oh-oh' – it's produced by a momentary closing of the muscles at the back of the throat. Diphthongs (combinations of vowels) are also common in Samoan, and are pronounced as they would be in English (eg in the words 'ear' or 'higher').

Vowels

a	as in 'at'
e	as in 'set'
i	as in 'sit'
o	as in 'hot'
u	as in 'full'

Consonants

f	as in 'far'
g	as in 'longing'
l	as in 'low'
m	as in 'may'
n	as in 'none'
p	as in 'pear'
r	as the 'r' in 'ring' (the tongue is flapped lightly against the the roof of the mouth, as in the Spanish 'para')
s	as the 's' in 'Samoa'
t	as the 't' in 'times'
v	as the 'v' in 'very'

Since their language is spoken only in the Samoas, the Samoans are both pleased and surprised when foreigners make an attempt to use it. The following are a few useful words and phrases to get you started:

Left: The Samoan male's traditional knee-to-waist *tatau*
Top: A *tufuga* (tatoo artist) and his apprentices at work
Middle: Workers in a cacao plantation
Bottom: Fresh hibiscus blossoms strung together to decorate fales

DORINDA TALBOT

DEANNA SWANEY

DEANNA SWANEY

SAMOA VISITORS BUREAU

DORINDA TALBOT

Top Left: Lobster claw heliconia
Top Middle: Hibiscus flower, Tanumapua
Plantation, Upolu

Top Right: Teuila (wild ginger blossom)
Middle: Poinciana tree, Savai'i
Bottom: Tanumapua Plantation

Greetings & Civilities

Hello.	*Malo.*
Goodbye.	*Tofa.*
Goodbye and farewell.	*Tofa soifua.*
Good morning.	*Talofa.*
Good evening.	*Talofa.*
Good night.	*Manuia le po.*
How are you?	*O a mai oe?*
I'm fine, thanks.	*Manuia, faafetai.*
Please.	*Fa'amolemole.*
Thank you. (very much)	*Fa'afetai. (tele)*
Welcome.	*Afio mai.*
Yes.	*Ioe.*
No.	*Leai.*
Maybe.	*Masalo.*
Excuse me.	*Tulou.*
I'm sorry.	*Ua ou sese.*
Forgive me.	*Malie.*

Essentials

Please write it down.	*Fa'amolemole tusi i lalo.*
Where are you going?	*Alu i fea?*
Please show me on the map.	*Fa'amolemole faasino mai ia te au i le fa'afanua.*
I understand.	*Ua ou Malamalama.*
I don't understand.	*Ou te le malamalama.*
I don't speak …	*Ou te le tautala …*
Do you speak English?	*Ete iloa Nanu?*
Is there anyone here who speaks English?	*E ai se isi e Nanu?*
How do you say …?	*E faapefea ona …?*
Where/what country are you from?	*Fea/O ai lou atunu'u?*
American Samoa	*Amerika Samoa*
Australia	*Ausetalia*
Canada	*Kanata*
France	*Falani*
Germany	*Siamani*
Great Britain	*Peretania*
Holland	*Holani*
Italy	*Italia*
Japan	*Iapani*
New Zealand	*Niu Sila*
Switzerland	*Suisilani*
USA	*Iuanaite Setete o Amerika*
Western Samoa	*Samoa i Sisifo*
I have a visa/permit.	*E iai lo'u visa/pemita.*
surname	*igoa faai'u*
given name	*igoa masani*
date of birth/place of birth	*aso fanau/nu'u na fanau ai*
nationality	*tagatanu'u*
age	*matua*
male/female	*tane/fafine*
passport	*tusi folau*

Small Talk

What is your name?	*O ai lo'u igoa?*
My name is …	*O lo'u igoa o …*
I'm a tourist/student.	*O a'u o le turisi/tama aoga.*
Are you married?	*Ua fai se aiga?*
How many children do you have?	*E to'afia tama'iti?*
How old are you?	*Fia ou tausaga?*
I'm … years old.	*Ua … o'u tausaga.*
Do you like …?	*E te manao i le …?*
I like it very much.	*O lo'u vaisu.*
Just a minute.	*Fa'atali mai lava.*
May I?	*E mafai?*
It's all right/no problem.	*Ua lelei.*
foreigner	*palagi*
boy	*tama*
boyfriend	*ma'amusa*
family	*aiga*
girl	*teine*
girlfriend	*ma'amusa*
little boy	*tama'iti'iti*
little girl	*teine'iti'iti*
father	*tama*
man	*tamaloa*
mother	*tina*
woman	*fafine*

Getting Around

I want to go to …	*Ou te fia alu i...*
I want to book a seat for …	*E fia totogi i lo'u pasese i le...*
Where does … leave from?	*O fea e alu ese mai ai le …?*
bus	*pasi*
train	*nofoa-afi*
boat/ferry	*va'a/va'a lau pasese*
yacht	*va'afaila*
canoe	*paopao*
longboat	*fautasi*
aeroplane	*va'alele*
What time does it leave/arrive?	*O le a le taimi e alu ese ai/taunuu ai le?*
How long does the trip take?	*O le a le umi a le malaga?*
What time is it?	*Ua ta le fia?*
Where do I catch the bus?	*O fea e fa'atali ai le pasi?*
Do I need to change buses?	*E tatau ona ou sui pasi?*
You must change buses.	*E tatau ona sui pasi.*
I'd like to hire a …	*E fia togipau se …*
bicycle/motorbike	*uila vili vae/uila-afi*
car	*ta'avale*
guide	*taiala*
horse	*solofanua*
petrol/gas	*penisini*
ticket	*pepa o le pasese*
ticket office	*ofisa tusi pasese*
timetable	*fa'asologa o malaga*

Directions

How do I get to …?	*Fa'apefe'a ona ou ali i …?*
Where is …?	*O fea …?*
street/road	*maga'ala/au'ala*
street number	*numera o le maga'ala*
suburb	*fuai'ala taulaga*
Is it near/far?	*E latalata/mamao?*
(Go) straight ahead.	*Alu (sa'o lava).*
(Turn) left	*(Liliu) itu tauagavale.*
(Turn) right	*(Liliu) taumatau.*

at the traffic lights	*i moli auala*
at the next/second/ third corner	*i le isi tulimanu/lona lua/lona tolu*
up/down	*luga/lalo*
behind/opposite	*tua/fa'afeagai*
east/west	*sasae/sisifo*
north/south	*matu/saute*
here/there/ everywhere	*i/io/soo se me'a*

Useful Signs

Campground	*Fanua e tolauapi ai*
Entrance	*Ulufale*
Exit	*Ulufafo*
Full	*Tumu*
Gents/Ladies	*Tane/Fafine*
Guesthouse	*Fale mo malo*
Hotel	*Fale talimalo*
Information	*Fa'amatalaga*
Open/Closed	*Tatala/Tapuni*
Police	*Leoleo*
Police Station	*Ofisa o leoleo*
Prohibited	*Fa'asa*
Do Not Enter	*Ua sa*
Rooms Available	*Potu avanoa*
Toilets	*Fale'ese*
Youth Hostel	*Fale nofo tumau*

Around Town

Where is the/a …?	*O fea le/se …?*
bank	*faletupe*
exchange office	*ofisa suitupe*
city centre	*nofoaga autu o le a'ai*
embassy	*ofisa o le amapasa*
entrance/exit	*ulufale/ulufafo*
hospital	*falemai*
market	*maketi*
police	*leoleo*
post office	*falemeli*
public toilet	*fale'ese faitele*
restaurant	*fale'aiga*
store	*faleoloa*
telephone office	*ofisi telefoni*
tourist information office	*ofisa a fa'amatalaga ta'u turisi*
I want to make a telephone call.	*E fia fai la'u telefoni.*

I'd like to change some money/ travellers cheques.	*E Fia sui a'u tupe/ siaki malaga.*

beach	*matafaga*
bridge	*ala laupapa*
cathedral	*malumalu*
church	*falesa*
hospital	*falemai*
island	*motu*
lake	*vaituloto*
laundry	*tagamea*
sea	*sami*

Accommodation

I'm looking for ...	*O lo'o ta'u su'e ...*
the camping ground	*nofoaga e tolauapi ai*
a hotel	*fale talimalo*
a guesthouse	*fale e mautotogi ai*
the manager/owner	*le pule/po'o le ona*

What's the address?	*O le a le tuatusi?*
Do you have a ... available?	*O i ai sau ... o avanoa?*
bed	*moega*
cheap room	*potu taugofie*
single/double room	*potu toatasi/toalua*
for one/two nights	*mo le tasi/lua po*

How much is it per night/person?	*E fia i le po/tagata?*
Is service/breakfast included?	*O aofia ai mea uma/ taumafataga o le taeao?*
Can I see the room?	*E mafai ona ou va'ai i le potu?*
Where is the toilet?	*Fea le fale'ese?*
It's dirty/noisy/ expensive.	*E palapala/pisa/ taugata.*
I'm/We're leaving now.	*O le a/matou o nei.*
Do you have ...?	*E i ai sau ...?*
a clean sheet	*'ie afu mama*
hot water	*vai vevela*
the key	*le ki*
a shower	*fale taele*

Plants & Animals

bird	*manulele*
chicken	*moa*
fish	*ia*
flower	*fuamatala*
mosquito	*namu*
pig	*pua'a*

Food & Drink

I'm hungry/thirsty.	*Ua ou fia ai/fia inu.*
I'd like the set lunch, please.	*Aumai se aiga masani o le aoauli fa'amolemole.*
I'm a vegetarian.	*Ou te le ai i aano o manu.*
I don't eat ...	*Ou te le 'ai ...*
I'd like some ...	*Aumai sau ... ma.*
Another, please.	*Se isi fa'amolemole.*

food	*mea taumafa*
breakfast	*aiga o le taeao*
lunch	*aiga o le aoauli*
dinner	*aiga o le po*
set menu	*mea'ai masani*
food stall	*fale'aiga fa'atau*
grocery store	*fale'oloa o mea'ai*
market	*maketi*
restaurant	*fale'aiga*
beer	*pia*
bread	*fala'oa*
chicken	*moa*
coffee	*kofe*
eggs	*fuamoa*
fish	*i'a*
fruit	*fuala'au aina*
liquor	*ava malosi*
meat	*fasi povi*
milk	*susu*
mineral water	*vai mama*
pepper	*pepa fai mea'ai*
pork	*fasi pua'a*
salt	*masima*
soup	*supo*
sugar	*suka*
tea	*ti*
vegetables	*fuala'au fai mea'ai*
water	*vai*
wine	*uaina*
hot/cold	*vevela/malulu*
with/without	*i ai fa'atasi/e leai se*

Shopping

How much is it?	*E fia le ta'u?*
I'd like to buy it.	*Ou te fia fa'atauina.*
It's too expensive.	*Taugata mo a'u.*
Can I look at it?	*E mafai ona ou va'ai i ai?*
I'm just looking.	*Sei ou matamata.*
I'm looking for …	*O lo'o su'e …*
the chemist	*fale talavai*
clothing	*lavalava*
souvenirs	*mea fa'amanatu*

Do you have another colour/size?	*E i ai se isi lanu/lapoa?*
big/bigger	*lapo'a/lapo'a atu*
small/smaller	*laititi/laititi teisi*
more/less	*tele/iti'iti*
cheap/cheaper	*taugofie/taugofie atu*

Other Useful Words & Phrases

bad	*leaga*
beautiful	*manaia*
fine	*manuia*
good	*lelei*
happy	*fiafia*
house	*fale*
journey	*malaga*
love	*alofa*
rain	*timu*
sun	*la*
village	*nu'u*
wind	*savili*

Health & Emergencies

Help!	*Fia ola*
Go away!	*Alu ese*
Call a doctor/the police.	*Vili se foma'i/leoleo.*
I'm allergic to penicillin/antiobiotics.	*Ele aoga ia te a'u tui penisini/vaila'au.*
I'm diabetic/epileptic/asthmatic.	*Ou te ma'i suka/ma'i maliu/ma'i sela.*

antiseptic	*vaila'au*
aspirin	*fuala'au aspirin*
condoms	*pa'u fai aiga*
contraceptive	*faiga e le ma'ito ai*
diarrhoea	*manava tata*
medicine	*vaila'au*

nausea	*fa'afaufau*
sunblock cream	*kulimi mo le vevela o le la*
tampons	*to'o o fafine*

Times & Dates

Sunday	*Aso Sa*
Monday	*Aso Gafua*
Tuesday	*Aso Lua*
Wednesday	*Aso Lulu*
Thursday	*Aso Tofi*
Friday	*Aso Faraile*
Saturday	*Aso Toana'i*

January	*Ianuari*
February	*Fepuari*
March	*Mati*
April	*Aperila*
May	*Me*
June	*Iuni*
July	*Iulai*
August	*Aukuso*
September	*Setema*
October	*Oketopa*
November	*Novema*
December	*Tesema*

What time is it?	*Ua ta le fia?*
It's …	*Ua ta le …*
1.15	*kuata e te'a ai le tasi*
1.30	*afa le tasi*
1.45	*kuata i le lua*
in the morning	*i le taeao*
in the evening	*i le afi'afi*

Numbers

1	*tasi*
2	*lua*
3	*tolu*
4	*fa*
5	*lima*
6	*ono*
7	*fitu*
8	*valu*
9	*iva*
10	*sefulu*
11	*sefulu-asi*
12	*sefulu-a*

13	*sefulu-tolu*	110	*selau sefulu*
20	*lua sefulu*	111	*selau sefulu-tasi*
21	*lua sefulu-tasi*	200	*lua selau*
30	*tolu sefulu*	1000	*afe*
40	*fa sefulu*	10,000	*sefulu afe*
100	*selau*	100,000	*selau afe*
101	selau tasi	one million	*tasi le miliona*

Facts for the Visitor

This chapter contains information relevant to both Samoas. For information specific to one or the other, such as details about visas, customs, money, etc, see the Facts for the Visitor chapter relating to the country or territory concerned.

PLANNING
When to Go

Weatherwise, the most comfortable time to visit the Samoas is between May and October, during the dry season. June, July and August are the driest months, December and January the wettest. See Climate in the Facts about the Region chapter for more detailed weather information.

Some of the more popular festivals are held towards the end of the year – the Teuila Festival, a week-long event featuring sporting competitions, music and dance, takes places in mid-September in Apia, Independent Samoa. In both Samoas the well-attended *fa'afafine* contests (see the Society & Conduct section in the previous chapter) are held from October onwards. See also Special Events in the regional Facts for the Visitor chapter and Activities later in this chapter.

What Kind of Trip?

Travelling solo through the Samoas is relatively safe and hassle-free but if it's solitude you're after you'd probably do better to head for the highlands of Scotland. Samoans are extremely social, family-orientated people who find it difficult to understand why anyone would deliberately choose to spend their time alone. Visitors walking by themselves in the streets may even be joined by total strangers who feel it their obligation to keep them company. (This won't happen in Pago Pago, however, where the locals have grown far too cool these days to even wave).

Organised tours can be an excellent way of learning about a place and seeing some of the best bits of a country, particularly in a place like Samoa which demands a certain amount of cultural awareness from visitors. Independent Samoa offers a number of interesting tours which focus on natural history and various 'eco-friendly' outdoor activities. See Organised Tours in the Getting Around chapter for a list of options.

Many visitors include Samoa as part of a wider tour of Pacific islands (most often Tonga and Fiji) and if you have the time and money to do so, it's a great way to get an insight into very different and rapidly changing island cultures. For suggestions see the Getting There & Away chapter.

Anyone going to the Samoas for more than just a short break should consider visiting both Independent and American Samoa – not only for the stunning scenery they both offer but for the opportunity to witness an ancient culture evolving in different directions. Though there are enough sights to see and things to do on the islands to keep you going for weeks if not months, most visitors will want to spend some time contemplating the state of Polynesia from beneath a palm tree. You might also consider seeing what a traditional healer can do for you.

Maps

The most up-to-date map of Independent Samoa is the 1:195,000 map published by South Pacific Maps in 1996 and distributed worldwide through Hema Maps (☎ 07-3290 0322; fax 07-3290 0478), PO Box 2660, Logan City DC 4114, Brisbane, Australia. The Visitors Bureau in Apia sells copies of the Hema map for ST10.

Local maps can also be purchased at the Department of Lands, Surveys & Environment, next to the New Zealand High Commission on Beach Rd, Apia. They will provide as concise topographic sheets as are available for around ST5 each. The department should also have copies of the NZ Department of Survey and Land's 1:250,000 map covering both Samoas.

The University of Hawaii publishes a larger scale map of both Samoas. In Apia, you can sometimes buy it at Aggie's Gift Shop; in Pago Pago, try the Transpac Store at the Nu'uuli Shopping Centre. The National Park Service publishes a very good map and guide to American Samoa. It's available from the National Park Visitor Information Centre (☎ 684-633 7082; fax 684-633 7084; NPSA-Administration@nps.gov), Pago Plaza, Pago Pago, American Samoa 96799-5137.

The US Geological Survey (USGS) mapping for American Samoa is available through the USGS, (fax 303-202 4693; infoservices@usgs.gov) PO Box 25286, Denver Federal Bldg, Denver, CO 80225, USA. For a catalogue of available US government nautical mapping for American Samoa, contact the National Ocean Service (☎ 1-800-638 8972), Distribution Division, Riverdale, Maryland 20737-1199, USA.

What to Bring

Given the consistently warm temperatures of the Samoas, the variety of clothing you'll need to bring can be kept to a minimum. Shorts (the knee-length, baggy variety) for men and knee-length cotton skirts for women, light cotton shirts and trousers, a beach towel, a hat, flip-flops (thongs), walking shoes, a swimsuit and a jumper, flannel shirt or light jacket will be about all anyone will need. This wardrobe can be supplemented as necessary at the Korean shops in Pago Pago or several inexpensive clothing stores around Apia.

Personal items such as sunblock cream, tampons, toothpaste, contraceptives, mosquito repellent and shampoos should probably be brought from home since the availability, quality and price of such things may be unpredictable. Film and camera equipment is also best brought from home, although US prices on some items are available in Pago Pago. A few paperbacks to read on the beach, a torch for exploring caves, a Swiss Army Knife, a universal-type drain plug, snorkelling equipment and rain gear will also be very useful.

If you're planning to camp out (there's nowhere much but a few official camp sites) or travel by ferry between Apia and Pago Pago, a sleeping bag and ground cover are essential. Music fans may also want to carry a tape recorder to record some of the magnificent Samoan voices and musical talent. Bring your own batteries, however, as they're quite expensive here, especially in Independent Samoa.

SUGGESTED ITINERARIES

Depending on the length of your stay and your particular interests, you might want to see and do the following things:

One week
  Tour the 'Big Island of Savai'i' – include an overnight stop in the banyan tree at Falealupo, a couple of days on the beach at Tanu or Satuiatua and a hike on the Tafua Peninsula

Two weeks
  Add to the above: a visit to Manono Island, an excursion into the Uafato Rainforest Conservation Area on Upolu, a couple of days on the beach at Aleipata and a visit to the Sa'anapu/Sataoa Mangrove Conservation Area.

Three weeks
  Extend any of the above and/or add: two or three days hiking in the Aopo Cloudforest Conservation Area on Savai'i or in the O Le Pupu-Pu'e National Park on Upolu.

One month
  Add to the above: a visit to the islands of Aunu'u and Ofu in American Samoa.

Two months
  Extend any of the above and add: a visit to the remote island of Ta'u and a tour of Tutuila. Consider touring the islands and then returning to your favourite spot.

HIGHLIGHTS

The following items are among Samoa's top attractions for visitors. These are, of course, in addition to the Samoan hospitality that so pleasantly pervades all the islands:

- Aleipata Beaches, Upolu, Independent Samoa – the place to go for some of the whitest sand and clearest water in the Samoas.
- Aunu'u Island, American Samoa – a beautiful and unusual island which presents a different face of American Samoa, just a few minutes by boat from Tutuila. Don't miss the lake of red quicksand, the crater lake full of eels and Ma'ama'a Cove, a wild cauldron of surf.

- Falealupo Peninsula, Savai'i, Independent Samoa – a remote area combining lovely wild beaches with a beautiful rainforest reserve which protects Samoa's unique vegetation as well as flying foxes and a variety of birds. An aerial walkway takes you through the rainforest canopy and up into a banyan tree.
- Fatumea Pool, Piula, Upolu, Independent Samoa – a clean freshwater cave pool which offers a cool and refreshing break on a hot day.
- Mt Matavanu, Savai'i, Independent Samoa – a gaping crater, which made its debut in 1911, and makes a wonderful and impressive day walk.
- Mulivai Waterways, Upolu, Independent Samoa – where an exotic tangle of freshwater streams meets the salt water and creates a unique region of rainforest and mangrove wetlands.
- Palolo Deep Marine Reserve, Upolu, Independent Samoa – a favourite with snorkellers, right on Apia's doorstep.
- Papaseea Sliding Rock, Upolu, Independent Samoa – an all-natural slippery slide which is better than Disneyland and just minutes from central Apia.
- Pulemelei Mound and Olemoe Falls, Savai'i, Independent Samoa – Polynesia's largest ancient monument and Samoa's most beautiful waterfall and tropical pool are to be found on the Letolo plantation on Savai'i.
- South Ofu Beach, Manu'a, American Samoa – art of the National Park of American Samoa, it offers the finest snorkelling in the territory. Some judge it to be the most beautiful beach in the world and it certainly is a contender.
- Tafua Rainforest Reserve, Savai'i, Independent Samoa – this reserve shelters a large colony of flying foxes and is also the last stronghold of the Samoan tooth-billed pigeon. There are several good walking tracks which would be ideal for day hikes.
- Taga Blowholes, Savai'i, Independent Samoa – among the world's largest and most impressive marine blowholes.
- The Robert Louis Stevenson Museum and Mt Vaea Scenic Reserve, Upolu, Independent Samoa – the exquisitely restored home of Robert Louis Stevenson, surrounded by gardens and forest and overlooked by Mt Vaea where the Stevenson's are buried.

INFORMATION

For information on Tourist Offices, Visas & Documents, Embassies, Customs, Money and on Post & Communications, see the Facts for the Visitor chapters for both Independent Samoa and American Samoa.

BOOKS

Most books are published in different editions by different publishers in different countries. As a result, a book might be a hardcover rarity in one country while it's readily available in paperback in another. Fortunately, bookshops and libraries search by title or author, so your local bookshop or library is best placed to advise you on the availability of the following recommendations. For information about bookshops and libraries in the Samoas, refer to the Independent Samoa and American Samoa Facts for the Visitor chapters.

Lonely Planet

If you'll be wandering beyond the Samoas in the Pacific, Lonely Planet also publishes books on Tahiti & French Polynesia, Fiji, Rarotonga & the Cook Islands, Vanuatu, New Caledonia, Tonga, Micronesia, the Solomon Islands, Papua New Guinea and New Zealand. The Galápagos Islands and Easter Island are covered in detail in the guides to Ecuador and Chile, respectively.

Guidebooks

Exploring Tropical Islands and Seas, by Fredric Martini, contains only bare-bones information about island groups. The real emphasis is on the natural history and environmental aspects of tropical islands in the Atlantic and Pacific. It is highly recommended. *Adventuring in the Pacific*, by Susana Margolis, isn't Sierra Club's best publication and contains very little meaty practical information about 'adventuring'. The National Park of American Samoa merits a small chapter of its own in the Sierra Club's parks guide *California, Hawaii & American Samoa*.

Travel

Transit of Venus – Travels in the Pacific, by Julian Evans, is a well-written account of the author's shoestring travels around the Pacific by boat and ship. It includes a very entertaining chapter on the Samoas and is probably the best modern travelogue about the Pacific.

The Pacific, by Simon Winchester, is an amusing but rather hastily assembled account of his journalistic travels around the great ocean.

Along similar lines is the book travellers love to hate, *The Happy Isles of Oceania – Paddling the Pacific* by Paul Theroux. This time, the perpetually miserable Theroux finds himself kayaking around in the South Pacific islands. Because his brother had served as a Peace Corps volunteer on Savai'i, Theroux gives the Samoas particularly high billing. Cynics will love the amusingly downbeat prose; Theroux's observations all seem to have been made through grey-coloured glasses and he utterly fails to notice any of the Samoas' favourable aspects. Just as well – in the end he concludes that thoroughly American Hawaii is the only real paradise on earth and he goes home.

A slightly earlier account of travel through the South Seas is *Slow Boats Home*, by Gavin Young. This is the sequel to his earlier *Slow Boats to China*. The two boooks recount the author's 1979 around-the-world voyage via a wide range of maritime transport. His witty and well-observed chapter on the Samoas is especially worthwhile.

Gavin Bell's *In Search of Tusitala – Travels in the Pacific after Robert Louis Stevenson* retraces the principal South Sea voyages of the Scottish writer, who settled on Upolu during the final four years of his life. Winner of the 1995 Thomas Cook/*Daily Telegraph* Travel Book Award, Bell's book succeeds in revealing something of Stevenson himself as well as the essential spirit of the islands that so captivated him.

History & Biography

The Fatal Impact, by Alan Moorehead, critically assesses the havoc wreaked on the Pacific by early European explorers and fortune-seekers. Although it doesn't deal with the Samoas directly, the issues are certainly relevant. *Slavers in Paradise*, by HE Maude, gives an enlightening account of the tragic events surrounding the kidnapping of Pacific islanders by the Peruvian slave traders in the early 1860s.

Samoa – A Hundred Years Ago and Long Before, by George Turner of the London Missionary Society, was first printed in Britain in 1884 and gives an interesting rundown of the myths, legends and social structure of the Samoan islands before the onslaught of outside influences. *Lagaga – A Short History of Western Samoa*, by Malama Meleisea and other contributors, is the definitive work and the best available source of information about the history of Independent Samoa, made even more credible by its Samoan authorship. It covers in detail the legends and prehistory of the country as well as the period of European influence. The same author has also written *The Making of Modern Samoa* which concentrates on traditional authority and colonial administration in Independent Samoa. *The War in Samoa, 1892: A Footnote to History*, by Robert Louis Stevenson, is the author's observations of the political unrest in Samoa in the early 1890s. *Amerika Samoa and its Naval Administration*, by Captain JAC Gray, is an interesting account of the years the territory was governed by the US Navy.

A Dream of Islands, by Gavan Dawes, deals with the lives and perspectives of island-inspired authors and artists, including Robert Louis Stevenson, who loved the Samoas. *Queen Emma*, by RW Robson, is an interesting biography of the daughter of a Samoan mother and an American father, who left the Samoas for New Britain Island in Papua New Guinea and there became an entrepreneur, landowner and pillar of high society, thus earning the title of 'Queen'.

Aggie Grey of Samoa, by Nelson Eustis, is a biography of the woman often called the 'first lady of Samoa' and the inspiration for Michener's 'Bloody Mary' in *Tales of the South Pacific*. This book, written in large print and short sentences, also includes a great deal of the history of Independent Samoa. *Tusitala of the South Seas*, by Joseph W Ellison, is the story of Robert Louis Stevenson, the *Tusitala* (teller of tales), and his time in the Samoas and the South Pacific. *My Samoan Chief*, by Faye Calkins Alailima, recounts the experiences of a California woman who married a Samoan man and returned with him to live in Samoa. The same author has also written *Aggie Grey – a Samoan Saga*.

Foreign Fiction

The Trembling of a Leaf, by W Somerset Maugham, is a collection of South Pacific short stories, including *Mackintosh*, *Red*, *The Pool* and the most famous, *Rain*, all of which take place in the Samoas. The protagonist of *Rain* is the infamous Sadie Thompson, whom residents of Pago Pago claim was an historical character. *Tales of the South Pacific*, *Rascals in Paradise* and *Return to Paradise*, by James Michener, are collections of short stories dealing with life in, and observations of, the South Pacific from WWII onward. Robert Louis Stevenson's novels *The Ebb-Tide* and *The Wrecker* and his short story *The Beach of Falesaá* were all written at the Vailima estate above Apia during the last four years of the author's life and they reflect well his attitudes toward the islands. All of Stevenson's South Sea fiction titles, plus a selection of prose and letters, appear in Canongate Books' *Tales of the South Seas*, edited by Jenni Calder.

Anthropology

Coming of Age in Samoa, by Margaret Mead, is perhaps the most famous work ever written about the Samoas. This controversial study was made on the island of Tau in the Manu'a group. Mead's theory was that cultural values determine adolescents' attitudes towards, and their abilities to face, the pressures of impending adulthood, particularly as they relate to sexuality, hypocrisy, education and authoritarian expectations. Although some claim that the study was tailored to fit the hypothesis, Mead found that casual attitudes toward life in Polynesian society fostered a healthy and stress-free transition from childhood to adulthood and promoted European acceptance of the age-old 'Polynesian myth' as regards sexuality in the South Sea islands.

Margaret Mead and Samoa: The Making

and Unmaking of an Anthropological Myth, by Derek Freeman, refutes Mead's study. While Freeman accuses Mead of employing flawed methods of data collection and discredits her findings on the basis of his own study, he is unable to formulate any convincing conclusions. As 50 years separates the two studies, it is unlikely that the dispute, regarding the Samoas anyway, will ever be settled to anyone's satisfaction.

Man's Conquest of the Pacific, by Peter Bellwood, discusses the arrival and migration of the Polynesian islanders from South-East Asia. Bellwood is the foremost authority on the subject.

Flora & Fauna

The *Field Guide to the Wildlife of Samoa*, by Meryl Rose Goldin, is a beautifully illustrated and very readable guide to all the indigenous creatures of Samoa (marine and terrestrial) which also includes sections on coral reefs, rainforests and the protected areas of the islands. Dr Arthur Whistler has spent more than 25 years studying the flora of the Pacific and has published a string of titles on the subject, including *Orchids of Samoa*, with Phillip Cribb; *Samoan Herbal Medicine*, an overview of the plants used and the ailments treated by traditional healers; *Wayside Plants of the Islands – a Guide to the Lowland Flora of the Pacific Islands*; *The Rainforests of Samoa* and *Flowers of the Pacific Island Seashore*.

Those interested in birdwatching in the Samoas should look out for *A Field Guide to the Birds of Hawaii and the Tropical Pacific*, by H Douglas Pratt, Phillip L Bruner and Delwyn G Berrett. Sea creatures are covered in Robert F Myers' book *Micronesian Reef Fishes – A Practical Guide to the Identification of the Coral Reef Fishes of the Tropical Central and Western Pacific*.

VIDEO SYSTEMS

If you want to record or buy video tapes to play back home, you won't get a picture if the image registration systems are different. American Samoa uses the North American and Japanese NTSC system; Independent

Samoa uses PAL which is compatible with Australian, New Zealand and European systems.

PHOTOGRAPHY & VIDEO
Film & Equipment
Film is normally more expensive in Samoa than it is in Europe, North America and Australasia so stock up before you leave home. There are photographic and processing shops only in the capitals. Remember to take spare batteries for cameras and flash units since they're quite expensive in Samoa. If you're shooting transparencies, you'll probably get the best results with Fujichrome 100, Velvia or Kodachrome 64. The cost of the film normally includes processing and you can mail the rolls to the labs in the envelopes provided. Rewrap the package to disguise it and send it registered if you don't trust the post. Useful accessories would include a small flash, a cable release, a polarising filter, a lens-cleaning kit (fluid, tissue, aerosol), and silica-gel packs to protect against humidity. Also, remember to make sure your equipment is insured.

Photography
Points worth remembering include the heat, humidity, very fine sand, tropical sunlight, equatorial shadows and the great opportunities for underwater photography. Don't leave your camera for long in direct sunlight and don't store used film for long in the humid conditions, as it will fade. The best times to take photographs on sunny days are the first two hours after sunrise and the last two before sunset. This brings out the best colours and takes advantage of the colour-enhancing long red rays cast by a low sun. At other times, colours will be washed out by harsh sunlight and glare, although it's possible to counter this by using a polarising filter.

If you're shooting on beaches, it's important to adjust for glare from water or sand; and keep your photographic equipment well away from sand and salt water. When photographing out of doors, take light readings on the subject and not the brilliant background

or your shots will all turn out underexposed. Likewise for people shots: dark faces will appear featureless if you set the exposure for background light.

You needn't invest in expensive underwater cameras in order to take shots of coral and fish – you can play around with waterproof throw-away cameras or use a standard camera with special waterproof housing and an underwater strobe flash, or on sunny days, with underwater slide film. Give preference to high shutter speeds to avoid camera shake and blurred fish. Water absorbs certain wavelengths and red filters can be used to reduce the exaggerated blue.

Video
Video cameras these days have very sensitive microphones and you might be surprised how much sound will be picked up. This can be a problem if there is a lot of ambient noise – filming by the side of a busy road might seem OK when you do it, but back home you might get a deafening cacophony of traffic noise. One good rule for beginners is to try to film in long takes, and don't move the camera around too much. If your camera has a stabiliser, you can use it to obtain good footage while travelling on various means of transport, even on bumpy roads. Make sure you keep the batteries charged and have the necessary charger, plugs and transformer for the country you are visiting. In most countries, it is possible to obtain video cartridges easily in large towns and cities, but make sure you buy the correct format. It is usually worth buying at least a few cartridges duty-free to start off your trip. Finally, remember to follow the same rules regarding people's sensitivities as for still photography – always ask permission first.

Photographing People
As in most places, the quest for the perfect 'people shot' will prove to be a photographer's greatest challenge. While many Samoans will enjoy being photographed, others will be put off and some people may be superstitious about your camera, suspicious of your motives or

simply interested in whatever economic advantage they can gain from your desire to photograph them. The main point is that you must respect the wishes of the locals, however photogenic, who may be camera shy for whatever reason. Ask permission to photograph if a candid shot can't be made and don't insist or snap a picture anyway if permission is denied. Often, people will allow you to photograph them provided you give them a photo for themselves, a real treasure in these countries (an excellent idea is to have copies laminated before sending them back). Understandably, people are sometimes disappointed not to see the photograph immediately materialise. If you don't carry a Polaroid camera, make it clear that you'll have to take their address and send the photo by post once it's processed. Photographing people, particularly dark-skinned people, requires more skill than snapping landscapes. Make sure you take the light reading from the subject's face, not the background. It also requires more patience and politeness.

TIME

Time really doesn't move more slowly in the South Pacific but it certainly seems that way. Sometimes – on Sundays for instance – it can even appear to grind to a halt. Visitors will need to get accustomed to an entirely different set of rules regarding punctuality. If a Samoan agrees to meet you at 9 am, you may be waiting until noon, three hours being a perfectly acceptable margin of lateness in the islands. Nothing is so pressing, they reason, that one should become flustered or inconvenienced. If it is not worth doing, it can wait until later, or even until tomorrow. If not worth doing, it can be conveniently forgotten.

The Samoas lie just east of the International Dateline, which means their dates are the same as those of North America. The local time is GMT/UTC minus 11 hours. Therefore, noon in the Samoas is 11 pm the same day in London; 3 pm the same day in Los Angeles; and 9 am the following day in Sydney.

WEIGHTS & MEASURES

While Independent Samoa uses the standard metric system, American Samoa uses the American version of the Imperial system, including miles, feet, inches for distances and measurements; the Fahrenheit scale for temperatures; and US pints, quarts and gallons for volume. For conversion information, see the table inside the back cover of this book.

TOILETS

Public toilets in Samoa are few and far between. In Apia and Pago Pago you'll probably have to rely on hotels, restaurants and cafes; if you're travelling off the beaten track you may, on occasion, have to nip behind a banyan tree (coconut trees can be hazardous due to falling coconuts). Though all toilets are of the Western sit-down variety, many villages won't have flush toilets (water is supplied in a separate container). Carry spare toilet paper with you. Sustainable development projects in several villages include the establishment of composting toilets.

HEALTH

Samoa is generally a healthy place for locals and visitors alike. Food and water are good, fresh, clean and readily available, there are few endemic diseases and the most serious problem that visitors are likely to experience is sunburn. Nevertheless, it never hurts to know some basic travel-health rules. Travel health depends on your predeparture preparations, your daily health care while travelling and how you handle any medical problem that does develop. Though basic medical care is available in the Samoas, travellers who come down with anything serious are advised to make arrangements to get to Hawaii, New Zealand or Australia. For more information about local services, see the following Medical Problems and Treatment section and under Health in the individual country Facts for the Visitor chapters.

Travel Health Guides

There are a number of books on travel health:

Staying Healthy in Asia, Africa & Latin America,
Dirk Schroeder, Moon Publications, 1994. Probably the best all-round guide to carry; it's compact, detailed and well organised.

Travellers' Health, Dr Richard Dawood, Oxford University Press, 1995. Comprehensive, easy to read, authoritative and highly recommended, although it's rather large to lug around.

Travel with Children, Maureen Wheeler, Lonely Planet Publications, 1995. Includes advice on health for those travelling with younger children.

There are also a number of excellent travel health sites on the Internet. There are links from the Lonely Planet home page (lonely planet.com/health/health.htm/h-links.htm) to the World Health Organisation, the US Center for Diseases Control & Prevention and Stanford University Travel Medicine Service.

Predeparture Planning

Health Insurance A travel insurance policy to cover theft, personal liability, loss and medical problems is a must. There is a wide variety of policies available and your travel agent will have recommendations. The international student travel policies handled by STA Travel or any other student travel organisations are usually good value. Some policies offer lower and higher medical-expense options – go as high as you can afford. Check the small print. Some policies specifically exclude 'dangerous activities' such as scuba diving, motorcycling or even trekking. A policy that pays doctors or hospitals directly may be preferable to one where you pay on the spot and claim later. If you have to claim later, make sure you keep all documentation. Some policies ask you to call back (reverse charges) to a centre in your home country where an immediate assessment of your problem is made. Check that the policy covers ambulances or helicopter rescue and an emergency flight home. If you have to stretch out you will need two seats and somebody has to pay for them!

Medical Kit Consider taking a basic medical kit including:

- Aspirin or paracetamol (acetaminophen in the US) for pain or fever.
- Antihistamine (such as Benadryl) – useful as a decongestant for colds and allergies, to ease the itch from insect bites or stings, and to help prevent motion sickness. Antihistamines may cause sedation and interact with alcohol so care should be taken when using them; take one you know and have used before, if possible.
- Antibiotics – useful if you're travelling well off the beaten track but they must be prescribed; carry the prescription with you. Ideally, antibiotics should be administered only under medical supervision and should never be taken indiscriminately. Overuse of antibiotics can weaken your body's ability to deal with infections naturally and can reduce the drug's efficacy on future occasions. Take only the recommended dose at the prescribed interval and continue using the antibiotic for the prescribed period, even if the illness seems to be cured earlier. Antibiotics are quite specific to the infections they are prescribed for. Stop taking them immediately if there are any serious reactions and don't use one at all if you are unsure that you have the correct one.
- Loperamide (eg Imodium) or Lomotil for diarrhoea; prochlorperazine (eg Stemetil) or metaclopramide (eg Maxalon) for nausea and vomiting.
- Rehydration mixture – for treatment of severe diarrhoea; particularly important for travelling with children.
- Antiseptic such as povidone-iodine (eg Betadine) – for cuts and grazes.
- Multivitamins – especially for long trips when dietary vitamin intake may be inadequate.
- Calamine lotion or aluminium sulphate spray (eg Stingose) – to ease irritation from bites or stings.
- Bandages and Band-aids.
- Scissors, tweezers and a thermometer (note that mercury thermometers are prohibited by airlines).
- Insect repellent, sunscreen, chap stick and water purification tablets.

Health Preparations Make sure you're healthy before you start travelling. If you are going on a long trip make sure your teeth are OK. If you wear glasses take a spare pair and your prescription. If you require a particular medication take an adequate supply, as it may not be available locally. Take part of the packaging showing the generic name, rather than the brand, which will make getting replacements easier. It's a good idea to have a legible prescription or letter from your doctor, to show that you legally use the medication, to avoid any problems.

Immunisations No vaccinations are required for entry into the Samoas unless you are arriving from an area infected with yellow fever. Most travellers from Western countries will have been immunised against various diseases during childhood but your doctor may still recommend booster shots against measles or polio, diseases still prevalent in many developing countries. Plan ahead for getting your vaccinations: some of them require more than one injection, while some vaccinations should not be given together. It is recommended you seek medical advice at least six weeks before travel. Record all vaccinations on an International Health Certificate, available from your doctor or government health department. Discuss your requirements with your doctor, but vaccinations you might consider include:

- *Hepatitis A* The most common travel-acquired illness after diarrhoea which can put you out of action for weeks. Havrix 1440 is a vaccination which provides long term immunity (possibly more than 10 years) after an initial injection and a booster at six to 12 months. Gamma globulin is not a vaccination but is ready-made antibody collected from blood donations. It should be given close to departure because, depending on the dose, it only protects for two to six months.

- *Typhoid* This is an important vaccination to have where hygiene is a problem. Available either as an injection or oral capsules.

- *Diphtheria & Tetanus* Diphtheria can be a fatal throat infection and tetanus can be a fatal wound infection. Everyone should have these vaccinations. After an initial course of three injections, boosters are necessary every 10 years.

- *Hepatitis B* This disease is spread by blood or by sexual activity. Travellers who should consider a hepatitis B vaccination include those visiting countries where there are known to be many carriers, where blood transfusions may not be adequately screened or where sexual contact is a possibility. It involves three injections, the quickest course being over three weeks with a booster at 12 months.

- *Polio* Polio is a serious, easily transmitted disease, still prevalent in many developing countries. Everyone should keep up to date with this vaccination. A booster every 10 years maintains immunity.

Basic Rules
Care in what you eat and drink is the most important health rule; stomach upsets are the most likely travel problem, but the majority of these upsets will be relatively minor. Don't become paranoid; trying the local food is part of the experience of travel.

Water The main water supply in Pago Pago, American Samoa, is OK to drink. Village water, however, isn't treated and should be avoided. Bottled water is widely available. In Independent Samoa, *don't drink the water* and that includes ice. If you don't know for certain that the water is safe assume the worst. Reputable brands of bottled water or soft drinks are generally fine, although in some places bottles may be refilled with tap water. Only use water from containers with a serrated seal – not tops or corks. Take care with fruit juice, particularly if water may have been added. In hot climates you should always make sure you drink enough – don't rely on feeling thirsty to indicate when you should drink. Not needing to urinate or very dark-yellow urine is a danger sign. Excessive sweating is another problem and can lead to loss of salt and therefore to muscle cramping.

Water Purification The simplest way of purifying water is to boil it thoroughly but you should consider purchasing a water filter for a long trip. There are two main kinds of filter. Total filters take out all parasites, bacteria and viruses and make water safe to drink. They are often expensive but they can be more cost effective than buying bottled water. Simple filters (which can even be a nylon mesh bag) take out dirt and larger foreign bodies from the water so that chemical solutions work much more effectively; if water is dirty, chemical solutions may not work at all. It's very important when buying a filter to read the specifications so that you know exactly what it removes from the water and what it doesn't. Simple filtering will not remove all dangerous organisms so if you cannot boil water it should be treated chemically. Chlorine tablets (Puritabs, Steritabs or other brand names) will kill many pathogens but not some parasites like giardia and amoebic cysts. Iodine is more effective in purifying water and is available in tablet form (such as Potable Aqua). Follow the directions carefully and remember that too much iodine can be harmful.

Food There is an old colonial adage which says: 'If you can cook it, boil it or peel it you can eat it ... otherwise forget it'. Vegetables and fruit should be washed with purified water or peeled where possible. Beware of icecream which is sold in the street or anywhere it might have been melted and refrozen; if there's any doubt (eg a power cut in the last day or two) steer well clear. Shellfish such as mussels, oysters and clams should be avoided as well as undercooked meat, particularly in the form of mince. Steaming does not make shellfish safe for eating. If a place looks clean and well run and the vendor also looks clean and healthy, then the food is probably safe. In general, places that are packed with travellers or locals will be fine, while empty restaurants are questionable. The food in busy restaurants is cooked and eaten quite quickly with little standing around and is probably not reheated.

Ciguatera The ciguatera toxin is found in some predatory fish, especially on reefs which have been upset by dredging or storms. The toxin is contained in algae, which is eaten by the smaller reef fish, which are in turn the prey of larger fish. The larger the fish the more likely it is to have higher concentrations built up over its lifetime. It is best to avoid eating big reef predators such as snapper, barracuda and groupers. Pelagic (open ocean) fish such as tuna, wahoo and mackerel are safe to eat. Diarrhoea, muscle and joint aches and pains, numbness and tingling around the mouth, hands and feet,

nausea, vomiting, chills, headaches, sweating and dizziness can all be symptoms of ciguatera poisoning. Seek medical attention if you experience any of these after eating fish. It's always wise to seek local advice before eating reef fish as any ciguatera outbreak will be well known.

Medical Problems & Treatment
Potential medical problems can be broken down into several areas. Firstly there are the problems caused by extremes of temperature or motion. Then there are diseases and illnesses caused by insanitation, insect bites or stings and animal or human contact. Simple cuts, bites and scratches can also cause problems. Self-diagnosis and treatment can be risky so wherever possible seek qualified help. Although we do give treatment dosages in this section, they are for emergency use only. Medical advice should be sought whenever possible before administering any drugs.

Medical care is limited in the Samoas and the type of care and standards of sanitation you're probably accustomed to in your home country simply aren't available. The LBJ Tropical Medical Centre in Pago Pago, American Samoa, was once highly regarded as the finest facility in the tropical Pacific, but staffing problems have taken their toll and it can now provide only marginal service.

In Independent Samoa, there is the large National Hospital in Apia and a fairly extensive system of rural hospitals, but they lack the staff and medications to treat anything but minor injuries and illnesses. There are private physicians in both Samoas but they will charge more than the hospital clinics. Travellers who come down with anything serious should make arrangements to get to Hawaii, New Zealand or Australia. Make sure your health insurance covers you for emergency transport out of the Samoas.

Environmental Hazards
Sunburn In the tropics you can get sunburnt surprisingly quickly, even through cloud. Use a sunscreen and take extra care to cover

areas which don't normally see sun – eg your feet. A hat provides added protection and you should also use zinc cream or some other barrier cream for your nose and lips. Take special care in situations where a cool breeze may disguise the power of the sun, such as when riding around in an open 4WD vehicle or travelling in an open boat. Calamine lotion is good for mild sunburn. Protect your eyes with good quality sunglasses.

Prickly Heat Prickly heat is an itchy rash caused by excessive perspiration trapped under the skin. It usually strikes people who have just arrived in a hot climate. Keeping cool, bathing often, drying the skin and using a mild talcum or prickly heat powder or resorting to air-conditioning may help until you acclimatise.

Heat Exhaustion Dehydration or salt deficiency can cause heat exhaustion. Take time to acclimatise to high temperatures, drink sufficient liquids and do not do anything too physically demanding. Wear loose clothing and a broad-brimmed hat. Salt deficiency is characterised by fatigue, lethargy, headaches, giddiness and muscle cramps and in this case salt tablets may help. Vomiting or diarrhoea can deplete your liquid and salt levels. Anhydrotic heat exhaustion, caused by an inability to sweat, is quite rare. Unlike other forms of heat exhaustion it is likely to strike people who have been in a hot climate for some time, rather than newcomers.

Heat Stroke This serious and sometimes fatal condition can occur if the body's heat-regulating mechanism breaks down and the body temperature rises to dangerous levels. Long, continuous periods of exposure to high temperatures and insufficient fluids can leave you vulnerable to heat stroke. You should drink lots of water and avoid excessive alcohol or strenuous activity when you first arrive in a hot climate. The symptoms are feeling unwell, not sweating very much (or at all) and a high body temperature (39°C to 41°C or 102°F to 106°F). Where sweating has ceased the skin becomes flushed and red.

Severe, throbbing headaches and lack of coordination will also occur and the sufferer may be confused or aggressive. Eventually the victim will become delirious or convulse. Hospitalisation is essential but, in the interim, get victims out of the sun, remove their clothing, cover them with a wet sheet or towel and then fan continually. Give fluids if they are conscious.

Fungal Infections Fungal infections occur more commonly in hot weather and are usually found on the scalp, between the toes or fingers (athlete's foot), in the groin (jock itch or crotch rot) and on the body (ringworm). You get ringworm (which is a fungal infection, not a worm) from infected animals or by walking on damp areas, like shower floors. To prevent fungal infections wear loose, comfortable clothes (avoid wearing artificial fibres), wash frequently and dry carefully. If you do get an infection, wash the infected area daily with a disinfectant or medicated soap and water and rinse and dry well. Apply an antifungal cream or powder like the widely available Tinaderm. Try to expose the infected area to air or sunlight as much as possible, wash all towels and underwear in hot water and change them often.

Motion Sickness Eating lightly before and during a trip will reduce the chances of motion sickness. If you are prone to motion sickness try to find a place that minimises movement – near the wing on aircraft, close to midships on boats, near the centre on buses. Fresh air usually helps; reading and cigarette smoke don't. Commercial motion-sickness preparations, which can cause drowsiness, have to be taken before the trip commences. Ginger (available in capsule form) and peppermint (including mint-flavoured sweets) are natural preventatives.

Jet Lag Jet lag is experienced when a person travels by air across more than three time zones (each time zone usually represents a one-hour time difference). It occurs because many of the functions of the human body (such as temperature, pulse rate and emptying of the bladder and bowels) are regulated by internal 24-hour cycles. When we travel long distances rapidly, our bodies take time to adjust to the 'new time' of our destination, and so we may experience fatigue, disorientation, insomnia, anxiety, impaired concentration and loss of appetite. These effects will usually be gone within three days of arrival, but to minimise the impact of jet lag:

- Rest for a couple of days prior to departure.
- Try to select flight schedules that minimise sleep deprivation; arriving late in the day means you can go to sleep soon after you arrive. For very long flights, try to organise a stopover.
- Avoid excessive eating (which bloats the stomach) and alcohol (which causes dehydration) during the flight. Instead, drink plenty of non-carbonated, non-alcoholic drinks such as fruit juice or water.
- Avoid smoking.
- Make yourself comfortable by wearing loose-fitting clothes and perhaps bringing an eye mask and ear plugs to help you sleep.
- Try to sleep at the appropriate time for the time zone you are travelling to.

Infectious Diseases

Diarrhoea A change of water, food or climate can all cause a mild bout of the runs; diarrhoea caused by contaminated food or water is more serious. Despite all your precautions you may still get a mild bout of travellers' diarrhoea, but a few rushed toilet trips with no other symptoms is not indicative of a major problem. Moderate diarrhoea, involving half-a-dozen loose movements in a day, is more of a nuisance. Dehydration is the main danger with any diarrhoea, particularly in children or the elderly as dehydration can occur quite quickly. Under all circumstances *fluid replacement* (at least equal to the volume being lost) is the most important thing to remember. Weak black tea with a little sugar, soda water, or soft drinks allowed to go flat and diluted 50% with clean water are all good.

With severe diarrhoea, a rehydrating solution is preferable to replace lost minerals and salts. Commercially available oral rehydration salts (ORS) are very useful; add them to boiled or bottled water. In an emergency you can make up a solution of eight teaspoons of sugar to a litre of boiled or bottled water and provide salted cracker biscuits at the same time. Stick to a bland diet as you recover. Lomotil or Imodium can be used to bring relief from the symptoms, although they do not actually cure the problem. Only use these drugs if absolutely necessary – eg if you *must* travel. For children under 12 years Lomotil and Imodium are not recommended. Under all circumstances, fluid replacement is the most important thing to remember. Do not use these drugs if the person has a high fever or is severely dehydrated.

In certain situations antibiotics may be required: watery diarrhoea with blood or mucous; watery diarrhoea with fever and lethargy; persistent diarrhoea not improving after 48 hours; severe diarrhoea, if it is logistically difficult to stay in one place. In all these situations, gut-paralysing drugs like Imodium or Lomotil should be avoided. The recommended drugs are norfloxacin 400mg twice daily for three days or ciprofloxacin 500mg twice daily for five days. These are not recommended for children or pregnant women. The drug of choice for children would be co-trimoxazole (Bactrim, Septrin, Resprim) with dosage dependent on weight. A five day course is given. Ampicillin or amoxycillin may be given in pregnancy, but medical care is necessary.

Giardiasis The parasite causing this intestinal disorder is present in contaminated water. The symptoms are stomach cramps, nausea, a bloated stomach, watery, foul-smelling diarrhoea and frequent gas. Giardiasis can appear several weeks after you have been exposed to the parasite. The symptoms may disappear for a few days and then return; this can go on for several weeks. Tinidazole, known as Fasigyn, or metronidazole (Flagyl) are the recommended drugs. Treatment is a 2g single dose of Fasigyn or 250mg of Flagyl three times daily for five to 10 days.

Dysentery This serious illness is caused by contaminated food or water and is characterised by severe diarrhoea, often with blood or mucus in the stool. There are two kinds of dysentery. Bacillary dysentery is characterised by a high fever and rapid onset; headache, vomiting and stomach pains are other symptoms. It generally does not last longer than a week, but it is highly contagious.

Amoebic dystenery is often more gradual in the onset of symptoms, with cramping abdominal pain and vomiting less likely; fever may not be present. It will persist until treated and can recur and cause long-term health problems. A stool test is necessary to diagnose which kind of dysentery you have, so you should seek medical help urgently.

Hepatitis Hepatitis is a general term for inflammation of the liver. There are many causes of this condition: drugs, alcohol and infections are but a few. The discovery of new strains has led to a virtual alphabet soup, with hepatitis A, B, C, D, E and others. These letters identify specific agents that cause viral hepatitis. Viral hepatitiis is an infection of the liver, which can lead to jaundice (yellow skin), fever, lethargy and digestive problems. It can have no symptoms at all, with the infected person not knowing that they have the disease.

Hepatitis A Transmitted by contaminated food or water, this is a very common disease in most countries, especially those with poor standards of sanitation. Most people in developing countries are infected as children; they often don't develop symptoms, but do develop life-long immunity. The disease poses a real threat to the traveller, as people are unlikely to have been exposed to hepatitis A.

The symptoms are fever, chills, headache, nausea, vomiting, abdominal pain, dark urine, light-colored faeces, jaundiced skin and the whites of the eyes may turn yellow. You should seek medical advice, but in general there is not much you can do apart from resting, drinking lots of fluids, eating lightly and avoiding fatty foods. People who have had hepatitis must avoid alcohol for some time after the illness, as the liver needs time to recover.

Hepatitis E is a very recently discovered virus, of which little is yet known. Spread in the same way as type A, it appears to be rather common in developing countries, generally causing mild hepatitis, although it can be very serious in pregnant women. At present it doesn't appear to be too great a risk for travellers.

Hepatitis B There are almost 300 million chronic carriers of this disease in the world. Hepatitis B, which used to be called serum hepatitis, is spread through contact with infected blood, blood products or body fluids, for example through sexual contact, unsterilised needles and blood transfusions, or contact with blood via small breaks in the skin. Other risk situations include having a shave, tattoo, or having your body pierced with contaminated equipment. The symptoms of type B are much the same as type A except they are more severe and may lead to irreparable liver damage or even liver cancer. Although there is no treatment for hepatitis B, a cheap and effective vaccine is available; the only problem is that for long-lasting cover you need a six-month course. People who should receive a vaccination include those who anticipate contact with blood or other bodily secretions, either as a healthcare worker or through sexual contact with the local population and particularly those who intend to stay in the country for a long period of time.

Hepatitis D Often referred to as the 'Delta' virus, this infection only occurs in chronic carriers of hepatitis B. It is transmitted by blood and bodily fluids. The risk to travellers is certainly limited.

Typhoid Typhoid fever is a dangerous gut infection caused by contaminated water and food. Medical help must be sought. In its early stages sufferers may feel they have a bad cold or flu on the way, as early symptoms are a headache, body aches and a fever which rises a little each day until it is around 40°C (104°F) or more. The victim's pulse is often slow relative to the degree of fever present –

unlike a normal fever where the pulse increases. There may also be vomiting, abdominal pain, diarrhoea or constipation. In the second week the high fever and slow pulse continue and a few pink spots may appear on the body; trembling, delirium, weakness, weight loss and dehydration may occur. Complications such as pneumonia, perforated bowel or meningitis may occur. The fever should be treated by keeping the victims cool and giving them fluids as dehydration should also be watched for. Ciprofloxacin 750mg twice a day for 10 days is good for adults. Chloramphenicol is recommended in many countries. The adult dosage is two 250-mg capsules, four times a day. Children aged between eight and 12 years should have half the adult dose and younger children one-third the adult dose.

Worms These parasites are most common in rural, tropical areas. The different worms have different ways of infecting people. Some may be ingested on food, including undercooked meat, and some enter through your skin. Infestations may not show up for some time and, although they are generally not serious, if left untreated some can cause severe health problems later. Consider having a stool test when you return home to check for these and determine the appropriate treatment.

Sexually Transmitted Diseases

Sexual contact with an infected partner spreads these diseases. While abstinence is the only 100% preventative, using condoms is also effective. Gonorrhoea, herpes and syphilis are among these diseases; sores, blisters or rashes around the genitals, discharges or pain when urinating are common symptoms. In some STDs, such as wart virus or chlamydia, symptoms may be less marked or not observed at all, especially in women. Syphilis symptoms eventually disappear completely but the disease continues and can cause severe problems in later years. The treatment of gonorrhoea and syphilis is with antibiotics. The different sexually transmitted diseases each require specific antibiotics. There is no cure for herpes or AIDS.

HIV & AIDS

HIV, the Human Immunodeficiency Virus, develops into AIDS, Acquired Immune Deficiency Syndrome, which is a fatal disease. HIV is a major problem in many countries. Any exposure to blood, blood products or body fluids may put the individual at risk. The disease is often transmitted through sexual contact or dirty needles – vaccinations, acupuncture, tattooing and body piercing can be potentially as dangerous as intravenous drug use. HIV/AIDS can also be spread through infected blood transfusions; some developing countries cannot afford to screen blood used for transfusions. If you do need an injection, ask to see the syringe unwrapped in front of you, or take a needle and syringe pack with you. Fear of HIV infection should never preclude treatment for serious medical conditions.

Insect-Borne Diseases

Dengue Fever Malaria does not exist in the Samoas but there have been occasional outbreaks of dengue fever. Dengue can be dangerous for the eldery and can be fatal in infants. There is no prophylactic available for this mosquito-spread disease; the main preventative measure is to avoid mosquito bites. A sudden onset of fever, headaches and severe joint and muscle pains are the first signs before a rash develops on the trunk of the body and spreads to the limbs and face. After a few more days, the fever will subside and recovery will begin. The patient should rest, drink lots of water to avoid dehydration, and take codeine to ease the aches. Depression is a symptom for some and dengue sufferers are notoriously grumpy and rude to their carers. Serious complications are not common but full recovery can take up to a month or more.

Filariasis This is a mosquito-transmitted parasitic infection which is found in many parts of Africa, Asia, Central and South America and the Pacific. Though quite rare, it does occur in Samoa from time to time. There is a range of possible manifestations of the infection, depending on which filarial parasite species has caused the infection. These include fever, pain and swelling of the lymph glands; inflammation of lymph drainage areas; swelling of a limb or the scrotum; skin rashes and blindness. Treatment is available to eliminate the parasites from the body, but some of the damage they cause may not be reversible. Medical advice should be obtained promptly if the infection is suspected.

Cuts, Bites & Stings
Cuts & Scratches Any puncture of the skin can easily become infected in the tropics and may be difficult to heal. Treat any cut with an antiseptic such as povidone-iodine or other protective antiseptic cream. Where possible, avoid bandages and Band-aids which can keep wounds wet; if you have to keep a bandage on during the day to protect the wound from dirt or flies, take it off at night while you sleep to let it get air. Coral cuts are notoriously slow to heal and if they are not adequately cleaned small pieces of coral can become embedded in the wound. Avoid coral cuts by wearing reef shoes or sneakers when walking on reefs (for the sake of the coral, it's best to avoid walking on reefs altogether) and try not to touch coral when swimming or snorkelling. If you do get cut, clean the wound thoroughly, get all the coral out and keep the wound clean and disinfected until it heals. Severe pain, redness, fever or generally feeling unwell suggest infection and the need for immediate antibiotics as coral cuts may result in serious infections.

Bites & Stings Mosquito attacks can be relentless, particularly in the wet season from November to April. To protect yourself, cover the body well with clothing and use insect repellent on exposed skin – the most effective will have 100% DEET. Sleep under mosquito nets at night or burn mosquito coils. If you're going walking in humid or densely-foliated areas, wear light cotton trousers and shoes, not shorts and sandals or thongs. Bee and wasp stings are usually painful rather than dangerous. However, in people who are allergic to them, severe breathing difficulties may occur and require urgent medical care. Calamine lotion or Stingose spray will give relief and ice packs will reduce the pain and swelling. Dogs can be a problem in Samoa, but more for their bark than their bite. A few well-aimed stones should keep aggressive dogs at bay. If you are bitten by a dog, you should have a tetanus vaccination within a few hours if you haven't had one during the past three years.

Jellyfish & Other Sea Creatures Jellyfish are not a big problem in Samoa because people mostly swim in protected lagoons and jellyfish are rarely washed in from the open sea. Stings from most jellyfish are simply rather painful. Dousing in vinegar will deactivate any stingers which have not 'fired'. Ammonia is also effective, but the folk remedy, used all over the world, is to apply fresh urine to the stings as soon as possible. This also neutralises the venom. Calamine lotion, antihistamines and analgesics may reduce the reaction and relieve the pain. Poisonous stonefish are rare but extremely painful for those unfortunate enough to step on one. These ugly and well-disguised creatures lurk on the sea floor and stepping on one forces poison up spines on the dorsal fin and into the victim's foot. Wear reef shoes or sneakers while walking through the water. If you do step on a stonefish, seek medical attention because there is an antidote available. Other stinging sea creatures found in Samoan waters include flame or stinging coral, anemones, crown-of-thorns starfish and sea urchins. Certain cone shells found in the Pacific can sting dangerously or even fatally. The best precaution against stings and cuts when snorkelling is to wear gloves, long pants and shirt. Don't touch anything unfamiliar and always wear reef shoes or sneakers while walking through the water.

Women's Health
Gynaecological Problems Poor diet, lowered resistance through the use of antibiotics for

stomach upsets and even contraceptive pills can lead to vaginal infections when travelling in hot climates. Maintaining good personal hygiene and wearing loose-fitting clothes and cotton underwear will help to prevent these infections. Yeast infections, characterised by a rash, itch and discharge, can be treated with a vinegar or lemon-juice douche, or with yoghurt. The usual treatment is Nystatin, miconazole or clotrimazole pessaries or vaginal cream. Sexually transmitted diseases are a major cause of vaginal problems. Symptoms include a smelly discharge, painful intercourse and sometimes a burning sensation when urinating. Male sexual partners must also be treated. Medical attention should be sought and remember, in addition to these diseases, HIV or hepatitis B may also be acquired during exposure. Besides abstinence, the best thing is to practise safe sex using condoms.

Pregnancy Most miscarriages occur during the first three months of pregnancy, so this is the riskiest time to travel. The last three months should also be spent within reasonable distance of good medical care. A baby born as early as 24 weeks stands a chance of survival, but only in a good, modern hospital. Pregnant women should avoid all unnecessary medication and vaccinations. Additional care should be taken to prevent illness and particular attention should be paid to diet and nutrition. Women travellers often find that their periods become irregular or even cease while they're on the road. A missed period doesn't necessarily indicate pregnancy.

See also Traditional Medicine in the Society & Conduct section of Facts About the Region chapter.

WOMEN TRAVELLERS

Thanks to Western and Asian videos, which are extremely popular in the Samoas, foreign women have a reputation for easy availability, whether or not they are single. Polite refusal of sexual attention by a non-Samoan woman will probably be taken to mean 'keep trying' by a hopeful Samoan man who may

have difficulty imagining why you wouldn't be interested, given the European, Asian, African, etc, promiscuity he sees portrayed on the screen (a sort of Polynesian myth working in reverse). The Samoan word for 'no' is 'leai' and it should be used firmly (of course, only if that's what you want to say). While frequent advances will be annoying, sober Samoans are unlikely to physically force the issue. To avoid the measure of attention that a lone foreign woman is likely to attract, modest dress is recommended. See how young Samoan women dress and do likewise. Don't turn up at a pub or disco alone unless you're expecting advances and ignore the inane remarks of adolescents who'll try to chat you up. Samoan custom requires men to ask permission of your male escort before requesting a dance so unwanted attention can be screened that way. Most of all, however, don't be paranoid or you'll miss out on some very pleasant (and platonic) friendships.

GAY & LESBIAN TRAVELLERS

Gays and lesbians will probably have to remain discreet in the Samoas. The obvious presence of the fa'afafine (effeminate Samoan men who sometimes dress as women and who are well integrated into society) belies the fact that homosexuality is technically illegal and is not openly accepted in Samoan society (this is just another of many Samoan paradoxes). There is no 'gay scene' as such and no specifically gay bars on the islands.

DISABLED TRAVELLERS

Unfortunately, travellers with restricted mobility will find little in the way of infrastructure designed to make it easier for them to get around in Samoa. Hotels and guesthouses are not used to receiving disabled guests and almost all forms of transport and island activities are geared for the 'able-bodied'.

TRAVEL WITH CHILDREN

The climate, natural setting, warm waters and lack of poisonous creatures make Samoa a paradise for children. Children are highly valued in Samoa and child care is seen as the responsibility of the extended family and community. Wherever you go, your children will be given lots of attention (not to mention plenty of sugary treats) and will be made to feel very much at home. Ensure that vaccinations are up to date and take health records.

Take a baby carrier, light clothes which cover the whole body and total-block sunscreen. Buy bottled mineral water and make your children drink frequently. Disposable nappies (diapers), formula and sterilising solution are available in Apia and Pago Pago. Never leave your child unsupervised near beaches or reefs. In the event of an emergency, you should be aware that medical facilities are limited in both Samoas. Make sure that your repatriation insurance also covers your child. Lonely Planet's *Travel With Children* has useful advice on family travel.

DANGERS & ANNOYANCES

See the preceding Health section for warnings about heat exhaustion and sunburn, the dangers of coral cuts and tropical ulcers, the importance of avoiding stepping on stonefish or sea urchins and warnings about things which bite or sting.

Swimming

Many of Samoa's beaches aren't great for swimming – lagoons and reefs can become very shallow at low tide. Even in the protected waters of a lagoon, swimmers and snorkellers should be aware of currents and tidal changes, particularly of the swift movement of water through a pass (*ava*) in the reef into the open sea. An ava can usually be spotted from an elevated location on shore as a width of darker (deeper) water extending out through the reef. Never swim or snorkel alone and aways seek local advice on conditions.

Theft & Violence

Violent crime and alcohol-related incidents seem to be more prevalent in American Samoa than in Independent Samoa, although the latter does have its share of minor crime and mischief, most of it perpetrated by bored juveniles. Theft isn't really a problem in the Samoas and you and your personal belongings are probably safer than in your home country but it's best not to strain the honesty of the people by leaving things (especially footwear) lying around unattended. Actually, it's not only honesty that's the issue here.

As mentioned under Society & Conduct in the Facts about the Region chapter, Samoan society is traditionally communal. This means that an article belonging to one person also belongs to others who may have need of it. 'Borrowing' your possessions or absconding with them altogether (essentially the same thing) will not violate any real social restrictions and will not cause severe strain on the Samoan conscience.

Visitors may also notice another practice that may become irritating at times but is perfectly innocent. There are really no beggars, per se, in the Samoas, but Samoans will habitually make requests of their well-off aiga members who are responsible for the welfare of the family. They also like to approach foreigners, whom they imagine to be inconceivably wealthy, and help them voluntarily part with some of their endless means before someone else does. They're not always after money, though some are. Many would be just as happy to get the book you're reading, your sunglasses or the shirt off your back. A polite explanation that you've already promised the item in question to someone is a good way to refuse.

If you suffer from guilt pangs for having so much cash and technology at your disposal, you could be cleaned out very quickly. Bear in mind that the Samoas are not poor and lack of monetary affluence and electronic gadgetry does not necessarily constitute poverty. Quite a few Samoans who migrate to other countries get caught up in Western materialism but many others return to the Samoas complaining foreigners are required to work too hard, that everyone abroad is in a big hurry and that good food is too difficult to come by. Many say they also miss contact with their traditions and the protection provided by their aiga.

Custom Fees

Each village in the Samoas is separately governed by a village council (the hierarchy of which is explained in the section on Society & Conduct) responsible for the affairs of associated aiga and for furthering the cause of the village as a whole. Outsiders, both foreigners and residents of other communities, are required to pay a fee to use resources belonging to one village or another. Such resources include beaches, mountains, caves and so on, and while this seems a fairly good way to supplement village coffers, there are a few scams involved.

Sometimes, custom fees are prominently signposted, or a collection booth is set up near the entrance to the attraction. On other occasions, however, visitors will merely be approached and requested to pay. Sometimes this is legitimate, but often, individuals who are in no way related to the village council get away with collecting money, sometimes in extortionate amounts, from unwary or foolish travellers.

Even authorised charges can sometimes be unrealistic. If you are in doubt about a particular fee, ask to see the pulenu'u (mayor) before paying. Never pay children and never pay after the fact unless there was no one around to collect a valid fee when you arrived. Standard custom fees range from ST2 to ST5 per person. In many places, charges are made per vehicle. All legitimate custom fees in force at the time of writing are outlined in this book but that doesn't mean prices won't change or new fees won't be introduced. Keep your wits about you and don't pay anything until you're certain it's legitimate; if you are charged unfairly, report the incident to the Visitors Bureau in Apia or the Office of Tourism in Pago Pago.

BUSINESS HOURS

As a general rule, banks are open Monday to Friday from 9 am to 4 pm. In Independent Samoa, government offices open from 8 am to noon and 1 to 4.30 pm. In American Samoa, they're more likely to open at 9 am and close at 5 pm. Shops in both countries remain open from 8 am to noon and from 1.30 or 2 pm to 4.30 pm. Restaurants and takeaway shops operate between 8 am and 4 pm if they serve breakfast and lunch or from 6 to 10 pm if they serve only the evening meal. Saturday shopping hours are from 8 am to 12.30 pm. On Sunday, everything not directly related to the tourist industry is closed, although ripples of activity appear around evening. Markets normally get underway by about 6 am. In American Samoa they close at about 3 pm, but the Maketi Fou in Apia is active 24 hours a day. The big market day is Saturday.

PUBLIC HOLIDAYS & SPECIAL EVENTS

Holidays celebrated only in Independent Samoa are followed here by (I). Those unique to American Samoa have an (A).

1 January
 New Year's Day
2 January
 Day after New Year's Day (I)
Third Monday in January
 Martin Luther King Day (A)
Third Monday in February
 President's Day (A)
17 April
 Flag Day (A)
25 April
 ANZAC Day (I)
April
 Good Friday (A & I), *Easter* (A & I)
 & *Easter Monday* (I)
First Monday in May
 Aso o Tina or *Mothers' Day* (W)
Last Monday in May
 Memorial Day (A)
1 to 3 June
 Independence Celebrations (I)
4 July
 Independence Day (A)
First Monday in September
 Labor Day (A)
4 August
 Labor Day (I)
Second Sunday in October
 White Sunday
Second Monday in October
 White Monday (I)

Second Monday in October
Columbus Day (A)
October or November
Palolo Day (I)
11 November
Veteran's Day (A)
November
Arbor Day (A)
25 December
Christmas Day
26 December
Boxing Day (I)

In American Samoa, the territorial holiday is Flag Day, which falls on 17 April. It commemorates the raising of the US flag over eastern Samoa on that day in 1900 and features an arts festival, performing arts and visual arts exhibits, and long-winded speeches by political figures. Accompanying the celebration are *fautasi* (longboat races), singing, dancing and traditional sports and skills competitions – coconut husking, basket weaving and fire building.

Independent Samoa celebrates its independence on the first three days of June with a number of well-attended events including fautasi and outrigger races, horse races, dancing, feasting and more of the traditional competitions mentioned in the discussion of Flag Day (yes, even the long-winded speeches by tulafale, the aptly named talking chiefs). Everything closes down for five days during this celebration, so don't be expect to transact business during this time! Independent Samoa actually gained independence on 1 January 1962. However, as New Year's Day is already a cause for merriment, Independent Samoans have decided to have another holiday in June.

White Sunday, the second Sunday in October, is anxiously awaited by children of both Samoas as this day is dedicated to honouring children. They dress in their finest whites and parade to church and sing and lead church services. Afterwards, the children are guests of honour at a feast that is prepared and served to them by adults.

A well-attended annual event is the Teuila Festival, which takes place from the first to the second week of September. The original

Traditional Samoan costume is often worn at festivals

objective of this lively festival, which combines a variety of cultural and sporting events, was to draw more tourists to Independent Samoa. However, it has also caught on with locals and is now quite a popular event, featuring choir, marching, dancing and brass band competitions; a mini-Olympic competition; traditional sports matches; *paopao* (canoe) races; arts and crafts demonstrations; Samoan cooking demonstrations; musical entertainment; talent shows; art exhibitions; a beauty pageant; and a number of tourism-related seminars and workshops. The festival is named after the *teuila* or red ginger *(Alpinia purpurata)*, which is Independent Samoa's national floral emblem. A similar but lower-key festival, Tourism Week, takes place in American Samoa in early July, with the highlight the crowning of Miss American Samoa.

ACTIVITIES

See Facts for the Visitor chapters for Independent Samoa and American Samoa

ACCOMMODATION

Compared to more developed Pacific islands such as Hawaii and Fiji, accommodation options in the Samoas are fairly limited. Independent Samoa offers a range to suit most budgets but budget accommodation is not necessarily cheap and, though there are several expensive resorts to choose from, don't expect anything too sophisticated. Good-value tourist accommodation in American Samoa is scarce.

Budget

On the islands of Upolu, Savai'i and Manono in Independent Samoa, the cheapest accommodation is to be found in basic beachside *fales* (open-sided, thatch-roofed shelters) where you'll pay a minimum of about ST15 per night plus the same again for two or three meals. Most of the fales are on Upolu.

In Apia's guesthouses and cheaper hotels, decent singles/doubles start at around ST44/55, though you can find dormitory beds for around ST20. In Independent Samoa, most places in this category offer cold-water facilities only.

In American Samoa, decent 'budget' accommodation starts at US$35 for a single room, though there are one or two places offering basic accommodation for less. Most places have hot water. At the time of writing there were no beachside fales to rent in American Samoa. Though there are a couple of designated camping areas on Upolu (and some guesthouses will allow camping in their grounds), unless you intend to hike up Mt Silisili on Savai'i or spend a couple of days in the O Le Pupu-Pu'e National Park on Upolu, it isn't really worth bringing camping gear to Samoa. More than 80% of Samoan land is under customary ownership and if you wish to camp on any of it – even a seemingly secluded beach – you must ask permission from the traditional owners.

Middle & Top End

In Independent Samoa there are quite a few smaller hotels and bungalow-style resorts in the middle bracket where singles/doubles rooms range from ST100/110 to around ST160/180. The bulk of these places are in Apia, with a few scattered over the two main islands. Standards tend to be quite variable in this category.

In American Samoa, there are only three or four hotels in this category with single/doubles starting at around US$60. You won't find any five-star hotels in Samoa but there are a couple of up-market hotels in Apia where prices range from ST200 for a standard double to more than ST300 for 'deluxe' rooms. There are two up-market resorts (in the Pacific, the term 'resort' can refer to any accommodation anywhere near the sea) on Upolu offering very comfortable standard rooms from ST200 and honeymoon-style luxury for around ST600. Savai'i has one similar, but more modest, resort. American Samoa's 'top-end' hotel is the notorious Government-owned Rainmaker Hotel, which has unspectacular (even grubby) rooms ranging from US$75 to US$150. If you are interested in a short stay in one place, it is often cheaper to prebook hotel or resort accommodation from home. Travellers in Independent Samoa should be aware that many hotels in the mid and top-end range quote prices in US dollars. This is not always clear and you may have to double check whether a rate is being quoted in *tala* (the local currency) or US dollars.

Staying in Villages

Samoan hospitality is legendary and sometime during their visit travellers may get the opportunity to stay in the home of a Samoan family. Not only will this provide outsiders with invaluable insights into the extremely complex culture of the islands, it will reflect a degree of honour upon the host in the eyes of other villagers.

No one in the Samoas, foreigner or otherwise, will ever be required to spend a night without a roof over their head. Those who would choose to do so – to camp outside, for instance, especially within sight of a village – might cast shame upon the village for failing to invite the strangers in. Be warned, however, that the hospitality of the people should not be construed as a cheap means of 'doing' the islands. Even the most welcome guest will eventually become a strain on a family's resources. It would probably be best to move on after a few days, but of course that will depend upon the individual situation.

When it's time to leave, gather the family together and offer your sincerest thanks for their hospitality, then leave a *mea alofa* (gift) as a token of your esteem. Don't call it 'payment' or your hosts may be offended that you may consider them guilty of selling their kindness and friendship. Perhaps you can say something like: 'Your kindness and hospitality are greatly appreciated. Please accept this gift as a symbol of my respect for you and of our mutual friendship.'

Gifts most gratefully received include money and goods that can't normally be obtained without money. Store-bought foodstuffs will always be appreciated. Samoans love *pisupo*. This is tinned corned beef, and before you say 'yuck' you should know that, years ago, palagis turned it into a national institution in the islands. Clothing such as printed T-shirts will also be enthusiastically accepted, as will photographs of the family, picture books, musical instruments, simple toys for the children or any type of gadgetry unavailable or expensive in the islands. As much as possible, try to choose a gift that reflects the value of food and accommodation you've enjoyed and the individual personalities of your friends.

In American Samoa, the Office of Tourism runs an official home-stay program known as *Fale, Fala ma Ti*, which means 'House, Mat and Tea'. In theory, it provides the option of staying with Samoan host families for US$25 to US$45 per night. For information and the most current listings of participants, contact the Office of Tourism (☎ 684-633 1091; fax 684-633 1094), PO Box 1147, Pago Pago, American Samoa 96799. In Independent Samoa, home and village stays can be organised through the Safua Hotel (☎ 51271; fax 51272) in Lalomalava on the island of Savai'i.

FOOD
Local Food
Traditional Samoan food, for the most part, is very good and some excellent dishes are derived from tropical crops. Meals consist mostly of such items as root vegetables, coconut products *(niu* and *popo)*, taro *(talo)*, breadfruit *(fuata)*, fresh fruit, pork *(pua'a)*, chicken *(moa)*, corned beef *(pisupo)* and fish *(i'a)*. The best way to sample the local cuisine is to stay in a village, be invited into a Samoan home or take part in an *umu* feast. An umu is a traditional Polynesian earth oven (made above the ground in Samoa) and some of the most interesting and delicious traditional concoctions are prepared in it. The midday Sunday meal *(to'onai)* is almost always cooked in an umu (on Sunday mornings the islands are thick with smoke from hundreds of umu fires) and one or two hotels offer excellent value to'onai's (the one at the Pasifika Inn in Apia is particularly recommended).

Feasts are held in honour of a festive event, such as a wedding, a birthday, an investiture of title, a holiday or the arrival of visitors. Typical feast foods include the ubiquitous chicken and fish, roast suckling pig and a variety of root vegetables, sweets and concoctions derived from coconut cream, such as *palusami* (baked coconut cream in taro leaves and banana leaf), *oka* (raw fish marinated in coconut cream, lemon juice, chili and onions), *supo esi* (papaya pudding) and *fa'ausi talo* (taro in coconut cream). Samoan seafood includes tuna (often served Japanese-style as sashimi) and other open sea fish, lagoon fish such as parrotfish and perch, lobster, squid, delicious freshwater crabs and prawns and a popular crunchy seaweed known as *limu*. Tropical fruits grown locally include bananas, papayas, pineapples and mangoes (in season from late September).

At home, Samoans generally sit on mats on the floor and eat with their hands. Prayers

A TASTE OF SAMOA
If you'd like to try Samoan cuisine, the following are some of the best traditional recipes.

Fa'ausi Talo
1 cup coconut cream
2 cups grated taro root
1 cup sugar

To make coconut cream, grate the meat of three to four mature coconuts and add one cup of hot water for each two cups of meat. Let stand for a quarter of an hour or so then pass through a cheesecloth or coconut sennit to extract the cream. Alternatively, use tinned coconut cream. Mix the coconut cream (reserving about one quarter of it for use later) with the grated taro root, wrap in foil and bake in a medium to hot oven for half an hour. Meanwhile, make a caramel syrup. In a saucepan, heat the remaining coconut cream and add the sugar, stirring until dissolved. Continue stirring until the mixture has thickened and darkened. Remove cooked taro mixture from foil and cut into cubes three or four cm in diameter. Pour the syrup over the taro cubes and serve hot.

Papaya Pudding
This is a deliciously refreshing and not-too-sweet dish that can be enjoyed any time of the day. Take as many papayas as required, remove seeds, scoop out the flesh and place in a saucepan. Add water to the level of the fruit and 1/2 teaspoon of sago to every cup of water. Simmer the mixture until the sago is cooked (the sago will turn clear). Add half a cup of coconut cream for every cup of water, sugar to taste if required, and one lime leaf. Cover pan and simmer for five minutes. Remove lime leaf and allow mixture to cool.

Oka
500g fresh skipjack or yellowfin tuna (or other reef fish such as mullet)
1 cup lemon or lime juice
1/2 cup coconut cream
1/2 cup finely chopped onion
1/2 cup finely chopped tomatoes
1/2 cup diced cucumbers
1 tsp chopped chilli peppers
salt to taste

Cut fish into cubes and rinse with cold water. Marinate in lemon or lime juice for at least two hours or overnight. Drain the juice and set aside. Mix together remaining ingredients, add some of the juice to taste and pour over fish. Serve chilled.

Palusami
12 young taro leaves
250g corned beef or shelled prawns,
or sweet potato (for vegetarians)
1 tin coconut cream
one onion, finely diced
salt to taste

Taro leaves

Mix the meat, prawns or sweet potato with the coconut cream, onion and salt. Divide the mixture into 12 portions and wrap each in a taro leaf. Wrap each parcel in foil, place in a baking dish and bake in a medium oven for one hour. ■

Coconut Kisses

There are countless versions of the origin of the coconut tree but this is one of the most romantic. The beautiful young woman Sina, who lived on Upolu, kept a pet eel called Tuna. When he grew to be as long as a man, Sina released him into the pool where she bathed every day. The two became such close friends that Sina's fiance became jealous of Tuna and sentenced him to death. Hearing of the plan to kill him, Tuna pleaded with Sina that she be the one to kill him.

'Plant my head in the sand on the seashore,' he said. 'From me a tree will grow that will provide for your every need. You will have food, water and shelter always. And every time you drink from my fruit, you will be kissing me.'

Next time you drink a coconut, you'll surely notice Tuna's tiny face looking up at you. ■

are said before every meal. Guests and the head of the household are served first, the rest of the family eat afterwards. Don't be surprised to be served an enormous quantity of food – you're not expected to eat it all and what you leave will be shared by the rest of the family. When invited to share a family meal, try to reciprocate by buying some groceries.

Fast Food

Local people, especially those in American Samoa, are facing serious health problems as junk foods and expensive supermarket items invade and replace the healthy diet to which Samoans have long been accustomed. Tinned meat and fish, white bread, artificial snack foods, sugary soft drinks and meat products with an excessively high fat content (turkey tails from the US and mutton flaps from New Zealand) are all very popular. In fact, it's difficult to find anything but fast food in American Samoa. In 1996 the first McDonald's opened in Apia.

Places to Eat

Most of Samoa's restaurants are to be found in Apia and Pago Pago, with Apia having the widest choice. Restaurants range from cheap cafes to upmarket places and menus tend to feature seafood, chicken and imported steak. Chinese food is very popular in both Samoas – with the more ordinary-looking places often having the better food. Reasonable Mexican and Korean food is available in American Samoa.

Vegetarians are not very well catered for; vegans, in particular, might find it difficult to maintain a decent protein intake. In Independent Samoa, a cheap meal costs from around ST10; an upmarket feed from ST25. In American Samoa, you'll pay US$5 for a cheap meal; US$30 for a splurge.

The cheapest food of all is to be found in the markets in Apia, Salelologa, on Savai'i, and Pago Pago where ST2 will get you doughnuts (called pancakes) and hot cocoa and ST3 a plate of fish and vegetables. Out of town, travellers will have to rely on hotel restaurants and home-cooked food provided by the proprietors of beachside fales. Some remote fales require visitors to bring their own food. Most fales provide barbecue areas for those who want to cook their own meals. It's often possible to buy fish from the locals to cook up yourself.

Stores in Apia and Pago Pago are pretty well stocked with goods, though some imported items, such as dairy products and wine, are very expensive. Every village has a small grocery store where you can buy basic goods such as bread, eggs, tinned fish, corned beef and local beer. Decent bread is difficult to come by in the Samoas with most of it being of the fluffy, white variety. Look out for sticky coconut buns, they're a delicious treat.

DRINKS
Nonalcoholic Drinks

The most refreshing drink available is the juice of the immature coconut, which is naturally carbonated and is quite delicious. After removing the fibre surrounding the coconut, the top of the nut is taken off with a machete. Drinking coconuts are cheap and available just about everywhere.

Despite the variety of fruit on hand, fresh juices aren't terribly popular. You're more likely to be served sugary cordial than freshly squeezed juice. Foreign soft drinks can be bought everywhere and locally produced bottled water is readily available. Most, if not all, milk available is longlife.

Another delicious Samoan drink is *koko Samoa*, a chocolate drink made with locally grown roasted cocoa beans, sugar and water. Because they lack the bitterness of beans produced elsewhere, Samoan cocoa beans are considered to be the best in the world. Real brewed coffee, some of it locally produced, can be found in quite a few places around the island, though it's often made very weak. Tea tends to be served black with lots of sugar. Fresh lemon grass tea makes a refreshing alternative.

An unusual hot drink you might come across is *vaisalo* which is made from coconut milk and flesh thickened with starch. Very rich and nourishing, it is traditionally the first food offered to women after they have given birth. You may see people drinking it early in the morning at the markets.

Alcoholic Drinks

Independent Samoa's locally brewed lager, Vailima, is very good and is available just about everywhere. A 750ml bottle costs ST5. Apia's restaurants and bars stock a range of imported alcoholic drinks, including wines from Australia and New Zealand. Talofa wine is brewed by Island Styles in the hills above Apia. It's made from local fruit products and is a cool and refreshing way to enjoy a drink. In American Samoa you can buy a range of American beers – Budweiser, Coors, Stroh's and the like – as well as Aussie Foster's and New Zealand Steinlager. Traditionally mixed by the virgin daughter of the highest chief, 'ava is the ceremonial drink imbibed at all important Samoan meetings.

Refer to the Society & Conduct section in Facts about the Region.

ENTERTAINMENT

Bars and nightclubs are immensely popular with urbanised Samoans and many foreigners enjoy getting in and partying with them. You can seek out quiet places to meet expats or enjoy conversation over a tropical drink. Apia has at least half a dozen nightclubs with many featuring live music. Pago Pago has one or two nightclubs and a couple of modern cinemas showing up-to-date mainstream movies. Outside the capital cities, evenings generally are pretty quiet. The bigger hotels on the islands stage regular *fiafia* nights – presentations of Samoan dancing and singing, usilly accompanied by a buffet dinner. The original fiafia was a local play or music program which amounted to a fund-raising effort for the performers. Though staged especially for tourists, today's fiafias are normally colourfully superb and good-value entertainment.

SPECTATOR SPORT

On weekday afternoons after school or work, young Samoans gather on a *malae* (village green) to play rugby, volleyball and a unique brand of cricket, *kirikiti* (see the Samoan Cricket aside). American Samoan secondary schools sponsor football teams and high school matches are among the most spirited and well-attended entertainment in the South Pacific. The dream of many young men in American Samoa is to play American football professionally or for a university team – and there are many success stories. Samoa's biggest competitive sport, however, is rugby and the country boasts several international stars. There are almost always several Samoan team members in the New Zealand All Blacks and the Samoan UK rugby union player Vaaiga Tuigamala ('the million dollar man') was the highest paid rugby union player in the world in the late '90s. The rugby union season runs from February to June; rugby league is played from June to November. Volleyball, basketball and soccer are also enthusiastically followed, played and

It's Just Not Cricket

Any discussion of Samoan sporting tradition wouldn't be complete without a mention of *kirikiti*, the national game. A bizarre version of cricket, kirikiti is played by apparently flexible rules known only to the players.

The balls are handmade of rubber and wrapped with pandanus. The three-sided bat also keeps things interesting – nobody, not even the batter, has a clue where the ball will go. In his book *In Search of Tusitala*, Gavin Bell is told the scoring system.

A ball struck to the boundaries (a nearby road, a church, and the front gardens of adjacent houses) scored one point; beyond the boundaries, two points; into a surrounding coconut plantation, four points; and out of sight, six points.

Lack of pads and face protection adds to the element of risk – disputed calls have resulted in death by cricket bat. This certainly isn't Lords!

Since everyone in the village will often want to be involved in a typical afternoon game, Samoans don't limit participation to 22. Serious competitions go on for days and, once a team has lost it can buy its way back into the match by paying a fee to the host village which is responsible for catering for the entire tournament.

The game is played year-round, with frequent Saturday matches throughout the year and practice games held practically every day. There are male, female and mixed teams. The main season for inter-village matches is from April to June while the national play-offs are held in August in preparation for the national championships. These take place during the Teuila Festival during the second week of September.

If you'd like to have a look at cricket, Samoan-style, or even participate in a game, wander through the rural villages of Upolu or Savai'i in the mid-afternoon. You'd be hard-pressed to find a malae where a match is not in progress. ■

supported. Among women, the most popular sport is netball; the Independent Samoan women's team is gaining outside recognition and has competed in several international tournaments. The main season is between late March and late May. In Independent Samoa, all major matches take place at Apia Park. Check the local papers for details. Golf can be played at the Royal Samoa Country Club at Fagali'i, just east of Apia in Independent Samoa, and at the Ili'ili Country Club just west of Tafuna Airport on Tutuila in American Samoa.

THINGS TO BUY

In Apia, there are several craft stores, a couple of interesting art galleries and a large flea market where you can look for local arts and crafts. Pago Pago has a few craft outlets, but prices are likely to be substantially higher than in Independent Samoa. Siapo, known elsewhere in the Pacific as tapa, is a type of 'cloth' made from the pounded bark of the paper mulberry tree and is one of the most typically Polynesian souvenirs you can buy. Prior to European arrival there were no woven materials in Polynesia and, since there were few land mammals, hides were not an alternative. Siapo, decorated with rich, earthy natural dyes, was used as clothing and coverings. Siapo rapidly disappeared when European cloth became available, but it is still produced for ceremonial use and for collectors. Samoan siapos are small in comparison to their Tongan counterparts, reaching only a few square metres in size. Consequently, they're more portable.

Woven mats of dried and treated pandanus are made by women in their spare time and serve as beds and carpeting in traditional fales. The *fala moe* (bedroll mats) are stored in the fale and used for sleeping. The *papa laufala* cover the floors of Samoan dwellings. The much more intricate *ie toga*, or fine mat, is made of pandanus leaves split into widths of just a couple of millimetre and, when completed, has the sheen and appearance of fine silk. An average one will take hundreds or even thousands of hours to weave, and the finest ones will merit heirloom value. Ie toga are given as gifts at weddings, births and investitures of title.

Baskets and other articles of woven pandanus are beautiful, inexpensive and make excellent souvenirs. Look out, too, for the round fish traps called *enu*. Made in a variety of sizes and used for catching smelt, they're beautifully woven from the bark of a local vine.

Carved wooden 'ava bowls are popular with visitors and are actually used in the islands. The multi-legged Samoan bowls come in more imaginative shapes than their counterparts in other South Pacific countries. Carved wooden weapons are to be found everywhere and there is plenty to choose from in the way of coconut shell jewellery. In order to help protect endangered of threatened species, don't buy items made from coral, whalebone or turtle shell.

Getting There & Away

The South Pacific is relatively expensive transport-wise and unless you have unlimited funds, some careful route-planning will be necessary. Remember that all visitors arriving in the Samoas need onward air tickets or a yacht-owner's guarantee that they will be departing on the same boat they arrived on.

AIR

The majority of the Samoas' visitors arrive on scheduled flights at Pago Pago airport at Tafuna on Tutuila in American Samoa, or at Faleolo airport 35km west of Apia on Upolo in Independent Samoa. (Faleolo was only opened to large trans-oceanic jets in 1985.) While the Samoas aren't exactly as remote or obscure a destination as Tuvalu or Kiribati, these islands are not as popular as Fiji or Tahiti either, and airfares often reflect that fact.

From New Zealand, Australia, Fiji, Tonga, Hawaii and Los Angeles, access to Samoa is fairly straightforward. From anywhere else, however, travelling to the Samoan islands will entail first reaching one of these connecting points. Auckland and Nadi/Suva seem to be the most convenient and best served runs.

AIRPORTS & AIRLINES

The major carriers are Air New Zealand and Polynesian Airways. Samoa Air flies between Independent and American Samoa as well as connecting the Samoas to the Vava'u group in Tonga.

The following airlines, most of which have offices in several countries, offer service to the Samoas.

Air New Zealand
Australia
(☎ 02-9223 4666) 5 Elizabeth St, Sydney 2000, NSW, Australia

Canada
(☎ 604-606 0199) Suite 1250, 888 Dunsmuir St, Vancouver, BC V6C 3K4, Canada
New Zealand
(☎ 09-366 2584) 139 Queen St, Auckland, New Zealand
Tonga
(☎ 676-21646; fax 676-21645) Tungi Arcade, Taufa'ahau Rd, PO Box 4, Nuku'alofa, Tonga
UK
(☎ 0171-839 1604) Ground Floor, New Zealand House, Haymarket, London SW1, UK
USA
(☎ 310-648 7000) 1960 East Grand Avenue, El Segundo, CA 90245, USA
Independent Samoa
(☎ 685-20825) Lotemau Centre, Apia, Independent Samoa

Air Pacific
Fiji
(☎ 679-304388; fax 679-304153) CML Building, Victoria Parade, Suva, Fiji
Independent Samoa
(☎ 22693; fax 20023) Beach Rd, Apia, Independent State of Samoa

Polynesian Airlines
American Samoa
Tafuna International Airport, (☎ 684-699 9126; fax 684-699 2109) PO Box 487, Pago Pago, American Samoa
Australia
(☎ 02-9299 1855; fax 02-299 1119) 50 King St, Sydney, NSW 2000, Australia
New Zealand
(☎ 09-379 4824; fax 09-307 3819) 283 Karangahape Rd, PO Box 68-423, Auckland, New Zealand
Tonga
(☎676-21565; fax 676-24225) Cnr Fatafehi & Salote Rds, Nuku'alofa, Tonga
USA
Suite 660, 5757 West Century Blvd, Los Angeles, CA 90045-6407, USA (☎ 310-670 1515; fax 310-338 0708)
Honolulu Reservations (☎ 1 800 644 7659)
Independent Samoa
NPF Bldg, Beach Rd, PO Box 599, Apia, Samoa (☎ 685-21261; fax 685-20023)

SAMOA VISITORS BUREAU

DORINDA TALBOT

DORINDA TALBOT

DEANNA SWANEY

Left: The Canopy Walkway in the Falealupo Rainforest Preserve on Savai'i
Top Right: Moving advertisement for one of Samoa's premier exports – beer

Middle: Traditional family fale, Upolu
Bottom: Aleipata, Upolu with Nu'utele in the background

Top: The Robert Louis Stevenson Museum in the hills above Apia
Middle: The road from Faleasao to Fiti'uta, Ta'u, Manu'a Islands
Bottom: Beach Road, Apia, Upolu

Samoa Air

American Samoa
    Main Office: Tafuna International Airport, PO
    Box 280, Pago Pago, American Samoa 96799
    (☎ 684-699 9106; fax 684-699-9751).
    Local Information/Reservations: Ofu, American
    Samoa (☎ 684-655 1103); Ta'u, American
    Samoa (☎ 684-677 3569)
Tonga
    Vava'u, Tonga (☎ 676-70477; fax 676-70221)
Independent Samoa
    Beach Rd, Apia, Samoa (☎ 685-22901; fax 685-
    23851); Faleolo Airport, Samoa (☎ 685-22606)

Buying Tickets

Your plane ticket will probably be the single
most expensive item in your budget and
buying it can be an intimidating business.
There is likely to be a multitude of airlines
and travel agents hoping to separate you
from your money and it is always worth
putting aside a few hours to research the
current state of the market.

Start early: some of the cheapest tickets
have to be bought months in advance and
some popular flights sell out early. Talk to
other recent travellers – they may be able to
stop you making some of the same old mis-
takes. Look at the ads in newspapers and
magazines, consult reference books and
watch for special offers. Then phone around
travel agents for bargains. (Airlines can
supply information on routes and timetables;
however, except at times of inter-airline war,
they do not supply the cheapest tickets.)

Find out the fare, the route, the duration
of the journey and any restrictions on the
ticket. Then sit back and decide which one is
the best for you.

You may discover that those impossibly
cheap flights are 'fully booked, but we have
another one that costs a bit more ...' Or the
flight is on an airline notorious for its poor
safety standards and leaves you in the
world's least favourite airport in mid-
journey for 14 hours. Or they claim only to
have the last two seats available for that
country for the whole of July, which they will
hold for you for a maximum of two hours.
Don't panic – keep ringing around.

Use the fares quoted in this book as a guide
only. They are approximate and based on the
rates advertised by travel agents at the time
of going to press. Quoted airfares do not
necessarily constitute a recommendation for
the carrier. If you are travelling from the UK
or the USA you will probably find that the
cheapest flights are being advertised by
obscure bucket shops whose names haven't
yet reached the telephone directory. Many
such firms are honest and solvent, but there
are a few rogues who will take your money
and disappear, to reopen elsewhere a month
or two later under a new name. If you are
suspicious about a firm, don't give them all
the money at once – leave a deposit of 20%
or so and pay the balance when you get the
ticket. If they insist on cash in advance, go
somewhere else and, once you have the
ticket, ring the airline to confirm that you are
actually booked on the flight.

You may decide to pay more than the
rock-bottom fare by opting for the safety of
a better known travel agent. Firms such as
STA which has offices worldwide, Council
Travel in the USA, or Travel CUTS in
Canada are not going to disappear overnight,
leaving you clutching a receipt for a non-
existent ticket, but they do offer good prices
to most destinations.

Once you have your ticket, write down its
number, together with the flight number and
other details and keep the information somewhere separate. If the ticket is lost or stolen,
this will help you get a replacement. It's
sensible to buy travel insurance as early as
possible. If you buy it the week before you
fly, you may find, for example, that you're
not covered for delays to your flight caused
by industrial action.

Travellers with Special Needs

If you have special needs of any sort – you've
broken a leg, you're vegetarian, travelling in
a wheelchair, taking the baby, terrified of
flying – you should let the airline know as
soon as possible so that it can make arrangements accordingly. You should remind them
when you reconfirm your booking (at least
72 hours before departure) and again when
you check in at the airport.

It may also be worth ringing around the airlines before you make your booking to find out how they can handle your particular needs. Airports and airlines can be surprisingly helpful, but they do need advance warning.

Most international airports will provide escorts from check-in desk to plane where needed, and there should be ramps, lifts, accessible toilets and reachable phones. Aircraft toilets, on the other hand, are likely to present a problem; travellers should discuss this with the airline at an early stage and, if necessary, with their doctor.

Guide dogs for the blind will often have to travel in a specially pressurised baggage compartment with other animals, away from their owner, though smaller guide dogs may be admitted to the cabin. All guide dogs will be subject to the same quarantine laws (six months in isolation, etc) as any other animal when entering or returning to countries currently free of rabies, such as the UK or Australia.

Deaf travellers can ask for airport and in-flight announcements to be written down for them.

Children aged under two travel for 10% of the full fare (or free on some airlines) as long as they don't occupy a seat. They don't get a baggage allowance in this case. 'Skycots', baby food and nappies (diapers) should be provided by the airline if requested in advance. Children aged between two and 12 can usually occupy a seat for half to two-thirds of the full fare and are entitled to a standard baggage allowance. Push chairs can often be taken as hand luggage.

The USA

The main hub for travel between North America and the Pacific is Honolulu and most travellers to the Pacific islands will have to pass through here. In the USA, the best way to find cheap flights is by checking the Sunday travel sections in major newspapers such as the *Los Angeles Times*, *San Francisco Chronicle*, *New York Times* and the *Boston Globe*. The student travel bureaus – STA or Council Travel – are also worth a

go but in the USA you'll have to produce proof of student status and in some cases be under 26 years of age to qualify for their discounted fares. North America is a relative newcomer to the bucket-shop traditions of Europe and Asia, so ticket availability and the restrictions attached to them need to be weighed against what is offered on the standard Apex or full economy (coach) tickets. Do some homework before setting off.

The magazines specialising in bucket-shop advertisements in London (see the discussion under Europe) will mail you copies so you can study current pricing before you decide on a course of action. Also recommended is the newsletter *Travel Unlimited* (PO Box 1058, Allston, Massachusetts 02134, USA) which publishes details of the cheapest airfares and courier possibilities for destinations all over the world from the USA.

In general, November and December are the most expensive and congested months to travel, while the northern summer, corresponding to the Samoan winter, is the cheapest and easiest time to get a booking – and is fortunately also the driest and most comfortable season to visit the equatorial Samoas.

Canada

As with US-based travellers, Canadians will find the best deals travelling to the Pacific region via Los Angeles/Honolulu. Qantas and Air Pacific fly to Nadi from Vancouver, with an intermediate stop in Honolulu. Travel CUTS has offices in all major Canadian cities. The *Globe & Mail* and *Vancouver Province* carry travel agents' ads. Travellers interested in booking flights with Canadian courier companies should obtain a copy of the *Travel Unlimited* newsletter mentioned in the USA section.

Australasia

Travelling to the Samoas from Australia or New Zealand is reasonably straightforward, but not necessarily inexpensive. Polynesian Airlines operates six weekly flights direct from New Zealand to Independent Samoa –

five out of Auckland and one from Wellington.

Air New Zealand flies three times weekly from Auckland and once a week from Wellington. Return fares from Auckland range from NZ$1200 to NZ$1400. Unfortunately there are no direct flights from Australia to Samoa. Polynesian Airlines has two weekly flights from Sydney to Apia, one via Auckland and one via Auckland and Tonga, plus one weekly flight from Melbourne to Apia via Wellington. Air New Zealand flies twice weekly from Sydney and once weekly from Melbourne and Brisbane, all via Auckland. Return fares from Australia range from A$1300 to A$1500.

If you're thinking of making Samoa part of a wider journey, Air New Zealand, in conjunction with Ansett and Singapore Airlines, operates a RTW ticket from Australia which allows unlimited free stopovers worldwide. Tickets are valid for one year and economy fares range from A$2349 to A$2999.

For a short break to the Samoas, a package deal may well be the cheapest option. Brisbane-based Pacific Unlimited Holidays (☎ 07-3229 5872; fax 07-3229 7073) offers various package deals to Independent Samoa. A return flight plus seven nights' accommodation in Apia or Savai'i can cost as little as A$1200. The Sydney-based Pacific Island Travel Centre (☎ 132 747; fax 02-9262 6318 in Sydney, 03-9663 4536 in Melbourne) offers similar package deals to both Independent and American Samoa.

Other Pacific Islands

Within the Pacific region, island-hopping isn't very difficult or expensive but some routes will present scheduling problems. Samoa Air flies between Pago Pago and the Vava'u group of islands in Tonga four times weekly for US$300 return. Royal Tongan Airlines operates weekly flights between Pago Pago and Nuku'alofa in Tonga for around the same price. Tickets can be booked through Samoa Air.

Polynesian Airlines flies once a week from Apia to Nuku'alofa. Between them,

Polynesian and Air Pacific run three weekly flights from Apia to Fiji for around US$300 return. Air New Zealand and Polynesian both have weekly flights from Apia to Honolulu for around US$600 return. To get to or from Niue, the Cook Islands or French Polynesia, you'll have to fly via New Zealand, Fiji or Hawaii. Though Polynesian Airlines offers a couple of good-value Pacific fares (see under Discounted Fare Deals), in general you'll get far better deals by applying through a travel agency specialising in independent travel rather than through package tour brochure jockeys or directly through the airlines. For some suggestions, see under USA, Canada, Europe and Australasia earlier in this chapter.

Europe

There is no straightforward way to get from Europe to the South Pacific. Europeans will have to get themselves to the North American west coast, Sydney or Auckland and work out a route from there. Considering the location of the South Pacific relative to Europe, a round-the-world ticket may be the most economical way to go (see the discussion of RTW tickets earlier in this section). Currently, the best fares to the South Pacific are with Air New Zealand from London. Fares remain the same whether your final destination is the Pacific islands, New Zealand or Australia. Tickets allow six free stopovers between London and Australasia, which may include Los Angeles, Hawaii, Samoa, Fiji, Tonga, the Cook Islands or New Zealand. From mid-April to mid-June return fares average around UK£750; during the remainder of the year fares range from UK£940 to UK1460. These tickets may be used in combination with another carrier as part of a RTW routing.

Discount Fares

Polypass Polynesian Airlines' Polypass is a popular option, open to those who don't mind limited time in a number of South Pacific destinations. It is good for 30 days and includes travel on Polynesian Airlines' flights to Independent Samoa, American

Samoa, Tonga, Fiji, Australia, New Zealand, Honolulu and Los Angeles. This is a good way to fill up your passport with stamps but actually see very little.

If you're planning to visit more than one Pacific destination from Australia, the Polypass will actually work out cheaper than a combination of individual flights. The adult Polypass costs US$1399 if you visit all eight destinations; US$999 excluding Honolulu and Los Angeles. Discounts are available for children under 12 years of age. A much more leisurely Polypass option is the Triangle Fare, which includes one circuit of the classic 'triangle' of Fiji, Tonga and Independent Samoa. It's valid for one year and costs US$448.

Round-the-World Tickets Round-the-world (RTW) tickets have become quite popular in recent years and are often very good value. Since Samoa is pretty much on the opposite side of the world from Europe and the North American east coast, it can work out no more expensive or even cheaper to keep going in the same direction right around the world rather than backtrack on your return.

The official airline RTW tickets are usually put together by a combination of two or more airlines and permit you to fly anywhere you want on those airlines' routes as long as you do not backtrack. For example, Air New Zealand can normally get you from London to New Zealand or Australia, allowing six free stopovers en route (Los Angeles, Honolulu, Samoa, Tonga, Fiji, Cook Islands), for as little as UK£375 one way or UK£750 return. The one-way option can be used in conjunction with a special fare on Thai, Malaysian or another Asian airline for the return route via Asia (currently less than UK£450). Restrictions are that you (usually) must book the first sector in advance and cancellation penalties then apply. The Air New Zealand ticket allows a 75% refund only if no sector of the route has been flown. Alternative RTW routings may be put together by specialised travel agents using a combination of discounted tickets. For some suggestions, see Finding a Discounted Ticket under Europe later in this chapter.

Circle Pacific Fares Circle Pacific fares are similar to RTW tickets and use a combination of airlines to formulate a circle route through the Pacific, including the Samoas and a combination of other countries. As with RTW tickets, there are advance purchase restrictions and limits to the number of stopovers allowed. Typically fares range between US$1000 and US$2000. Your best bet will be to organise your itinerary through an agency which specialises in independent travel.

Student Travel Worldwide, there are a number of student travel organisations which offer bargain-basement airfares to out-of-the-way destinations the world over, including the Pacific. Organisations which offer student services include:

Australia
    STA Travel (☎ 03-9349 2411; fax 03-9349 537), 222 Faraday St, Carlton, Victoria, 3053
    STA Travel (☎ 02-9212 1255; fax 02-9281 4183), 855 George St, Ultimo, Sydney 2007, NSW
Canada
    Travel CUTS (☎ 416-977 5228; fax 416-977 7112), 187 College St, Toronto, Ontario M5T 1P7
France
    Voyages Wasteels (☎ 01-43 43 46 10; fax 01-43 45 75 40), 2 Rue Michel Chasles, 75012 Paris
Germany
    STA Travel (☎ 30-311 0950; fax 30-313 0948), Goethestrasse 73, 10625 Berlin
    STA Travel (☎ 69-430191; fax 69-439858), Bergerstrasse 118, 60316 Frankfurt/Main
Italy
    Viaggi Wasteels (☎ 06-474 55 52; fax 06-488 16 47), Via Barberini 87-89, 1-00187 Rome
Japan
    STA Travel (☎ 03-5391 2922; fax 03-5391 2923), 7th Floor, Nukariya Bldg, 1-16-20 Minami-Ikebukuro, Toshima-Ku, Tokyo 171
New Zealand
    STA Travel (☎ 09-309 0458; fax 09-309 2059), 10 High St, Auckland
    STA Travel (☎ 03-379 9098; fax 03-365 7220), 90 Cashel St, Christchurch
    STA Travel (☎ 04-385 0561; fax 04-385 8170), 233 Cuba St, Wellington

UK
> Council Travel (☎ 0171-437 7767), 28A Poland St, London W1
> STA Travel (☎ 71-361 6262; fax 0171-938 4755; help@statravelgroup.co.uk), 86 Old Brompton Rd, London SW7 3LQ 01

USA
> STA Travel (☎ 212-627 3111; fax 212-627 3387), 10 Downing St, New York, NY 10014
> STA Travel (☎ 415-391 8407; fax 415-391 4105), 51 Grant Ave, San Francisco, CA 94108

SEA

Cargo Ship

Many travellers come to the South Pacific with grand dreams of island hopping aboard cargo ships, but few actually do. The truth is that the days of working or bumming your way around the world on cargo ships are just about over. All sorts of insurance and freight company restrictions have made such travel difficult. Those who are serious about trying to take this route should approach the captain of a ship in port. On some freight lines the captain has the option of deciding who goes and who doesn't. The newspapers in Pago Pago, Apia, Nuku'alofa, Suva and Honolulu (the most difficult of all) list sailing schedules and routes of the various lines up to three months in advance. Agencies in American Samoa include Polynesia Shipping Services (☎ 633 1211; fax 633 1265), PO Box 1478, Pago Pago 96799 and Samoa Pacfic Shipping (☎ 633 4665; fax 633 4667), Pago Pago 96799. The once-monthly cargo ship that sails between Apia and the remote Tokelau Islands, however, provides Tokelau's only passenger link with the rest of the world. For sailing dates and fares, contact the Office of Tokelau Affairs (☎ 20822) in Apia, Independent Samoa.

Yacht

Between the months of May and October the harbours of the South Pacific swarm with cruising yachts from all over the world. Almost invariably they'll be following the favourable winds west from the Americas. Routes from the US west coast take in Hawaii and Palmyra before following the traditional path through the Samoas, Tonga, Fiji and New Zealand. From the Atlantic and Caribbean, yachties will be able to access this area via Venezuela, Panama, the Galaápagos Islands, the Marquesas, the Society Islands and Tuamotus, possibly making stops at Suwarrow in the northern Cook Islands, Rarotonga or Niue en route.

Because of the cyclone season, which begins in late November, most yachties will want to stay clear of Fiji or Tonga and be on their way to New Zealand by the early part of that month, (Cyclone Val struck on 6 December, 1991).

Access to the Samoas is almost always from the northern Cook Islands or directly from French Polynesia. Often, yachts will anchor in Pago Pago Harbor to stock up on provisions at one of the local supermarkets because American Samoa has the lowest grocery prices between Venezuela and South-East Asia. From there, most of them stop at Apia and a few cruise around Savai'i before moving on to the Tongan groups. The significance of all this is that the yachting community is very friendly, especially toward those who display an interest in yachts and other things nautical. Often they are looking for crew, and for those who'd like a bit of low-key adventure, this is the way to go. Most of the time, crew members will only be asked to take a turn on watch – that is, scan the horizon for cargo ships, stray containers and the odd reef – and possibly to cook or to clean up the ship. In port, they may be required to dive and scrape the bottom, paint or make repairs. In most cases, sailing experience is not necessary and crew members have the option to learn as they go. Most yachties will charge crew US$15 to US$20 per day for food and supplies.

The best places to secure a passage on a cruising yacht are, naturally, east of the Samoas. The west coast of the USA is a prime hunting ground – San Francisco, Newport Beach, San Diego and Honolulu are all good. Likewise, it shouldn't be too difficult to crew on in Papeete or Rarotonga. The best way to make known your availability is to post a notice on the bulletin board of the yacht club in the port (both Apia and Pago

Pago have yacht clubs). It would also be helpful to visit the wharfs or wait at the dinghy dock and ask people if they know anyone setting off on a cruise, around the time you'd like to go, who might be looking for crew members.

It may be a matter of interest that the most successful passage-seekers tend to be young women who are willing to crew on with male 'single-handers' – those who sail alone. Naturally, the bounds of the relationship should be fairly well defined before you set out. For sanity's sake, bear in mind that not everyone is compatible with everyone else. Under the conditions of an ocean voyage, rivalries and petty distress are magnified many times, so only set out on a long passage with someone you can feel relatively comfortable with. Remember that, once aboard, the skipper's judgement is law. If you'd like to enjoy some relative freedom of movement on a yacht, it's a good idea to try to find one that has windvane steering. Nobody likes to spend all day and all night at the wheel staring at a compass, and such a job would go to the crew members of the lowest status more often than not. Comfort is also greatly increased on yachts that have a furling jib, a dodger to keep out the weather, a toilet (head) and a shower. Those that are rigged for racing are generally more manageable than simple liveaboards. As a general rule, four metres of length for each person aboard affords relatively uncrowded conditions. For those not interested in cruising, yachties have a mind-boggling store of knowledge about world weather patterns, navigation and maritime geography and are a good source of information regarding such things.

Arriving by Yacht There are a number of rules and regulations to observe if you are arriving by yacht.

Apia Harbour Yachts arriving in Apia Harbour should pull up inside the basin rather than outside where they may block large freighters. The entrance fee is ST15. Customs will want you to pull up alongside the wharf at Apia Harbour with the quarantine flag raised. Port quarantine officials will come aboard first and will probably check for yellow fever vaccination certificates, although these aren't officially required unless you're coming directly from Africa or South America. When the yellow flag is lowered, customs officials will board and check documentation, which must include a certificate of clearance from your previous port of call and five copies of the crew list.

Crew members must be guaranteed onward passage with the yacht or have an air or ferry ticket away from Independent Samoa. (An air ticket out of Pago Pago will normally also suffice.) Visits to other harbours in Independent Samoa will require permission from the Prime Minister's office.

Pago Pago Harbor The anchorage at Pago Pago Harbor is free for seven days. After that you are charged about US$15 per month, more or less, depending on the length of your yacht. Those arriving by yacht from Hawaii must present a US customs clearance document from Honolulu. Yacht people have mixed feelings about the anchorage in Pago Pago Harbor but most agree it's not the most pleasant in the South Pacific. Though improved filtering has cut down the nose-wrenching fumes from the tuna canneries, boats leave the 'fertile' harbour covered with a worm-like tubular scum that grows to unbelievable thicknesses in a matter of days and fouls depth sounders, anchor chains, through-the-hull fittings and propellers after only a short visit. Having said all that, Pago Pago is the safest anchorage in the South Pacific, although when a stiff wind howls up and funnels in from the sea, you'll wonder.

DEPARTURE TAX

There is a departure tax of ST20 for every person flying out of Western Samoa, payable at the airport at the time of check-in. The American Samoa departure tax is US$3 but it's included in the price of airline tickets.

ORGANISED TOURS

See Getting Around chapter.

WARNING

The information in this chapter is particularly vulnerable to change: prices for international travel are volatile, routes are introduced and cancelled, schedules change, special deals come and go, and rules and visa requirements are amended. Airlines and governments seem to take a perverse pleasure in making price structures and regulations as complicated as possible. You should check directly with the airline or a travel agent to make sure you understand how a fare (and ticket you may buy) works. In addition, the travel industry is highly competitive and there are many lurks and perks.

The upshot of this is that you should get opinions, quotes and advice from as many airlines and travel agents as possible before you part with your hard-earned cash. The details given in this chapter should be regarded as pointers and are not a substitute for your own careful, up-to-date research.

Getting Around

This chapter contains information relevant to both Samoas. There are separate Getting Around sections at the beginning of the chapters dealing with the individual islands of Independent Samoa and American Samoa.

AIR

The main inter-island transport in the Samoas is provided by Samoa Air and Polynesian Airlines. The former flies between Apia (from Fagali'i airport just east of town) and Pago Pago; between Pago, Ofu and Ta'u and between Pago and Savai'i. Polynesian flies between Pago Pago, Apia and Savai'i. Inter-island transport is all on small planes, mainly De Havilland Otters. Samoa Air runs three to six daily flights between Apia and Pago Pago. Flight time is one hour and 15 minutes. From Apia, the one-way/return fare at the time of writing was ST120/189.50. From Pago the fare is US$69/$93. Polynesian Airlines also flies daily between Apia and Pago Pago for the same price. Polynesian does the 20-minute hop from Apia's Fagali'i airport to Savai'i's Maota airport on the south-east side of the island three times daily for ST34/60.50 one way/return. Polynesian Airlines also flies once a day to Savai'i's new airport at Asau on the northwest side of the island. The flight takes 30 minutes and costs ST55/90 one way/return. Samoa Air flies twice weekly between Pago Pago and Maota airport.

BUS

Travelling by public bus is the most common method of getting around both Samoas and is an experience that shouldn't be missed. The buses are vibrantly coloured, woodenseated vehicles that blast reggae music at volumes that, depending upon your opinion of reggae music, inspire you to either get up and dance or become ill with a throbbing headache. The biggest problem with bus travel in Independent Samoa is that bus ser-

vices operate at the whim of the drivers. If your driver feels like knocking off at 1 pm, he does, and passengers counting on the service are left stranded. Never, under any circumstances, rely on catching a bus after about 2 pm.

In American Samoa, the island of Tutuila is served by small aiga buses (pick-up trucks with a bus frame attached at the back). The buses theoretically run until early evening, but if you want to head back to town after visiting outlying villages, make sure you leave by 3.30 or 4 pm at the latest. It's difficult to find transport after about 2 pm on Saturday, and on Sunday the only buses running are those taking people to church.

In Independent Samoa, buses are scarce on Saturday afternoons and Sundays. Paying the fare will go more smoothly if you have as near to the exact change as possible. The buses make so many stops and starts that the going is slow anyway, but a driver having to dig for $19.50 in change will hold things up considerably.

To stop a bus in either Samoa, wave your hand and arm, palm down, as the bus approaches. To signal that you'd like to get off the bus, either knock on the ceiling or clap loudly. Pay the fare to the driver or leave the money on the dash as you leave. Although most visitors don't notice it at first, there is a seating hierarchy on Samoan buses, and a great deal of amusement can be derived from observing the manner in which Samoans seat and stack themselves. Unmarried women normally sit together. Foreigners and older people must have a seat and sit near the front of the bus. Don't worry about arranging this yourself – the Samoans will see to it that everything is sorted out. When all the seats are full (or a young woman boards and there is no other woman to sit with), people begin stacking up. Women sit on laps of women, men on men (although some mixed stacking now goes on occasionally) and sometimes they are stacked up to four high. When this resource is exhausted, people sit on kero tins and sacks in the aisle. If someone in the rear of the bus is blocked by those seated, everyone systematically files off the bus, lets them off, and reboards without a word. You get the feeling they've been doing this for a long time.

Details about specific routes and fares are provided in the Getting Around sections of the chapters dealing with individual islands.

BOAT
Ferry
Ferries and launches connect all the main Samoan islands except Manu'a. The largest car ferry, the *Queen Salamasina* owned by the Samoa Shipping Corporation, runs between Pago Pago Harbor and Apia once a week. It leaves Apia for Pago Pago on Wednesday at 10 pm and returns on Thursday at 4 pm. The trip takes about eight hours each way. The fare from Apia to Pago Pago is ST40 but it's US$30 in the opposite direction (about twice as much) so if you're making a return trip, it's better to purchase a return ticket from Apia and a one-way ticket from Pago Pago. Cars cost ST240/480 one way/return from Apia and US$213/426 from Pago Pago.

In Apia, buy tickets from the Samoa Shipping Corporation, on the corner of Vaea and Convent Sts, opposite the Lotemau Centre (☎ 20935; fax 22352). In Pago Pago, tickets must be purchased at least one day in advance from Polynesia Shipping (☎ 633 1211), which is on the dock in Fagatogo.

Samoans are usually not very good sailors (neither are a lot of travellers) and the ship isn't all that clean to begin with. The sight of people puking and the general smell and trashy nature of the ship may have effects even on those not usually prone to seasickness. You'd be advised to drop a seasick pill three hours or so before the voyage or pop on a scopolamine patch 12 hours before sailing if you want to avoid the worst of it. The toilets on board the *Queen Salamasina* aren't very exciting either.

Travellers on overnight ferries should carry a ground cover and sleeping bag if they plan to do any sleeping on the boat. If it's windy or rainy, you may wind up sleeping under the tables in the stuffy lounge, but if the weather is fair, stake out a space on the upper deck and hope that a squall doesn't blow up in the middle of the night. Food and drinks are not usually available on board so bring some goodies, too, if you think you'll be able to eat. For information on the ferry between Upolu and Savai'i, see Getting There & Away at the end of the Savai'i chapter.

Yacht
The yachtie route through the Samoa islands begins in Pago Pago and runs west to Apia Harbour and to the three anchorages on Savai'i. August, September and October are the best months to go yacht hitchhiking around the Samoas. Details about crewing on a yacht are outlined in the earlier Getting There & Away chapter. Private yacht owners who intend to cruise around Savai'i should apply for a cruising permit at the Prime Minister's office in Apia. The permit will be issued in one or two days. If you're sailing out of Western Samoa from Savai'i, check out of the country in Apia before leaving the harbour or you'll have to sail back against prevailing winds to do so.

CAR
In either of the Samoas, hiring a car (at the time of writing, there were no agencies offering motorcycles for hire) will give you the opportunity to see the sights around the main islands quickly and comfortably but will also rob you of some of the unique cultural experiences that can be gained on public transport and without the liability of a vehicle.

Getting around by car in Upolu and Savai'i in Independent Samoa or Tutuila in American Samoa is quite straightforward and won't require a daring demeanour or any special skills. You'll normally get by using your driving licence from home but occasionally visitors to Independent Samoa will be required to pay ST10 to have their licence endorsed at the police station in Apia.

Road Rules

In both American and Independent Samoa vehicles drive on the right. The speed limit within the Apia area and through villages is 40km/h; outside populated areas, it's 55km/h. In American Samoa, the speed limit is 15mph (24km/h) through villages and (25mph) 40km/h outside populated areas.

While you're out exploring the islands, never leave a car unattended in a village or it's quite possible that some sort of mischief will befall it. If you hit a domestic animal on the road, some travellers advise you to keep driving. If you stop, they say, you may experience the wrath of the offended village and possibly risk personal injury, or the destruction of your vehicle. Instead, you could note the name of the village and arrange to make fair restitution through the police.

Rental in Independent Samoa

There are at least 20 car rental agencies in Apia and a couple in Saleloga on Savai'i (these are listed under Getting Around in the Upolu and Savai'i chapters). You must be at least 21 years of age to hire a car in Independent Samoa and tariffs on hire cars are regulated by the government. The most popular vehicles are small Suzuki 4WD jeeps which cost from around ST100 per day including insurance, tax and unlimited km. The price usually drops to ST80 per day if you hire the car for seven days or more.

When hiring a vehicle, check for any damage or scratches before you get into the car and note everything on the rental agreement, lest you be liable for the damage when the car is returned. Furthermore, fend off requests to leave your passport or a cash deposit against possible damages. Petrol costs about ST1.20 per litre. There are occasional shortages when the islands are awaiting tanker supplies.

On Upolu, you'll find petrol stations only in Apia, at Faleula (10km west), Vailele (5km east) and at Nofoalii (about 5km east of Faleolo airport). The LA Traders store at Lalomanu sells petrol, at a price, should you find yourself running low on the south side of the island. On Savai'i, petrol is available

at Saleologa and Lalomalava on the south-east of the island and at Avao and Auala on the north side.

Rental in American Samoa

In American Samoa, hiring a car will be the best way to reach the more remote parts of Tutuila if you don't have an unlimited amount of time. While the aiga buses frequently ply the main roads, few traverse the passes over to the north coast of the island where some of the most interesting villages and nicest beaches are found. There are half a dozen car-rental agencies in the Pago Pago area (listed under Getting Around in the Tutuila chapter), but you'll pay standard US mainland prices (from US$55 per day). Few tourists spend more than a stopover here and it doesn't pay rental firms to offer discounts and specials on hire cars. Petrol is readily available and costs about 36 cents per litre.

BICYCLE

For fit, experienced cyclists, touring Upolu and Savai'i by bicycle is certainly possible – some would even say it's the best way to appreciate the islands. The roads are generally in very good condition and traffic is minimal. The major roads encircling the islands are all sealed except for the small section on the south side of Upolu between Le Mafa Pass Road and the South Coast Road. The longest stretch between accommodation options would be about 45km on Savai'i.

The island of Tutuila in American Samoa is much less suitable for cycling. Though smaller than Upolu and Savai'i, Tutuila is more mountainous, traffic is heavier and a complete circuit of the island is impossible since there are no roads across the rugged north coast of the island.

A primary consideration on a cycling tour is to travel light, but you should take a few tools and spare parts, including a puncture repair kit and an extra inner tube (you won't find any bicycle shops on the islands). You'll need to carry plenty of water and some basic food supplies, too. Panniers are essential to balance your possessions on either side of the bike frame. Take a good lock and always use it when you leave your bike unattended.

The biggest challenge will be dealing with the heat. Even during the coolest months of the year (July, August, September) afternoon temperatures will still reach the high 20s. Plan your expedition carefully to avoid cycling long stretches in the heat of the day. Also bear in mind that buses are unlikely to be able to accommodate bicycles should you run out of leg power.

Maps are available from the Department of Lands, Surveys & Environment in Apia. There are a couple of places in Apia which rent bicycles (see the Upolu Island chapter), but if you're planning a serious tour you'll need to bring your own.

HITCHING

Hitching is never entirely safe in any country and we don't recommend it. Travellers who decide to hitch should understand that they are taking a small but potentially serious risk. People who do choose to hitch will be safer if they travel in pairs and let someone know where they plan to go.

The main difficulty with hitching in the Samoas is that rides won't generally be very long, perhaps only from one village to the next, and it could take you a good while to go a longer distance. Still, given the sorry state of the bus service on Savai'i, hitching is one way to see that island and it will give you an out if you're caught in the nether lands of Upolu or Tutuila after the buses have stopped running for the night. You might be expected to pay a small fee for a ride so offer what you think the ride is worth – never more than about ST2 or ST3 per person – although offers of payment will normally be refused.

ORGANISED TOURS

Independent Samoa offers a good range of local tours – from laid-back beach trips on Sunday (when there's nothing to do but pray, eat and sleep) to serious seven-day adventure holidays where visitors get to kayak through mangroves, eat traditional Samoan food and stay in local villages. You can also meander round the islands in air conditioned splend-

our or even take in the sights by helicopter. Tours start at about ST50 per person per day.

Organised tour offerings in American Samoa are much more limited in scope and about twice the price. The following agencies operate tours around the islands:

Annie's Tours (☎ 21550; fax 20886), PO Box 4183, Matautu, Apia, Independent Samoa, offers full and half-day tours around Upolu and Savai'i.

Coconuts Beach Club Tours (☎ 23914; fax 20071), PO Box 3684, Apia, Independent Samoa, runs snorkelling and dive tours, boat cruises into the mangrove estuary and can also put together custom tours based upon individual interests.

Eco-Tour Samoa (☎ /fax 22144; ecotour@talofa.net), PO Box 4609 Matautu-uta, Independent Samoa, offers an action-packed, seven day Samoan Safari (US$137 per person per day) that takes visitors (maximum of 15) to Upolu, Manono and Savai'i. Five nights are spent in villages. Eco-Tour also runs a seven-day Samoan Soft Adventure, with five nights in hotels and two nights in villages; sea kayaking tours (maximum of three people); and educational tours.

Jane's Tours & Travel Ltd (☎ 20218; fax 22680), PO Box 70, Apia, Independent Samoa, offers sightseeing tours around Upolu Island.

Oceania Travel & Tours (☎ 24443; fax 22255), PO Box 9339, Apia, Independent Samoa, operates one and two day tours to Savai'i and Pago Pago, American Samoa. The one day tours cost US$99 and US$135 respectively.

Outrigger Adventure Tours (☎ /fax 20042; outrigger@talofa.net), PO Box 4074, Apia, Independent Samoa, runs three tours a week: a visit to Manono Island; a trip to Togitogiga Falls in the national park plus barbecue at Paradise Beach; a Sunday tour to south-east Upolu where guests enjoy a traditonal umu. All tours cost ST40 per person including food. Children up to 12 go free.

Retzlaff's Tours (☎ 21724; fax 23038), PO Box 1863, Saleufi, Apia, Independent Samoa, also offers sightseeing tours around Upolu Island.

Safua Tours (☎ 51271; fax 51272), Lalomalava, Savai'i, Independent Samoa, provides excellent cultural, educational and scenic tours, including a look at siapo making, a half day tour to Pulemelei Mound and an excellent clifftop walk from Cape Paepaeoleia on the Tafua Peninsula.

Samoa Scenic Tours (☎ 26981; fax 26982; aggiegrey@talofa.net), PO Box 669, Apia, Independent Samoa, runs full and half day tours around Apia and Upolu.

Samoa Tours & Travel (☎ 633 5884; fax 633 1311), PO Box 727, Pago Pago, American Samoa 96799, offers tours around Tutuila Island, village visits and island feasts.

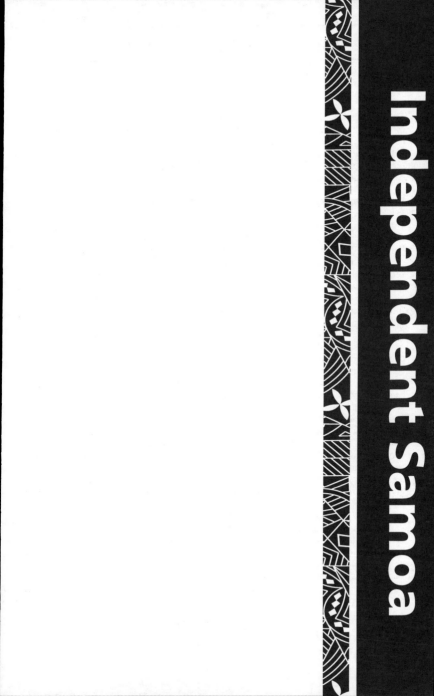

Independent Samoa

Facts about Independent Samoa

HISTORY

The Independent State of Western Samoa officially changed its name to the Independent State of Samoa in July 1997.

For a discussion of events prior to 1900, see the Facts about the Region chapter at the beginning of the book.

Early Colonial Period

In February 1900, after the bitter colonial power struggle between the US, Britain and Germany left the latter in control of Western Samoa, Dr Wilhelm Solf was appointed governor and the new caretakers of the colony settled in to rule. The German trading company DHPG (see History in the Facts about the Region chapter) began to import foreign labour to Western Samoa. At least 7000 Melanesians were brought from German claims in New Guinea and the Solomons to work on the plantations and soon Chinese were also being brought to the colony as labourers.

As would be expected in such a situation, health and working conditions were deplorable but, of the two groups, the Chinese seemed to fare better because they were actually paid a wage, however minimal, for their labour. In 1908, a Chinese consul was appointed to oversee their affairs in Samoa and the Chinese were given the official and legal status of Europeans. They were also given the freedom to work for whomever they chose, while the Melanesians were restricted to employment with the DHPG.

Although the Germans had agreed to rule 'according to Samoan custom', they hardly kept their word. Upon assuming the governorship, Solf deposed the king at the time, Tupu Samoa, and determined that the highest power to be in charge of local affairs would be an *ali'i* (paramount chief). His next act was to disarm the people and, at the end of his first year of rule, all the gift rifles distributed during the dispute between the three powers were confiscated.

In 1903, Solf established a Lands & Titles Commission, ostensibly to determine land ownership and settle conflicts. What it actually determined, however, was that 35% of arable Samoan land had already been sold to Europeans.

Early 20th Century

Although the first decade of the 20th century was more peaceful than the previous decades had been, Solf continued to ignore Samoan tradition in favour of personal and European interests, causing a breakdown in communications between the Samoans and their colonial rulers. In matters of dispute, the governor assumed the role of dictator.

By 1908 many Samoans had decided they could take it no longer. An official resistance force, the Mau a Pule (Mau Movement), was organised on Savai'i by Namulau'ulu Lauaki Mamoe, the talking chief of Fa'asalele'aga district. Its members tried by all peaceful means available to persuade the Germans to see things from a Samoan viewpoint but Solf was unmoving. Fearing violence, Germany sent warships and in January 1909 Namulau'ulu and company were exiled to the Micronesian island of Saipan in the Mariana Islands (at the time a German colony).

While all this was going on, nature was wreaking havoc on Savai'i. In 1905, Mt Matavanu exploded and the entire island heard and felt the eruption that devastated the north coast, destroying villages and crops and polluting the water supply. Fortunately, there was enough warning to evacuate the area before it disappeared under the river of boiling lava that surged down from the mountain and no-one was killed. The Mormon and Catholic churches in the area were flattened but the flow 'miraculously' separated and spared the Methodist church.

Eruptions continued until 1910 and the German administration acquired land on

Upolu on which to resettle the displaced and famine-stricken Savai'i people.

When Archduke Franz Ferdinand was assassinated in Sarajevo in 1914 and Austria-Hungary declared war on Serbia, Germany was involved in a rush to colonise as many countries as possible before the entire world was swallowed up by other powers. German imperialism, however, was thwarted by Germany's alliances with Austria. When Russia allied itself with Serbia, Germany declared war on Russia. Britain, France and the USA joined Russia and WWI ensued.

At the outbreak of war, Britain persuaded nearby New Zealand to seize German Samoa. Preoccupation with affairs on the home front prevented Germany from resisting.

New Zealand occupation continued peacefully under the military leadership of Colonel Logan until 30 April 1920. When the Mau Movement leaders in Saipan heard of the New Zealand takeover they decided it would be necessary to learn English if they wanted to deal with the new administration at home. The leader at the time, I'iga, built an outrigger canoe on Saipan and escaped to the American colony on Guam, arriving after only two days at sea. In honour of this crossing, the strait between Saipan and Guam became known as I'iga Pisa. Finally, I'iga was allowed to return home and was invited by Colonel Logan to serve as the Secretary of the Office of Samoan Affairs, a position that he held until 1954.

It was during Logan's rule that the ship *Talune* was carelessly permitted to dock in Apia Harbour. Shortly afterwards, 8500 Western Samoans – 22% of the population – died of Spanish influenza. During the crisis, the New Zealand administration refused offers of medical assistance from American Samoa.

Although the Mau Movement's leaders had been exiled, the organisation continued at home and by the 1920s tolerance for New Zealand rule was growing thin. It remained a peaceful organisation and many European residents of the Samoas also joined. The administration became tense about its popularity and had several of its European affiliates banished.

The growing hostility between the factions came to violence on 28 December 1929. One of the exiles, a Mr Smyth, was enthusiastically greeted in Apia by the Mau upon his return after three years. Armed police took the opportunity to nab some wanted Mau members and a fight resulted. The authorities fired a machine gun into the crowd of unarmed people, killing 11, including the movement leader, Tupua Tamasese Lealofi III.

The Mau were officially disbanded and a New Zealand warship was sent to enforce the policy of the increasingly paranoid administration. When a Labour government came to power in New Zealand in 1935, the conflict cooled down and relations between Samoans and the government improved.

Independence

During WWII, US marines stationed on Upolu were involved primarily in public works that might have been useful in the case of attack. When they left, the Kiwi grip on Samoa was relaxed and the islands acquired the status of a United Nations Trust territory under the administration of New Zealand.

In 1947, the Council of State was established to serve as the executive body of local government, although it was still subservient to the United Nations Executive Council. It consisted of the New Zealand High Commissioner, who was president, and two Samoan chiefs, who were advisers. A legislative assembly was established simultaneously.

Seven years later a constitutional convention met and in 1957 the entire government of Western Samoa was reorganised, obviously in preparation for the independence of the country. In September 1959 a prime minister, Fiame Mata'afa, was appointed and the following year a formal constitution was adopted.

A proposal of independence was put before the United Nations in January 1961. This resulted in a referendum that asked all Western Samoans whether or not they approved of the constitution. It also asked whether or not they wanted independence on 1 January 1962. Of course, the overwhelming response was in favour of freedom from foreign rule. This was the first and last time that the Western Samoan commoner was allowed a say in government matters until 1990, when universal suffrage was adopted. Until that time, only *matais* were permitted to vote in elections.

The two high chiefs who had served with the New Zealand High Commissioner on the Council of State, Tupua Tamasese and Malietoa Tanumafili II, became joint heads of state. The death of the former, on 5 April 1963, left the latter as the sole head of the newly independent state of Western Samoa.

The official economic plan was to proceed slowly from a subsistence economy towards a cash economy but, by 1965 the vision of imminent prosperity had faded. Labour disputes and a devastating cyclone in 1966 did nothing to improve the situation. Numerous Samoans emigrated to New Zealand and many more made plans to do so.

Western Samoa became increasingly dependent on foreign economic aid during the 60s and 70s and the idea of promoting foreign investment and tourism began to take hold. Roads were sealed, the airport was improved, and the Tusitala Hotel (it has since been taken over by Japanese interests and is now known as the Hotel Kitano Tusitala) was opened to accommodate business visitors and holiday-makers. Though tourism continues to be an important growth industry, the government still relies heavily on foreign aid and overseas borrowing.

In February 1990 and December 1991, the islands were struck by Cyclones Ofa and Val; 32 people were killed, villages were destroyed and crops and forestry plantations were devastated. Little evidence of the damage remains but some crops, such as coffee and cocoa, have never fully recovered.

In 1993 and 1994, the country's biggest export crop, taro, was wiped out by a virulent fungal blight.

In 1997, only a tiny amount of taro was being grown for domestic consumption.

The past few years have seen an increase in taxation, a decrease in agricultural subsidies, rising foreign debt and continued high levels of government corruption. In 1997, the country made international news with a scam involving the sale of Samoan passports for up to $HK26,000 in Hong Kong.

GOVERNMENT & POLITICS

The national government of Independent Samoa operates under a British-based parliamentary system which has been revised to accommodate local custom and Christian principles.

Although the constitution provides for a head of state to be elected by the *fono* (the parliament or legislature) every five years, that provision won't take effect until the current holder of that position, Malietoa Tanumafili II, retires from office. Malietoa Tanumafili II was one of the two initial heads of state designated to hold that title for life when the country gained its independence.

The position of head of state, known as O le Ao O le Malo, is titular only, but its holder does have the power to appoint or remove the prime minister and to grant pardons. All official acts, however, are subject to the approval of the fono. Future heads of state will be chosen from the Tama'aiga – the four royal families of Samoa.

The 49-seat fono is comprised of 47 members of parliament, headed by a speaker. The remaining two seats in the fono are held by members elected by a small body of naturalised Samoans and, in theory, represent the interests of ethnic Europeans and Chinese who are citizens of Independent Samoa but are not members of any *aiga*. The beehive-shaped *Fale Fono* (the fono building), opened in June 1972, is on the Mulinu'u Peninsula near Apia.

Until recently, voting rights in the country were restricted to the 20,000 official matais but, unfortunately, their selections were often influenced more by cronyism, obligation or family ties than by professed beliefs, policies or ability. Universal suffrage by all citizens 21 years of age or over was adopted by referendum in 1990, but only matais have the right to stand for election.

There are currently two political parties represented in the fono – the ruling Human Rights Protection Party (HRPP) under Prime Minister Tofilau Eti Alesana and the opposition Samoan National Development Party (SNDP) led by Tupua Tamasese Lealofi IV, the son of the Mau leader murdered by New Zealand police in 1929.

Elections in 1996 returned the HRPP with a slim majority. Shortly afterwards, the government's term of office was increased from three years to five years.

The prime minister selects 12 cabinet ministers from the fono. The constitution also provides for a Council of Deputies to serve as a resource for 'backup' heads of state to act in an official capacity in the absence of the title-holder.

The judicial branch of government comprises four courts – the Supreme Court, the Magistrate's Court, the Lands and Titles Court and the Court of Appeals. Although court proceedings are held in English, they are always simultaneously interpreted into Samoan. Although the system is based on the British, Samoan tradition is also considered in cases where it becomes an issue.

Local governments include administrative districts that oversee the operation of educational and medical facilities, agricultural offices and police. Villages are still governed by the matai system.

Land held in trust for aiga by respective matais comprise 80% of Western Samoa. It is called customary lands and can be leased to, but never purchased by, other aiga. Although there is still alienated land within the country, the Berlin Act of 1889 disallowed any land claims based upon trade with Europeans for alcohol or firearms. Mission land and that currently held by outside corporations and individuals occupy only about 8% of the territory. The remainder is held by the state.

For more information on local government, see the discussion of the Matai System under Society & Conduct in the Facts about the Region chapter.

ECONOMY

Since Independence, Samoa has concentrated on developing a modern economy based on traditional village agriculture and primary products. Subsistence agriculture still supports around 75% of the population. The primary sector employs more than half the workforce and accounts for 50% of GDP and about 80% of export earnings. About 30% of the workforce is employed by the government. Despite huge investments in agriculture, fisheries and forestry, however, there has been a continuing decline in the export of primary products and, at the same time, a rise in imports. Low commodity prices, poor management in the agricultural sector, the effects of Cyclones Ofa and Val, and the recent taro blight are all partly to blame for the decline in agricultural exports.

The economy continues to depend heavily on foreign aid, provided by New Zealand, Australia, the European Economic Community, Japan and China. Remittances from Samoans working overseas is another important source of foreign exchange.

Emigration to Australasia and North America remains high, and though this provides much-needed foreign exchange, it also results in a loss of skilled workers. Those who leave often find it difficult to adjust to the stress of living in a fast-paced, materialistic society.

Wages in Independent Samoa are extremely low relative to local living costs: the minimum legal wage for employees of private companies is ST$2.50 per hour. It's understandable then that many Independent Samoan workers find it difficult to resist trading their professional jobs for drudgery work at the tuna canneries in American Samoa or an unsettling life in the fast lanes of New Zealand, Australia or the USA.

Tourism is of increasing importance to the economy of Independent Samoa and in recent years the government has promoted the development of light manufacturing industries.

Agriculture

Coffee, bananas and copra have historically

The World in Your Palm

It's not surprising that Samoans, like other Pacific islanders, revere the coconut palm. The rich milk that is squeezed from the silky white flesh of the coconut is used as the basis of Polynesian cooking and coconut water is a delicious and refreshing liquid, so pure that it can be used medicinally.

But there's even more to be gained from the 'milkbottle on the doorstep of mankind'. The dried meat of mature coconuts – copra – is used as the basis for making coconut oil, for many years an economic mainstay of island economies. Sun-drying is the usual means of making copra but commercial operations involve placing the wet meat in a large kiln and using the shells as fuel. It has been estimated that over 800 products are derived from coconut oil alone.

In Samoa, women use coconut oil and *moso'oi* flowers to make a healing, scented oil.

The shells can be used as drinking vessels and, when burned, make excellent charcoal. Polished shell can also be fashioned into jewellery.

The stringy coconut husk is braided into rope and used for scrubbing brushes in the home. Coconut leaves are woven to make thatching, blinds, baskets and trays for serving food; sweeping brooms are made from the strong stalks of the leaves.

The trunk of the tree is used for timber – posts for *fales*, fences, roof tiles and firewood.

Trees live to over 70 years of age and will produce about 60 coconuts a year. If the nuts are not cut down they eventually fall, which is why you should always check for coconuts before settling in for a nap beneath a palm tree, or parking your car under one. ■

---

been the most important export crops and for a while, cocoa was the star on Independent Samoa's economic horizon. In 1980, US$5 million worth of cocoa was produced and throughout the 1980s, the export amount increased steadily every year. In the 1990s, cyclone damage, coupled with a waning enthusiasm for this crop, caused exports to plummet. Plantations still cover parts of Savai'i but most of the cocoa (which is said to be the best in the world) is for domestic consumption. The Wilex chocolate factory in Apia, however, does produce a range of chocolate products for the Pacific market. Farmers are reluctant to plant cacao (the tree that produces cocoa beans) because the trees take at least five years to mature.

Independent Samoa's banana export business, which was decimated in the late 1950s by disease, cyclone damage, mismanagement and competition from Latin America, was revived somewhat in mid-1993 when the 12-hectare plantation of the Agricultural Store Corporations began exporting four container loads of bananas to New Zealand each month. Bananas are still exported to New Zealand but growers can't produce enough to satisfy demand. Currently, the African tree snail, first noticed in Apia three or four years ago, poses a threat to banana plantations.

Coconuts and small quantities of coconut oil are exported to Australia and elsewhere. Until recently, the largest coconut plantation in the southern hemisphere was at Mulifanua, 40km west of Apia. It was first owned by the German government and then by the New Zealand administration. The plantation was maintained by the Western Samoa Trust Estates until the mid-1990s. The government-controlled Samoa Land Corporation has since bought much of the land and is in the process of selling and leasing it as private land.

Independent Samoa has traditionally been one of the world's largest producers of *taro niue* (a tasty and easily stored strain of taro), exporting ST$6.9 million worth of the root crop annually, mainly to expatriate populations in New Zealand, Australia and the USA. In July 1993, however, a virulent fungal blight, *Phytophthora colocasiae*, was discovered in the Samoas. (This infestation is a close cousin of the infamous potato blight which destroyed Ireland's potato crops in the 1840s, leading to the starvation of almost a third of the country's population.) By the end of 1994, it had wiped out crops throughout Upolu and Savai'i. Taro crops have still not recovered and taro must now be imported.

Though ta'amu, or 'big taro', is grown in place of taro, and sweet potato and cassava have been grown as experimental crops, nothing has filled the export gap.

Independent Samoa no longer exports timber, but there are four local saw-milling companies operating on the island of Savai'i.

Fishing

Subsistence agriculture has traditionally gone hand in hand with fishing and it has been estimated that about 60% of farming households are engaged in subsistence fishing within lagoon waters. Methods involve fishing from traditional outrigger canoes, spearfishing and collecting shellfish from the reefs.

It is thought that overfishing, nonselective fishing techniques and the use of poisons and dynamite (now illegal) have led to a decline in lagoon fish stocks in Upolu. An increasing number of local fishers are becoming involved in commercial fishing, attracted in the main by the very high prices being paid for tuna by the two big canneries in Pago Pago, American Samoa. However, unlike the Korean, Peruvian and American fleets, which operate longliners and purse-seiners, Independent Samoan fishers go out in twin-hulled aluminium craft with outboard motors.

Manufacturing & Foreign Investment

Independent Samoa has several small-scale manufacturing concerns. Its best known product, Vailima beer, has been turning up

Skipjack Tuna are fished commercially

not only in American Samoa, but also in Hawaii and further afield. Since 1993, Vailima has been canned under licence in New Zealand. Majority shares in the brewery, which was established in 1978, are held by the government with a management contract run by German firm Haase Braurei of Hamburg.

Yazaki Samoa is a fairly large Japanese joint venture which manufactures automobile components. The Wilex chocolate factory exports a range of chocolate products to other Pacific countries and Rothmans exports tobacco to the USA, American Samoa and other islands.

In order to make itself more appealing to foreign investment and joint ventures, Independent Samoa has introduced tax breaks for foreign manufacturers who export at least 95% of their production. So far, the keenest takers have been the Japanese. The country is also setting itself up as an offshore banking centre, providing a tax haven for Asian, European and North American businesses. The Chinese are becoming increasingly involved in small businesses on the islands and China has recently provided funding for the new Women & Youth Activity Centre in Apia.

INDEPENDENT SAMOA

Facts for the Visitor

TOURIST OFFICES
Local Visitors Bureau Office
The Samoa Visitors Bureau (☎ 20180; fax 20886), PO Box 2272, Apia, is housed in a modern *fale* on the reclaimed area behind Beach Rd. Bureau staff are quite helpful and can provide you with up-to-date information on hotels and happenings around the country. The office is open from 8 am to 4.30 pm Monday to Friday and on Saturday from 8.30 am to noon. The bureau publishes a free monthly newspaper, *The Visitor*, which contains advertising by most of Independent Samoa's tourist-related businesses as well as background articles on the country and the society.

Visitors Bureau Offices Abroad
Independent Samoa has Visitors Bureau Offices in the following countries:

Australia
> Level 67, MLC Centre, 19 Martin Place, Sydney, NSW 2000 (☎ 02-9238 6113; fax 02-9221 1987)

Belgium
> Rue Americaine 27, 1050 Brussels, Belgium (☎ 2-538 2930; fax 2-538 2885)

France
> 13 Rue d'Alembert, 3800 Grenoble (☎ 04-76 70 06 17; fax 04-76 70 09 18)

Germany
> Dirkenstrasse 40, 1020 Berlin, Germany (☎ 30-2381 7628; fax 30-2381 7641)

New Zealand
> Level 1 Samoa House, 283 Karangahape Rd, PO Box 68423, Newton, Auckland (☎ 09-379 6138; fax 09-379 8154)

UK
> 375 Upper Richmond Rd, London SW14 7NX (☎ 0181-392 1838; fax 0181-392 1318

USA
> Lake Blvd 475, PO Box 7740, Tahoe City, CA96145 (☎ 916-538 0152; fax 916-583 0154)

VISAS & DOCUMENTS
Visitors entering Independent Samoa will require a valid passport and an onward ticket. You'll also be required to provide a contact address within the country, so have the name of a hotel ready upon arrival. Vaccinations for yellow fever may be required if you are coming from an infected area. Tourist visas of 30 days are automatically granted on arrival. Yachts must be cleared by immigration, health and customs; those intending to visit Savai'i need to apply for a permit from the Prime Minister's office in Apia. If you intend driving, a licence from home is normally sufficient but occasionally visitors will be required to pay ST10 to have their licence endorsed at the police station in Apia.

Visa Extensions
Visas may be extended by several weeks at a time by the Immigration Office in Apia. Take along your passport, wallet, two passport-sized photos and don't make any other plans for the rest of the day. You may also need to have proof of hotel accommodation, onward transport and sufficient funds for your requested period of stay. Those intending to stay longer than 30 days can also apply for a Visitor's Permit (valid for up to six months) from their home country – allow between one and three months for processing. Permanent immigration to Independent Samoa is quite difficult – even for spouses of citizens – but teachers and people with medical and other expertise are always in demand for temporary contract jobs.

EMBASSIES
Samoan Embassies
In countries without Samoan diplomatic posts, Independent Samoa is represented by New Zealand and British diplomatic missions. Samoa has diplomatic representation in the following countries:

Australia
> PO Box 3274, 13 Culgoa Circuit, O'Malley, ACT 2606 (☎ 06-286 5505; fax 06-286 5678)

Belgium
> 95 Avenue Franklin Roosevelt, 123-Bte 14, B-1050 Brussels (☎ 02-660 8454; fax 02-675-0336)

Germany
    Spaldingstrasse 210, D2000 Hamburg 1 (☎ 40-234 155; fax 40-234 158)
Hawaii
    94-537 Waipahu St, Waipahu, Hawaii 96797 (☎ 808-677 7197; fax 808-523 2928
Japan
    Marunouchi Bldg, 4-1 Marunouchi, 2-Chome, Chiyoda-Ku, Tokyo 100 (☎ 813-211-7604; fax 813-214-7036)
New Zealand
    High Commission: 1A Wesley Rd, Kelburn, PO Box 1430, Wellington (☎ 04-720 953; fax 04-712 479)

    Consulate General: Samoa House, 3rd Floor, PO Box 68-147, Karangahape Rd, Auckland (☎ 09-303 1012; fax 09-302 1168)
United Nations Mission
    820 2nd Avenue, Suite 800, New York, NY 10017 (☎ 212-599 6196; fax 212-599 0797)

Foreign Embassies in Independent Samoa
Refer to the Upolu chapter for details.

CUSTOMS
Visitors can bring in a 1L bottle of spirits and up to 200 cigarettes duty free. Any sexually explicit publications or other material the officials consider objectionable will be confiscated. As usual, it's illegal to import live animals. Plant material, vegetables or meat may not be imported without a permit from the Quarantine Section of the Department of Agriculture.

MONEY
Costs
Independent Samoa is one of the cheapest places to travel in the South Pacific, placing it in a particularly good position to attract budget travellers. In Apia, which many people use as a base while exploring the main island of Upolu, pleasant singles/doubles start at ST44/55 and dormitory beds can be found for around ST20. Beachside fales on Upolu and Savai'i cost as little as ST15. In Apia, you'll pay from ST10 for a decent meal; three times as much in an up-market restaurant. If you're prepared to use public transport you can travel anywhere on Upolu for less than ST2 and can get to Savai'i for ST6. The fare from the Salelologa ferry landing to anywhere on Savai'i will be less

than ST3. With car hire, medium-range accommodation and up-market eating (not that there's a great deal of it), two people could travel in Samoa on a minimum of about ST160 each per day.

Carrying Money
Theft is not a major problem in Samoa but it can happen. Avoid becoming suddenly destitute by keeping your money in inside pouches and secret stashes and by not carrying your wallet in your back pocket. Don't put all your eggs in one basket – carry a combination of cash, travellers' cheques and credit cards. It would also be a good idea to take travellers' cheques in a variety of small and large denominations to avoid being stuck with lots of cash when leaving. When travelling around the islands, be sure to carry cash in small denominations. In Apia, most middle to upper range hotels, car rental agencies, upmarket restaurants and craft shops will accept major credit cards.

Currency
The Samoan *tala* (dollar), which is divided into 100 *sene* (cents), is the unit of currency in use. Bank notes currently in circulation come in denominations of ST2, 5, 10, 20, 50 and 100. Coins come in 1, 2, 5, 10, 20 and 50 sene and ST1. Because of Independent Samoa's proximity to American Samoa, the most acceptable foreign currency is the US dollar, which is normally negotiable in shops, restaurants and hotels (indeed, some hotels quote their rates in US dollars so they don't sound so expensive!).

Currency Exchange
Each morning the banks receive the daily exchange rates by fax and changing money is straightforward. They'll exchange just about any 'solid' currency but most preferable are US, New Zealand and Australian dollars, and pounds sterling. Travellers' cheques will generally fetch about 4% more than cash. No one will try to get the best of you here and there are no black-market-related hassles to contend with.

When you're leaving Independent Samoa,

excess tala may be re-exchanged for foreign currency (normally limited to US, New Zealand and Australian dollars) in the banks or at the exchange branches at Faleolo airport. As of March 1997, tala can be exchanged for local currency in Australia, New Zealand, Fiji, Tonga and American Samoa. At the time of writing, the exchange rates were as follows:

Australia	A$1	=	ST1.76
Canada	C$1	=	ST1.67
Fiji	F$1	=	ST1.63
France	1FF	=	ST0.45
Germany	DM1	=	ST1.15
Japan	¥100	=	ST2.14
New Zealand	NZ$1	=	ST1.55
Tonga	T$1	=	ST1.88
UK	UK£1	=	ST3.73
USA	US$1	=	ST2.44

Changing Money

The three main banks in Independent Samoa and those that change travellers' cheques and foreign currency are the Bank of Samoa, the Pacific Commercial Bank and the new National Bank of Samoa. All have their main branches in central Apia. There are subsidiary offices in Salelologa on Savai'i. They're open weekdays from 9 am to 3 pm. The National Bank of Samoa has a branch near the main market in Apia which is open on Saturday from 8.30 am to 12.30 pm. There are also currency-exchange branches at Faleolo airport which are open to coincide with incoming and outgoing flights. All the banks charge a small commission for changing travellers' cheques. The Bank of Samoa provides Visa and Mastercard cash advances and the Pacific Commercial Bank gives Mastercard cash advances. There are no ATMs in Samoa. In a pinch or on weekends, cash and travellers' cheques can be exchanged at Aggie Grey's Hotel, the Tusitala and the Vaisala Beach Resort. Some travel agencies will exchange US dollars.

Tipping & Bargaining

Tipping is not part of everyday life in Polynesia and is not expected or encouraged in Independent Samoa. The Pacific is not like Asia: bargaining isn't the norm on any of the islands and the price listed is the price you're expected to pay.

Consumer Taxes

There is a hotel tax of ST1 per person per night but it is normally included in the quoted price of the room. There's also a 10% GST on goods and services which is usually included in marked prices.

POST & COMMUNICATIONS

The main post office is on Beach Rd, Apia, one block east of the clock tower. It was consolidated with the communications office (International Telephone Bureau, or just ITB) after the old post office was destroyed in a suspicious fire in 1986. Postal services are available between 9 am and 4.30 pm. The counter selling souvenir envelopes and first-day covers is closed at lunchtime.

Postal Rates

To post an item to anywhere in the Pacific islands, including Australia and New Zealand, the rate is 70 sene for up to 10g, ST1.05 for up to 20g and ST2.10 for 50g. To North America or Asia, it's 90 sene for 10g, ST1.40 for 20g and ST2.90 for 50g. To Europe, the Middle East and Latin America, you'll pay 95 sene for 10g, ST1.55 for 20g and ST3.35 for 50g. Postage to the rest of the world is ST1.20 for 10g, ST1.90 for 20g and ST5.50 for 50g. Aerogrammes to anywhere in the world cost 85 sene. An air mail parcel weighing 1kg costs ST21.55 to New Zealand; ST24.20 to Australia; ST20.70 to North America; ST37 to the UK; and from ST46 to Europe.

Receiving Mail

Poste restante is located in a separate office just down Post Office St behind the main lobby. If you're to receive mail in Apia, have it addressed to you with your surname underlined to: Poste Restante, Chief Post Office, Apia, Samoa.

Telephone, Telex & Fax

The ITB is open for phone and telex services from 8 am to 10 pm daily. Fax services are available upstairs from 8 am to 4.30 pm Monday to Friday. There are two pay phones in the office – these are the only public telephones on the islands, so be prepared for long waits. A three minute local call costs 50 sene. A three minute station-to-station call to Hawaii, Europe, the UK and the USA costs ST13.50; the same to Australia or New Zealand costs ST9. The country code for Independent Samoa is 685. A one page fax to the Pacific region and Australasia costs ST9.50; to Asia, Hawaii, Europe, the UK and the USA, ST14.

BOOKS

See Facts for the Visitor chapter.

NEWSPAPERS & MAGAZINES

There are a handful of local papers which provide minimal coverage of international news and rather more comprehensive treatment of local politics and sports. The *Samoa Observer* (☎ 23078; fax 21195), PO Box 1572, Apia, comes out Tuesday to Friday and also on Sunday. The *Sunday Newsline* is published weekly and the government run paper *Savali* comes out twice a week. The local news magazine *Taluma*, PO Box 1321, Apia, is published monthly. Magazines which cover the Pacific in general include *Le Pasefika*, a new travel and lifestyle magazine; *Pacific Magazine* and *Pacific Islands Monthly*. Weekend Australian and New Zealand newspapers are available from Lynn Netzler's Store and Le Moana Cafe in Apia.

RADIO & TV

Independent Samoa has two radio stations. Magic 98FM, which broadcasts from 6 am to midnight, plays a good range of popular music. The government run AM station Radio 2AP operates on two channels – the English language channel broadcasts from 5 pm to 11 pm Monday to Friday; the Samoan channel from 6 am to 11 pm daily. WVUV comes in from American Samoa, as do short-wave broadcasts from the BBC and Voice of America. TV Samoa, operated in conjunction with Television New Zealand, mainly broadcasts overseas programs. Limited US network programming is available on station KVZK Pago Pago, due to the proximity of American Samoa. Cable programming is also available in the big hotels. Cable TV was due to be introduced across the islands in 1998.

ELECTRICITY

The area around Apia is served by hydro and diesel-generated power that emerges at 240V, 50Hz AC. Outlets accept the three-pronged plugs used on New Zealand and Australian appliances. Use of American appliances would require mutilation of the plug (or an adapter) as well as a voltage converter. Power fluctuations can damage electronic items. Anyone planning to use a laptop computer or similar may want to invest in a surge protector just to be on the safe side.

LAUNDRY

In Samoan laundries there are usually attendants who will wash, dry and iron your clothes but prices are quite high relative to other costs within the country. Most middle and upper-range hotels offer same-day laundry services. For specifics, see under Apia in the Upolu chapter.

HEALTH

The National Hospital in Apia is inland, on Ifiifi St in the village of Leufisa (about five minutes by taxi from the centre of town). Health treatment is free to Samoan citizens and legal residents but foreigners must pay a small fee.

Before you settle in for that long wait to see the doctor, be sure to visit the 'booking' window and check in so they'll know you're there. Then proceed to the clinic waiting room, but don't forget to bring a book to read while you wait. If you can't spend a day waiting to see the hospital doctor you'd do well to shell out a bit more money and visit a private practice. For recommendations, see under Apia in the Upolu chapter.

INDEPENDENT SAMOA

Prescription medicines are available at the hospital dispensary for a nominal fee. Keep in mind, though, that some pharmaceutical companies ship expired supplies to places such as Samoa and the drugs you receive there may not retain their full potency, especially if they're more than one or two years out of date. Check the dates before buying. There is also a chemist opposite the public library on Beach Rd, but supplies are limited.

Although the staff at the National Hospital are fairly well-equipped to handle tropical diseases, infections and minor injuries, the health-care budget of Samoa is minimal and just doesn't stretch to include the equipment and expertise you can expect in Europe, North America or Australasia. If you come down with a serious ailment and can't get home easily, your best bet would be to fly to New Zealand or Hawaii for diagnosis and treatment. The latter, however, can be extremely expensive.

ACTIVITIES
Samoa has plenty of outdoor activities to offer visitors, but whatever you do – whether it's exploring the rainforests, snorkelling in the lagoons or even surfing offshore breaks – be sure to ask the local owners beforehand for permission to use to be able to take advantage of their land/beach/lagoon. See the Dos & Don't section in the Facts about the Region chapter.

Snorkelling
There is no shortage of snorkelling possibilities in Independent Samoa, but not many

places hire out gear. If you'd like to explore the reefs a bit, it's well worth bringing along your own mask and snorkel. One of the best and easiest places to catch a glimpse of the underwater scene is at Palolo Deep near Apia (you can hire gear here), but you will also find countless other opportunities all over the country.

Although just about any stretch of reef with more than a metre of water over it will qualify as a snorkelling site, the best areas for inexperienced snorkellers are along the Aleipata coast on the far eastern end of Upolu and around the islands of Manono and Apolima on the far western end. Just off the south coast, near Poutasi, is Nu'usafe'e Islet, which offers some of the most diverse corals and fish around Upolu. Strong swimmers and snorkellers can also tackle the turbulent waters en route to the excellent snorkelling around Nu'utele and Nu'ulua islands and between Malaela village and Namu'a Island, all in the Aleipata district.

Be extremely wary of the pounding surf and the sometimes overpowering current that ploughs through this area. There is less coral off Savai'i because recent volcanic flows have covered reef areas. The best snorkelling is at Vaisala in the north-west and at Tuasivi on the east coast.

The dive centres mentioned below offer organised snorkelling trips to sites around Upolu. Expect to pay around ST40 per person.

Diving
Although diving in Samoa isn't as spectacular as in some other Pacific countries, it's still

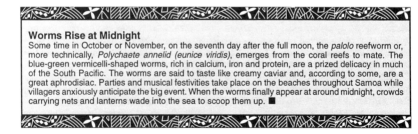

Worms Rise at Midnight
Some time in October or November, on the seventh day after the full moon, the *palolo* reefworm or, more technically, *Polychaete annelid (eunice viridis)*, emerges from the coral reefs to mate. The blue-green vermicelli-shaped worms, rich in calcium, iron and protein, are a prized delicacy in much of the South Pacific. The worms are said to taste like creamy caviar and, according to some, are a great aphrodisiac. Parties and musical festivities take place on the beaches throughout Samoa while villagers anxiously anticipate the big event. When the worms finally appear at around midnight, crowds carrying nets and lanterns wade into the sea to scoop them up. ■

Considerations for Responsible Diving

The popularity of diving is placing immense pressure on many sites. Please consider the following tips when diving and help preserve the ecology and beauty of reefs:

- Do not use anchors on the reef, and take care not to ground boats on coral. Encourage dive operators and regulatory bodies to establish permanent moorings at popular dive sites.
- Avoid touching living marine organisms with your body or dragging computer consoles and gauges across the reef. Polyps can be damaged by even the gentlest contact. Never stand on corals, even if they look solid and robust. If you must secure yourself to the reef, only hold fast to exposed rock or dead coral.
- Be conscious of your fins. Even without contact the surge from heavy fin strokes near the reef can damage delicate organisms. When treading water in shallow reef areas, take care not to kick up clouds of sand. Settling sand can easily smother the delicate organisms of the reef.
- Practise and maintain proper buoyancy control. Major damage can be done by divers descending too fast and colliding with the reef. Make sure you are correctly weighted and that your weight belt is positioned so that you stay horizontal. If you have not dived for a while, have a practice dive in a pool before taking to the reef. Be aware that buoyancy can change over the period of an extended trip: initially you may breathe harder and need more weighting; a few days later you may breathe more easily and need less weight.
- Take great care in underwater caves. Spend as little time within them as possible as your air bubbles may be caught within the roof and thereby leave previously submerged organisms high and dry. Taking turns to inspect the interior of a small cave will lessen the chances of damaging contact.
- Resist the temptation to collect or buy corals or shells.
- Ensure that you take home all your rubbish, and any litter you may find as well. Plastics in particular are a serious threat to marine life. Turtles will mistake plastic for jellyfish and eat it.
- Resist the temptation to feed fish. You may disturb their normal eating habits, encourage aggressive behaviour or feed them food that is detrimental to their health.
- Minimise your disturbance of marine animals. In particular, do not ride on the backs of turtles as this causes them great anxiety. ■

very good and there are two or three outfits offering diving charters.

One of these options is the well-established Samoa Marine (☎ 22721; fax 20087; pmeredith@samoa.net), PO Box 4700, Apia, located on Beach Rd opposite the main wharf. The proprietor, Peter Meredith, charges around ST135 for one-tank dives and ST160 for two, which includes the hire of all equipment. Snorkellers are welcome to come along if there's space but, naturally, only certified divers have access to the diving equipment.

A typical four hour trip is to the main reef off Faleula, 30 minutes by boat from Apia. Charters to Aleipata and Apolima can also be arranged for negotiable rates; the price will depend largely on the season and the number of divers interested.

Pacific Quest Divers (☎ 24728; pqdivers@ samoa.net) operates from Beach Rd, Apia, across from Aggie Grey's Hotel and out of Coconuts Beach Resort (☎ /fax 23914), on the south coast of Upolu. Diving trips along the south coast reefs with a qualified diver cost ST127 per person, including all equipment. If, however, you have your own equipment, you will only have to pay ST87 per person.

If you're not a certified diver but are interested in learning, one day resort courses, including instruction, equipment and one dive, are available for ST224 per person. A five day full certification course costs ST750. Sqvama Divers (☎ /fax 24858; tourism@ samoa.net), PO box 843, Apia, has an office above the Pasifika Inn and offers one-tank dives from ST96 per person; a whole range of diving courses starting at ST219 and all-day dives with lunch included for ST317.

Moonlight, Sea and Sex like Fireworks

Sex may be infrequent for coral but it is certainly spectacular.

Although the mass spawning which creates new coral only takes place once a year, the build-up to the big night lasts for six months or more. During that time the polyps ripen their eggs.These are initially white but later turn pink, red, orange and other bright colours. At the same time, male coral develops testes and produces sperm.

Some colonies of coral polyps are all male or all female, while polyps of other colonies are hermaphrodite – both male and female. In a few types of coral, hermaphrodite polyps can produce their own young, which are released at various times over the year. In most cases, however, the sperm of these polyps cannot fertilise their own eggs or other eggs from the same colony.

The big event comes in late spring or early summer. It begins a night or two after a full moon and builds to a crescendo on the fourth, fifth and sixth nights. At this time, water temperatures are ideal and there's a minimum of tidal variation. The eggs and sperm from the hermaphrodite coral are bundled together and half an hour prior to spawning time, the bundles are 'set'. This means they are held ready at the mouth of the polyp, clearly visible through the thin tissue.

Suddenly, right across the reef these tiny bundles are released and are allowed to float upward towards the surface. Remarkably, this spawning takes place simultaneously across the reef. Different colonies release their egg and sperm bundles; single-sex polyps eject their sperm or their eggs and everything floats upward. The egg and sperm bundles, large enough to be seen with the naked eye, are spectacular. Those who have seen the event describe it as like a fireworks display or an inverted snowstorm. Since it can be so accurately predicted, divers are often able to witness the mass spawning.

Once at the surface, the bundles break up and the sperm swim off in search of eggs of the same coral species. Obviously, corals of the same species must spawn at the same time in order to unite sperm and eggs of different colonies. Amid the swarm, it's obviously not easy for an individual sperm to find the right egg, but biologists believe that by spawning all at once they reduce the risk of being consumed by the numerous marine creatures which would prey on them. In addition, spawning soon after the full moon, when the tidal variation is reduced, means there is more time for fertilisation to take place before waves and currents sweep everything away.

Once fertilisation has occurred, the egg cells begin to divide, and within a day have become swimming, coral larvae known as planulae. These are swept along by the current but after several days sink to the bottom and, if the right spot is found, the tiny larvae become coral polyps and a new coral colony is begun. ∎

Surfing

Shallow waters, sharp reefs, treacherous currents and inconsistent breaks make surf conditions in Samoa tricky, to say the least. The surf, however, can be excellent and the islands are only just beginning to be 'discovered' by surfers en masse. The wet season (November to April) brings swells from the north; the dry season (May to November) brings big swells from the south. Well known surf spots on Upolu include Solosolo, 10km east of Apia; the break near Nu'usafe'e Islet on the south coast and nearby 'Boulders' break off Cape Niuato'i. Two of the best spots on Savai'i are at Fagamalo on the north coast and at Satuiatua on the south-west coast.

For local advice and tips about surfing spots and information on how to get there, talk to Cyril Curry, the owner of the Seaside Inn in Apia.

Hiking

There are plenty of opportunities for hiking on all the islands – rugged coastal areas, sandy beaches, lush rainforests and volcanoes all invite exploration on foot. Even on short walks, however, the sun and the almost perpetually hot, humid conditions can take their toll. Be sure to carry insect repellent to ward off mosquitoes, sufficient water and salty snacks to replenish body elements lost to heavy sweating and always protect yourself from the sun with a hat and an effective sunblock cream.

Hiking possibilities on Upolu include the coastal and rainforest walks in O Le Pupu-Pu'e National Park; the coastal route from

Falefa Falls to Fagaloa Bay; the rugged hike between the village of Uafato and Tiavea; the short but steep walk to the summit of Mt Vailima to see the graves of Robert Louis and Fanny Stevenson; and the muddy but rewarding trek to Lake Lanoto'o in the central highlands.

On Savai'i, there's even more scope. Shorter possibilities include the hike to Olemoe Falls and the mysterious Pulemelei Mound, to the blowholes south of Salelologa or into the rainforest at Sasina. Longer day-hikes might include exploration of the Mt Matavanu area, the Tafua Peninsula Rainforest Preserve or the Falealupo Rainforest Preserve (with an overnight stop in a banyan tree).

For more of an expedition, you can hire a guide and climb up into the Cloud Forest Preserve on Mt Silisili, the highest point in the Samoas. It will be heavy going through dense vegetation, so plan on at least three days for this trip. Guided walks (among other activities) are offered on tiny, traditional Manono Island. Visitors can stroll peacefully through villages which are entirely free from both dogs and cars!

Kayaking & Canoeing

Sea kayaking is an excellent way to explore the islands and one of the only ways to access some of the more remote parts of the coastline. Tours, for a maximum of three people only, are available with Eco-Tour Samoa (☎ /fax 22144; ecotour@samoa.net) for around ST334 per day per person, including all meals and accommodation. A number of villages offer traditional outrigger canoe tours – from Manono Island, you can take a trip out to uninhabited Nu'ulopa Island for ST40 and in the Sa'anapu Conservation Area, canoe tours through the mangroves are available for ST20. The Samoan Outrigger Hotel, in Apia, has a couple of outrigger canoes which guests can use. Sinalei Reef Resort and Coconuts Beach Club, on the south coast of Upolu, offer a variety of organised boat tours.

Fishing

The reefs and their fishing rights are owned by villages so you can't just drop a line anywhere; seek permission first. If you'd like to go fishing with the locals, enquire at your hotel or beach fale or speak to the *pulenu'u* (mayor) of the village concerned.

Samoa Marine (see under Diving) operates pricey, deep-sea fish charters on a no-fish-no-pay scheme. Game fishing seems to be becoming more popular in the islands.

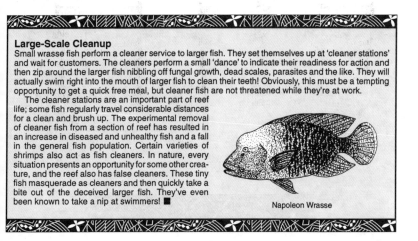

Large-Scale Cleanup
Small wrasse fish perform a cleaner service to larger fish. They set themselves up at 'cleaner stations' and wait for customers. The cleaners perform a small 'dance' to indicate their readiness for action and then zip around the larger fish nibbling off fungal growth, dead scales, parasites and the like. They will actually swim right into the mouth of larger fish to clean their teeth! Obviously, this must be a tempting opportunity to get a quick free meal, but cleaner fish are not threatened while they're at work.

The cleaner stations are an important part of reef life; some fish regularly travel considerable distances for a clean and brush up. The experimental removal of cleaner fish from a section of reef has resulted in an increase in diseased and unhealthy fish and a fall in the general fish population. Certain varieties of shrimps also act as fish cleaners. In nature, one situation presents an opportunity for some other creature, and the reef also has false cleaners. These tiny fish masquerade as cleaners and then quickly take a bite out of the deceived larger fish. They've even been known to take a nip at swimmers! ■

Napoleon Wrasse

The Samoa International Gamefishing Tournament, first held in 1996, takes place on Upolu during the first week of August.

THINGS TO BUY

Apia's Flea Market is a good place to look for craft items such as siapo, fine mats and kava bowls. You'll also find an amazing variety of coconut shell jewellery, items woven from coconut fronds, coconut oil, bouncy kirikiti balls, lavalavas and printed T-shirts. Aggie's Gift Shop and Kava & Kavings, both on Beach Rd, sell locally produced crafts and artwork but their prices will generally be a bit higher than at the market. Kava & Kavings probably sells the largest variety of kava bowls, and if you have the time you can have one custom-made in just about any shape you'd like.

The village of Uafato, on the east coast of Upolu, also is a good place to buy kava bowls and see local carvers at work. The Tiapapata Art Centre, off the Cross Island Rd just south-west of the Baha'i Temple, sells beautiful traditional and contemporary arts and crafts including carvings, prints and pottery. The centre also offers workshops and demonstrations in traditional arts.

Island Styles factory and principal outlet on the Cross Island Rd (the continuation of Falealili St), not far from Vailima. It sells Stevenson's Coconut Cream Liqueur (a delicious mixture of coconut cream, vanilla and Fijian rum) for ST35 a bottle, passionfruit and papaya fruit wine for ST8.50, souvenir T-shirts, hand-printed clothing and colourful lavalavas.

The larger supermarkets, such as Chan Mow and the Molesi Store (formerly Morris Hedstrom), also sell Stevenson's liqueur as well as packets of local coffee and superb Samoan cocoa. Look out, too, for locally-made coconut soap. Herman Bartley's, on Beach Rd, almost opposite the flea market, sells a good selection of fabrics; you can have a lavalava made up for less than ST10. The CKK store in Apia sells a huge amount of second-hand clothing as well as a selection of second-hand paperbacks.

Upolu's international airport has a small duty free shop and an expensive gift shop. Coconuts Beach Club and Sinalei Reef Resort, on the south coast of Upolu, both have gift shops stocked with an interesting selection of local work.

Upolu Island

With a land area of 1115sq km, cigar-shaped Upolu is the second-largest island of Samoa, yet it has, by far, the largest population – over 115,000.

About 40% of the island is characterised by relatively gentle volcanic slopes rising to crests of around 1000m. The highest peak is Mt Fito (1158m), which lies within the O Le Pupu-Pu'e National Park. The interior of the island is covered in indigenous rainforest, which accounts for about 20% of the total land area.

Around 30% of Upolu is customary land (ie, owned by extended families and unable to be transferred or made freehold), the bulk of which is cultivated for subsistence agriculture. Crops are grown to a maximum height of about 300m. Though most of Upolu's villages lie along the coast, there are several villages and settlements scattered around the central highlands.

The island stretches 72km from east to west and up to 24km from north to south. A fairly good system of roads makes all parts of the island easily accessible from the national capital and hub of activity, Apia, which is situated roughly in the centre of the north coast.

In general, the climate of the north coast – the leeward side – is drier and more comfortable than that of the windward south coast. Overall, the sunniest and coolest time to visit is between May and October.

Getting There & Away

Flights for Savai'i and Pago Pago leave from Fagali'i airport, a few kilometres east of Apia. If you're going to Faleolo Airport from Apia, take any bus marked Faleolo, Mulifanua or Falelatai. The bus fare between the airport and Apia is ST1.50. Airport buses, which are run by Schuster Tours, meet arriving and departing flights at Faleolo airport. The fare is ST6 per person for the 45 minute trip between the airport terminal and the major hotels.

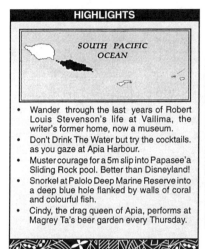

HIGHLIGHTS

SOUTH PACIFIC OCEAN

- Wander through the last years of Robert Louis Stevenson's life at Vailima, the writer's former home, now a museum.
- Don't Drink The Water but try the cocktails. as you gaze at Apia Harbour.
- Muster courage for a 5m slip into Papasee'a Sliding Rock pool. Better than Disneyland!
- Snorkel at Palolo Deep Marine Reserve into a deep blue hole flanked by walls of coral and colourful fish.
- Cindy, the drag queen of Apia, performs at Magrey Ta's beer garden every Thursday.

Alternatively, you can flag down a public bus just outside the airport gate. As you face the highway, Apia-bound buses will be coming from your right (although some buses coming from your left will actually turn around at the airport gate and return to Apia).

Taxis between Apia and Faleolo airport cost ST30 each way, which is quite high by local standards. Taxis between Fagali'i

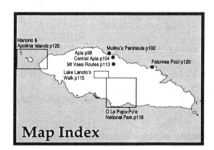

Manono &
Apolima Islands p125

Apia p98
Central Apia p104
Mt Vaea Routes p113

Mulinu'u Peninsula p102

Fatumea Pool p120

Lake Lanoto'o
Walk p115

O Le Pupu-Pu'e
National Park p118

Map Index

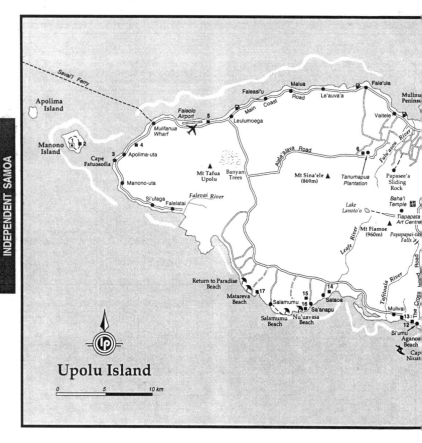

Upolu Island

0   5   10 km

---

airport and central Apia cost ST5. By bus it's 60 sene. To get to this airport, take any city bus marked Fagali'i.

Getting Around

Travelling around Upolu is an easy but time-consuming matter. There are lots of options to choose from, but if you're relying on public transport, don't try to visit too many points of interest in a single day. A good rule of thumb is to allow an entire day for each excursion to a point of interest beyond the environs of Apia.

Bus Buses connecting Apia with other parts of Upolu leave from the main market, the Maketi Fou, off Fugalei St, and from the bus area behind the Flea Market. Just because the bus has left the market, however, doesn't mean you're underway. Buses will travel between the main market areas and around central Apia as many times as the driver deems necessary to fill the bus or until he realises that it's no longer economically feasible to waste fuel making the circuit. If he decides that he hasn't inspired sufficient interest in the trip, it is cancelled altogether.

Keep in mind that buses tend to begin

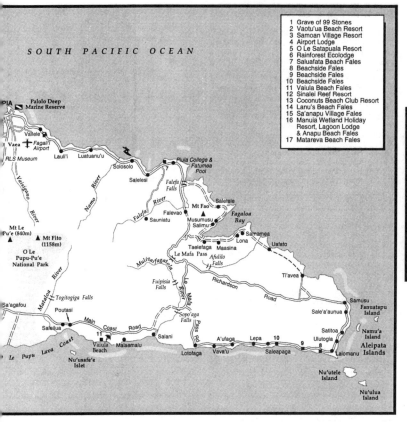

1 Grave of 99 Stones
2 Vaotu'ua Beach Resort
3 Samoan Village Resort
4 Airport Lodge
5 O Le Satapuala Resort
6 Rainforest Ecolodge
7 Saluafata Beach Fales
8 Beachside Fales
9 Beachside Fales
10 Beachside Fales
11 Vaiula Beach Fales
12 Sinalei Reef Resort
13 Coconuts Beach Club Resort
14 Lanu's Beach Fales
15 Sa'anapu Village Fales
16 Manuia Wetland Holiday
   Resort, Lagoon Lodge
   & Anapu Beach Fales
17 Matareva Beach Fales

running early and stop running in the early afternoon – and that Upolu by bus seems much larger than Upolu on the map! If you'd like to visit a remote spot – say Lefaga or Aleipata – and return the same day, be at the Maketi Fou in Apia by 6 or 7 am.

Fares range from 40 sene to ST3 and cover transport from Apia to just about any part of the island.

All buses prominently display the name of their destination in the front window. No tickets are necessary – just pay the driver at your destination.

Any bus with the sign 'Pasi o le Va'a' in the window will be passing Faleolo airport and going on to Mulifanua Wharf, from where the Savai'i ferry departs. If it also says 'Falelatai' or 'Manono-uta', it will be going beyond to the Manono ferry dock or to the south-western end of the island. Catch the Mulifanua bus at least an hour before you plan to catch the Savai'i ferry. Manono-bound launches leave whenever people are waiting to go.

To reach the Aleipata district and the eastern end of the island, catch the Lalomanu bus, which takes Richardson Rd. Alternatively, take the Lotofaga bus via Le Mafa

How a Lazy Lad put Upolu on the Map

There are a number of ancient stories about the origin of the name Upolu. The most interesting one tells of the marriage of an earthly chief called Beginning, to Timuateatea, a daughter of the god Tagaloa.

The couple had a son whom they named Polu. Like many young boys, he grew bored and lazy during his teenage years. Being a typical father, Beginning thought his son ought to get a job and looked around for something for the boy to do. When he looked over towards nearby Savai'i, he realised that it might be a good idea to send Polu over there to see if the island had any inhabitants. So he called Polu and instructed him to pay a visit to his heavenly grandfather, who would provide him with carpenters to help him build a canoe for the journey. Polu initially refused but Beginning insisted and the boy finally agreed to do the job.

Up in heaven, the god Tagaloa loked down and noted that the initially reticent Polu had found the carpenters uninterested and lazy, but he had nevertheless managed to urge them to build his canoe. Thus, Tagalao decided to honour his grandson and name his island Upolu – 'The Urging of Polu'. ■

Pass Rd and change there to an eastbound bus running along the south coast. Heading east along the north coast (to Piula, for instance), take the Falefa, Lufilufi, Faleapuna, Fagaloa or Lotofaga bus.

For any point along the main Cross Island Rd (to the Robert Louis Stevenson Museum, the Baha'i temple, the turn-off to Lake Lanoto'o and Papapapai-tai Falls), take either the Mulivai or the Salani bus. To Togitogiga and O Le Pupu-Pu'e National Park, take the Tafatafa or Salani bus from the Maketi Fou.

If you're going to Papasee'a Sliding Rock, the Tafa'igata bus will drop you several kilometres away, so it's better to take the Se'ese'e bus and let the driver know where you want to go. He'll drop you within 2km of the rocks and provide directions to the entrance.

From Apia, fares to the western end of Upolu (Mulifanua and Manono-uta) or Mulivai are ST1.50. To Si'umu or Lefaga

they're ST2 and to Aleipata, ST3. Getting around Apia and its environs will cost between 40 and 80 sene.

Car The Main Coast Rd follows the coast most of the way around Upolu but cuts off abruptly at Falelatai in the south-west and breaks at Salani in the south-east. To continue on from Salani, take the 5km dirt track which runs between the southern Main Coast Rd and Le Mafa Pass Rd.

Three good cross-island roads pass over the east-west central ridge and divide the island roughly into quarters. The central one begins in Apia at Falealili St before becoming The Cross Island Rd further south. The north-eastern section of Upolu is the most rugged; you'll need a 4WD to negotiate the track to Fagaloa Bay. The Fagaloa Bay track and the tracks leading off the southern main Coast Rd down to Aganoa Beach, Nu'uavasa Beach and Matareva Beach can get pretty muddy after heavy rain.

Petrol availability is limited; see the Getting Around chapter for details.

You can take rental cars on the ferry to Savai'i; there are also a couple of rental agencies over there (see the following section). Following is a list of car rental agencies in Apia. Prices start at around ST100 per day for a 4WD Suzuki jeep. Discounts are offered for longer term rental. There are plenty of agencies, so ring around for the best deal.

Apia Rentals
  (☎ 24244; fax 26193; apia rentals@samoa.net)
Avis Car Rentals
  (☎ 20486; fax 26069)
Billie's Car Rentals
  (☎ 25363; fax 23038)
Budget Car Hire
  (☎20561; fax 22284)
Emka Rentals
  (☎23266)
Funway Rentals
  (☎22045; fax 25008)
G & J Rentals
  (☎/fax 21078)
Hibiscus Rentals
  (☎ 27039; fax 20162)

DORINDA TALBOT

DORINDA TALBOT

DORINDA TALBOT

DEANNA SWANEY

Top Left: Beachside fale, Aleipata area, Upolu
Middle: View of Lalomanu Beach, Upolu Island
Right: Ancient grinding stones (*foaga*) south-west coast of Tutuila
Bottom: *Paopao* (canoes), Asau Harbour, Savai'i

DORINDA TALBOT

DORINDA TALBOT

DEANNA SWANEY

DORINDA TALBOT

DEANNA SWANEY

DEANNA SWANEY

Top Left: Polynesia, American style
Top Right: Dancing in the street during the
annual Teuila Festival, Apia
Middle: Tamagali blossoms

Bottom Left: Local children
Bottom Right: Better than Disneyland,
Papase'a Sliding Rock

J & S Car Rentals
  (☎ 24503; fax 24504)
Juliana's Car Rentals
  (☎ 23009)
Le Car Rentals
  (☎ /fax 22754)
Lima-Oueni Enterprises
  (☎ /fax 25495)
Mikaele Rentals
  (☎ /fax 25114)
Mt Vaea Rentals
  (☎ 20620)
P & F Schuster Transport
  (☎ 23014; fax 23626)
P & K Filo Rentals
  (☎ 26797; fax 25574)
Paradise Car Rentals
  (☎ 26575; fax 21144)
Pavitt's U-Drive
  (☎ 21766; fax 24667)
Reliance Rentals
  (☎ 21828; fax 20087)
Schani Rentals
  (☎ 21519; fax 25182)
South Pacific Rentals
  (☎ /fax 22074)
Teuila Rentals
  (☎ 20284; fax 24179)

Taxi Apia's taxis are cheap and plentiful, if slightly worse for wear. To travel anywhere between Aggie's and the post office will cost ST2; to anywhere else in Apia, the charge is ST3. The standard fare for a trip to or from the airport is ST30.

It's still possible for foreigners to get a fair price in Samoa, but the temptation for taxis to overcharge is great, so if you know the correct fare, stand your ground. Be sure you agree on a price with the driver before you climb in. Taxis are convenient for day-tripping around Upolu. You'll pay around ST40 for half a day's sightseeing for up to four or five people. This is a particularly useful option if you'd rather avoid anxiety about catching the last bus back to Apia. The following companies are recommended:

Airport City Cabs (☎ 25420/21600)
Magic 98FM Taxis (☎ 20808)
  corner of Beach Rd and Mata'utu St
Samoan Lager Taxis (☎ 25909)

Bicycle The Seaside Inn (☎ 22578), on Beach Rd, and the Rainforest Cafe (☎ 25030),

also on Beach Rd, have bicylces to rent from around ST15 per day. For information on cycling around the islands see the Getting Around chapter.

Apia

With its rundown colonial buildings, big old pulu trees and easy-going pace, Apia still retains a certain shabby and romantic charm. This is Michener's *Tales of the South Pacific*, Maugham's *MacIntosh* and *The Pool* and everything else that is the legacy bequeathed to Samoa by early European missionaries, trading companies and rogues. The modern world is well and truly here, too, as evidenced by the rapidly increasing number of private vehicles, the outsized Samoa Central Bank, the extraordinary seven storey government building, McDonald's, cable television, mobile phones and email. Polynesia proper, however, is only 10 minutes away by slow bus and, before you head off to explore the villages and lagoons beyond, it is worth wandering around Apia. Highlights include the Robert Louis Stevenson Museum, just outside town, Palolo Deep Marine Reserve and cocktails at Don't Drink the Water.

Orientation

Apia is the only place in Samoa that could conceivably be called a city but it would be more accurately described as an agglomeration of urbanised villages. From the centre of town, Apia's neat villages spread west along the level coastal area and climb up the gentle slopes towards the hills and into the valleys. Apia is the service centre of Independent Samoa and it is here and only here that you'll find shops, supermarkets, communications offices, tourist information, travel agencies and so on. The bulk of the islands' hotels and restaurants are located in Apia, too.

The main drag is Beach Rd, which follows the curve of the wide, pleasant harbour. Most of the activity is centred along Beach Rd between Aggie Grey's Hotel and the Flea

INDEPENDENT SAMOA

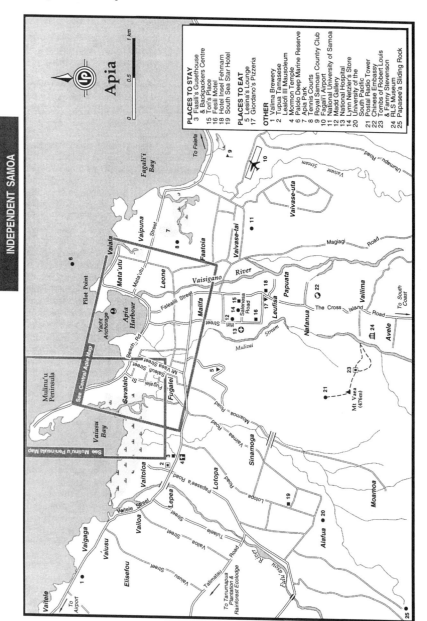

Apia

0   0.5   1 km

PLACES TO STAY
3   Fiasili's Guesthouse
    & Backpackers Centre
15 Tori's Place
16 Fesili Motel
18 Hotel Insel Fehmarn
19 South Sea Star Hotel

PLACES TO EAT
5   Lesina's Lounge
17 Giordano's Pizzeria

OTHER
1   Vailima Brewery
2   Tupua Tamasese
    Lealofi III Mausoleum
4   Mormon Temple
6   Palolo Deep Marine Reserve
7   Apia Park
8   Tennis Courts
9   Royal Samoan Country Club
10 Fagali'i Airport
11 National University of Samoa
12 Madd Gallery
13 National Hospital
14 Lynn Netzler's Store
20 University of the
    South Pacific
21 Postal Radio Tower
22 Chinese Embassy
23 Tombs of Robert Louis
    & Fanny Stevenson
24 RLS Museum
25 Papasee'a Sliding Rock

Market, with the business district spreading south from the clock tower into the area known as Chinatown. The main market and main bus station are a couple of blocks south of the clock tower, between Fugalei and Saleufi Sts. The wharf lies at the eastern end of the harbour. Palolo Deep is just beyond the wharf.

Information
Tourist Office The Samoa Visitors Bureau (☎ 20878; fax 20886; wsvb@samoa.net) is housed in a large Samoan *fale* on the reclaimed area on the northern side of Beach Rd (above the remains of the German warship *Adler*, destroyed in the 1889 typhoon). The staff are quite friendly and if you're not in a hurry, they can help with most queries. A good map of Independent Samoa, which includes a plan of Apia, is available for $ST10. The office is open from 8 am to 4.30 pm Monday to Friday and from 8.30 am to noon on Saturday.

Foreign Embassies & Consulates Following is a list of foreign consulates and embassies in Apia.

Australian High Commission
NPF Building, Apia (☎ 23411)
British Consul
Bob Barlow, NPF Building, 2nd Floor, Apia (☎ 21895)
Chinese Embassy
Vailima (☎ 22474)
French Consul
Norman Samuel Paul, Gold Star Building, 2nd Floor (☎ 22711)
German Consul
William Keil, Taufusi, above South Pacific Paints (☎ 22695)
New Zealand High Commission
Tamaligi, Apia (☎ 21404)
South Korean Consul
Gary Carruthers, Carruthers Building (☎ 21414)
Swedish Consul
Papalii John Ryan, Mata'utu opposite Harbour Light Hotel (☎ 20345)
The Netherlands Consul
Terence Betham, John Williams Building, 4th Floor (☎ 24337)
USA Embassy
John Williams Building (☎ 21631)

Money Samoa's three main banks, the Bank of Samoa (☎ 22422), the Pacific Commercial Bank (☎ 20000) and the new National Bank of Samoa (☎ 23076) are open from 9 am to 3 pm Monday to Friday. The National Bank branch near the market is open from 8.30 am to 12.30 pm on Saturday. Aggie Grey's Hotel and the Hotel Kitano Tusitala offer currency-exchange services.

Post & Communications The main post and telephone office is on Beach Rd just one block east of the clock tower. Postal services are available at the counter between 9 am and 4.30 pm. For poste restante, go to the separate office two doors down Post Office St from the main lobby. The telephone office (which has the only two public telephones on the islands) is open from 8 am to 10.30 pm daily. Fax services are available upstairs from 8 am to 4.30 pm Monday to Friday. The telephone area code for Samoa is ☎ 685.

Travel Agencies Two recommended local agencies are Island Hopper Vacations (☎ 26940; fax 26941), PO Box 2271, in the Lotemau Centre, and Oceania Travel & Tours (☎ 24443; fax 22255), PO Box 9339, near the Hotel Kitano Tusitala. For a list of local tour operators, see Organised Tours in the Getting Around chapter.

Bookshops A small selection of new books, including some dealing with the subjects of Polynesia, Pacific issues and the Samoas in general, is available at the Wesley Bookshop in the Wesley Arcade, with branches in Salelologa and Asau on Savai'i and in Pago Pago, American Samoa. You'll also find a limited number of titles at the Educational Bookshop, near the corner of Mt Vaea and Vaitele Sts, and at Aggie's Gift Shop, on Beach Rd. If you're only after pulp reading material, the CCK Family Shopper store in Apia (look for the brightly coloured flags) is a good place to pick up inexpensive second-hand paperbacks.

Libraries The Nelson Public Library, on Beach Rd just by the clock tower, has an excellent collection of Pacific titles. Travellers may borrow books for ST5 plus a ST15 refundable deposit. The library is open from 9 am to 4.30 pm Monday to Thursday; from 8 am to 4 pm Friday; and from 8.30 am to noon Saturday. Another library of interest is the lovely air-conditioned waiting room on the ground floor of the New Zealand High Commission, also on Beach Rd. There is a vast amount of literature on New Zealand and a fair amount dealing with Polynesia in general.

Campuses Originally established in 1984, the National University of Samoa (☎ 20072; fax 20938; nus@samoa.net) opened a new campus in 1997 at Malifa, just south-east of the town centre. The new campus includes an enormous traditionally made fale which can seat 400 people. The university offers courses in arts, commerce, education, nursing and science. The University of the South Pacific, which is based in Suva, Fiji, has its Agriculture Department (☎ 21671) in Alafua, on the outskirts of Apia.

Laundry The most convenient of the several laundrettes in Apia is Sapolu's Laundry & Legal Services on Mata'utu St near Beach Rd, only five minutes walk from town. It charges ST2.50 to wash and ST4 to dry; washing powder costs ST1. Lily's Laundromat, also on Mata'utu St, is a bit cheaper. Other laundry services include the Three Corners Laundromat, at the top of Mt Vaea St; Faupepa's Laundromat, near the National Hospital; and the laundrette opposite the Mormon temple.

Medical Services The following private medical and dental services have been recommended by the Samoa Visitors Bureau. All of the following are in the Apia area:

Apia Medical Clinic (☎ 20942)
Faletoese Clinic (☎ 23344)
Dr John Atherton (☎ 26113)
Dr Kome Kuresa (☎ 20365)
LTP Surgery (☎ 21652)
So'onalole Dental Surgery (☎ 21145)
T&T Medical Centre (☎ 24946)

Emergency In an emergency, call one of the following:

Ambulance (☎ 999)
Fire (☎ 994)
Police (☎ 995)
National Hospital (☎ 996)

Markets

Maketi Fou The main market, between Fugalei and Saleufi Sts a couple of blocks south of Beach Rd, is the centre of activity in Apia and has the biggest and best selection of fresh produce as well as the lowest prices in the South Pacific. It hums 24 hours a day and to have a stall there is so prestigious that family members take turns staying the night so as not to lose their privileged spots. The busy, crowded atmosphere is enlivening at just about any time.

Every kind of meat and produce available in Samoa is sold in this vibrant and colourful place. Here, *matais* gather to chat and drink 'ava and the general public comes to socialise. You'll find drinking coconuts for sale, kiosks selling ready-made *palusami*, *fa'ausi* pudding, cakes and *koko Samoa*. You can also order cheap meals of meat and traditional vegetables. At the back of the main market are shops selling tinned foods, bread and other dry goods. Right next to the market is the central bus terminal serving the entire island of Upolu, where colourfully painted wooden buses blast reggae music and compete for passengers on their seemingly endless cycles around the market square.

Flea Market Apia's Flea Market is housed in the old central market building down on Beach Rd, to the west of the clock tower. Here you'll find cheap clothing and craft stalls selling everything from *siapo* and 'ava bowls to coconut shell jewellery. Tucked beyond the craft stalls, on the northern side of the Flea Market, is a row of cheap food stalls; the harbour breeze blowing through makes this a pleasant spot for a snack and a rest. Buses also gather in the area behind the Flea Market.

INDEPENDENT SAMOA

Fish Market The Fish Market is in a separate building to the east of the Flea Market. It's open every day, but Sunday morning is the busiest time with everyone rushing in to buy fish for the Sunday *umu* before hurrying off to attend church. Look out for Coca-Cola bottles full of sea slug innards (a Samoan delicacy) and the bright green seaweed that looks like bunches of tiny grapes.

Churches

Christianity plays a major role in Samoan life and the churches of Apia reflect the fact that there's also a great deal of financial responsibility associated with churchgoing. Clean and well kept, they dominate the skyline of Apia nearly as much as they dominate the skylines of small villages.

The landmark of the city's waterfront is the chunky Madonna-topped **Catholic cathedral** (☎ 20400) on Beach Rd; before the government building and the Samoa Central Bank were constructed in front of it, the cathedral could be seen up to 20km out to sea. Construction of the cathedral began in 1885 and finished 20 years later. The **Wesleyan church** nearby is also an imposing structure.

A lovely and unassuming building is the **Anglican church**, the only one in Samoa, which is on Ifiifi St not far from the National Hospital. Although it's not an old building, it has some beautiful stained-glasswork in the windows. The cornerstone inscription states that it was laid on '3 December 1944, the 50th anniversary of the falling asleep of Tusitala'.

When the Reverend John Williams of the London Missionary Society was killed on 20 November 1839, on Erromanga in Vanuatu, he was subjected to the cannibalistic traditions of the Melanesians of the day. His bones were recovered, however, and buried on the site where the **Congregational Christian church** (☎ 24414) now stands, on the corner of Beach Rd and Falealili St. Of all Apia's churches, its old-style wooden architecture is the simplest and most pleasant. It is also one of the best places to hear Samoan voices practising hymns and choral

presentations. Across the street is the monument to Williams and his 'martyrdom'. It was erected in 1930, commemorating 'the first hundred years of Christianity in Samoa'.

On Sunday, everyone dresses in sparkling white and attends a morning church service. Most churches have several services on this day, some of which are conducted in English.

Clock Tower

The clock tower in the centre of town is a landmark for anyone who's ever tried to give directions around Apia. It was originally constructed in memory of those who fought and were killed in WWI. It was built on the site of an old bandstand where sailors on incoming warships were serenaded by their compatriots. Its clock and chimes were a gift to the city from one of Samoa's most successful early businesspeople, Mr Olaf Frederick Nelson, whose father had come from Sweden in 1868 and opened a chain of trading companies around the country. It was donated in memory of Olaf Nelson's only son, Ta'isi, who died in the influenza epidemic introduced to the islands by the New Zealand ship SS *Talune* in 1918.

Just to the south-east, on the harbour side of Beach Rd, is another monument – this one 'in memory of our sons who served overseas in the World War of 1939-1945'. More than 60 are listed. It was donated by the Mothers Club of Samoa, whose members are listed opposite the names of the soldiers.

Government Buildings

The most imposing addition to the Apia skyline is the seven-storey **government office building**, a product of Chinese benevolence, which towers above the area, reclaimed from the sea, behind the Samoa Visitors Bureau. Built in 1993, its universally unpopular design was only slightly improved by the addition of the Samoan fale – a last minute concession to *fa'a Samoa* – which forms its top floor. On the reclaimed area behind the clock tower is the Pulenu'u Fale where Samoa's *pulenu'u* (village mayors) meet.

Next to the Flea Market is the **Women**

INDEPENDENT SAMOA

and Youth Activity Centre, also financed by the Chinese government. Opened in 1997, the centre houses the Ministry of Women's Affairs.

The two-storey knocked-about colonial building on the corner of Beach Rd and Ifiifi St is home to the **Supreme Court**. It was on the street here that the bloody clash between the formerly peaceful Mau (Samoa for Samoans) Movement and the New Zealand police brought about the deaths of 11 Samoans, including the Mau leader, Tupua Tamasese Lealofi III, on 28 December 1929.

The **police station** is just around the corner on Ifiifi St and at 7.45 am every weekday, the Police Band of Samoa marches from here to the government building. Vehicle and pedestrian traffic is stopped and the national anthem is played while the flag is raised. It's a great way to start the day, especially in the 'winter', when the sun is low and the long rays cast a serene morning glow over the harbour.

Samoa's new parliament building, the **Fale Fono**, is towards the end of the Mulinu'u Peninsula, a prominent spit of land extending from the western end of Apia. Resembling a large beehive, the Fale Fono was opened on 31 May 1972. The **Lands and Titles Court**, housed in the old parliament building nearby, is the entity that settles land rights cases in the event of the death of a traditional owner or a dispute over unverified ownership of land. Until recently, land titles were not recorded on paper and land rights were handed down by oral tradition. This method of determining ownership, however, has understandably become rather subjective of late. This is chiefly because Samoan landowners have a distinct advantage, automatically inheriting the office of matai and becoming eligible to stand for election to public office.

Madd Gallery

One of Samoa's best known contemporary painters, Momoe von Reiche, set up the Madd Gallery (☎ 25494), on Ifiifi St opposite the hospital, in 1984, as a place to inspire and ecourage those with an interest in the

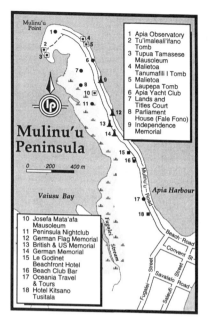

1 Apia Observatory
2 Tu'Imaleali'ifano Tomb
3 Tupua Tamasese Mausoleum
4 Malietoa Tanumafili I Tomb
5 Malietoa Laupepa Tomb
6 Apia Yacht Club
7 Lands and Titles Court
8 Parliament House (Fale Fono)
9 Independence Memorial

10 Josefa Mata'afa Mausoleum
11 Peninsula Nightclub
12 German Flag Memorial
13 British & US Memorial
14 German Memorial
15 Le Godinet Beachfront Hotel
16 Beach Club Bar
17 Oceania Travel & Tours
18 Hotel Kitsano Tusitala

arts. Among other things, Madd (which stands for Motivational Art, Dance and Drama) exhibits paintings and siapo, offers workshops, stages modern dance and hosts poetry readings. The gallery is open from 9 am to 4 pm Mondy to Friday and from 9 am to noon Saturday.

Monuments & Memorials

The Mulinu'u Peninsula, which extends from the western end of Apia, seems to serve more than anything else as a repository for political monuments. As you walk along the peninsula from the Hotel Kitano Tusitala, the first monuments you'll see (on your left) are **naval memorials**, one erected by Germany and the other jointly by Britain and the USA. The latter was constructed in memory of those European personnel killed in the civil strife at the close of the 19th century. The German monument is a memorial to those aboard the *Olga* killed in the naval battle on 18 December 1888.

A bit further on is the **German Flag Memorial**, erected in 1913 just one year before the New Zealand takeover of Western Samoa. It commemorates the raising of the German flag over the islands on 1 March 1900.

On the lawn in front of the Fale Fono is the **Josefa Mata'afa Mausoleum**. Josefa Mata'afa was the puppet paramount chief supported by the Germans after they annexed Western Samoa in 1899. The grave is not of Samoan design and it seems that the Germans constructed it, hoping to undermine the pride the locals had in their leaders by altering their age-old burial customs. The Tupua Tamasese dynasty mausoleum, also on the peninsula, is similar.

The **Typhoon Monument** commemorates the 145 German and US personnel killed in the 1889 typhoon.

The relatively elaborate **Independence Memorial** was built to mark the independence of Western Samoa granted on 1 January 1962.

The **Apia Observatory** was built by the Germans as a weather station in 1902. On fine days, the surrounding green lawns offer opportunities for picnics.

On the eastern side of the peninsula, near the observatory on Mulinu'u Point, are the **tombs of Malietoa Tanumafili I and Malietoa Laupepa**, the father and grandfather, respectively, of the present ceremonial head of state. Gardens are planted around the tombs as a mark of respect. At the very end of the peninsula are two more tombs, the **mausoleum of Tupua Tamasese** and the magnificent seven-tiered **tomb of the Tu'imaleali'ifano dynasty**.

Near the Mormon temple, south-west of the centre, is the German bandstand that was used as the headquarters of the Mau Movement. **Tupua Tamasese Lealofi III's tomb** is not far from the bandstand and reflects the respect Samoans still hold for his chiefly titles and his many contributions to the cause of Samoan sovereignty.

Palolo Deep National Marine Reserve
Past the wharf on Beach Rd, near the palagi enclaves of Mata'utu and Vaiala, is Palolo Deep National Marine Reserve. There is excellent snorkelling in Palolo Deep, as well as shady and comfortable fales for picnicking and relaxing. If you're going out on the reef or to the viewing platforms at low tide, you'll need some sort of foot protection against the rough coral. At high tide you can just snorkel out.

The real attraction at Palolo Deep is the sudden drop from the shallow reef into a deep blue hole flanked by walls of coral and densely populated by colourful species of fish. After one afternoon there, you'll want to return again and again. The reserve is open between 8 am and 6 pm daily. Admission is ST2 per person. The rental fee for snorkelling gear also includes admission. A snorkel, mask and fins cost ST10 per day. Just the mask and snorkel cost ST6; flippers alone cost ST4. Palolo is about a 15 minute walk from Aggie Grey's Hotel.

Places to Stay
Apia offers a reasonable range of accommodation options, from cheap backpacker dorms to quiet rainforest retreats – there's even an urban village option where you can experience traditional Samoan life within walking distance of town. Except where stated that tax is included, all prices are subject to the addition of 10% GST. It's always worth asking whether a hotel offers reduced rates for families, groups or weekly stays.

Places to Stay – bottom end
The *Samoan Outrigger Hotel* (☎ /fax 20042; outrigger@samoa.net), PO Box 4074, is a spacious old colonial house at Vaiala Beach, a short walk from Palolo Deep. The hotel opened in December 1994 and two years later won the Kodak Excellence Award for best budget hotel in the South Pacific. Bookings are advised. Dorm beds (two rooms containing three bunks each) cost ST22; singles/doubles without shower will cost you ST44/55; and double or triple rooms (large airy rooms with sea breeze) with shower and toilet are ST88, including tax. Breakfast of

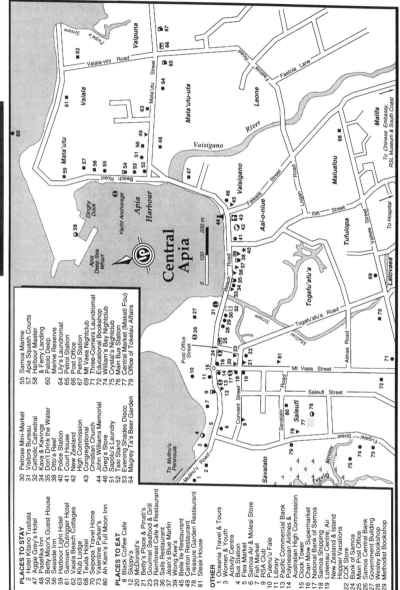

PLACES TO STAY
2 Hotel Kitano Tusitala
47 Aggie Grey's Hotel
48 Pasefika Inn
50 Betty Moor's Guest House
56 Seaside Inn
59 Harbour Light Hotel
61 Samoan Outrigger Hotel
62 Vaiala Beach Cottages
63 Teula Hotel
68 Seipepa Travel Home
70 Valentine Parker's
73 Ah Kam's Full Moon Inn
80

PLACES TO EAT
8 Black Coffee Cafe
12 Skippy's
20 McDonald's
21 Betty's Place & Pinati's
23 Gourmet Seafood & Grill
33 Rainforest Cafe & Restaurant
36 Sails Restaurant
37 Jean's Blue Marlin
39 Wong Kee's
45 Belle Ile Restaurant
49 Canton Restaurant
78 Treasure Garden Restaurant
81 Steak House

OTHER
1 Oceania Travel & Tours
3 Women & Youth
   Activity Centre
4 Bus Station
5 Flea Market
6 Samoa Air & Moelsi Store
7 Fish Market
9 RSA Club
10 Puleru'u Fale
11 Library
13 Pacific Commercial Bank
14 Polynesian Airlines &
   Australian High Commission
15 Clock Tower
16 Chan Mow Supermarket
17 National Bank of Samoa
18 Samoa Shipping
19 Lotemau Centre; Air
   New Zealand & Island
   Hopper Vacations
22 CCK Store
24 Bank of Samoa
25 Main Post Office
26 Samoa Central Bank
27 Government Building
28 Wesley Bookshop
29 Methodist Bookshop

30 Pelrose Mini-Market
31 Visitors Bureau
32 Catholic Cathedral
34 Kava & Kavings
35 Don't Drink the Water
38 Otto's Reef
40 Police Station
41 Court House
42 New Zealand
   High Commission
43 Congregational
   Christian Church
44 John Williams Memorial
46 Greg's Store
51 Sapolu's Laundry
52 Taxi Stand
53 Evening Shades Disco
54 Magrey Ta's Beer Garden

55 Samoa Marine
57 Apia Squash Courts
58 Harbour Master
   & Ferry Landing
60 Palolo Deep
   Marine Reserve
64 Lily's Laundromat
65 Petrol Station
66 Post Office
67 Petrol Station
69 Mt Vaea Nightclub
71 Three-Corners Laundromat
72 Educational Bookshop
74 William's Bay Nightclub
75 Crystal's Nightclub
76 Main Bus Station
77 Central Market (Maketi Fou)
79 Office of Tokelau Affairs

toast, fruit and coffee or tea is included. There is no hot water as yet, but there are plans to install solar panels. The hotel has a fully equipped kitchen with two big dining tables, a reading room with maps and pool table, a laundry room (ST4 for a load of washing) and two outrigger canoes which guests can use for a small fee. Snorkelling gear is available for hire, there's a telephone and fax service and cold Vailima's for sale. The manager of the hotel, Claus Hermansen, also runs three local tours each week (to Manono Island, Aleipata and Paradise Beach) for ST40 per person, including food.

Around the corner from the Outrigger, on Beach Rd, is the *Harbour Light Hotel* (☎ 21103; fax 20110), PO Box 5214, where somewhat grubby singles/doubles/triples with air-conditioning, shower (hot) and toilet cost ST45/56/67. Breakfast is included.

The *Seaside Inn* (☎ 22578; fax 22918), PO Box 3019, Apia, continues to be a popular choice with budget travellers. With its outdoor terrace and small, friendly bar, it's a good place to meet and mix with other travellers. On Beach Rd, opposite the wharf, the guesthouse is just a 10 minute walk from town. It has 20 rooms and two dormitories. Dorm beds cost ST25, while clean singles/doubles/triples with shower (cold) and toilet cost ST45/55/65. Breakfast is included. The Seaside has a kitchen which guests can use, laundry facilities, fax and telephone service, bicycles for ST15 per day and Suzuki jeeps from ST100 per day. The manager, Cyril Curry, is an excellent source of knowledge on surfing and is happy to provide advice on where to find the best surf spots, how to get there and so on. Advance room bookings are advised.

Betty Moors Guest House (☎ /fax 21085), just off Beach Rd on Mata'utu St, is basic and cheap. Betty's been running the place for 18 years and is quite a character. Cubicle-like rooms, some without windows, cost ST20 per person. Breakfast is not included.

Further up Mata'utu St is *Klub Lodge* (☎ 25611; fax 25610), PO Box 2201, with attached fitness centre and cafe. Cramped rooms with air-conditioning, shower (cold)

and toilet cost ST46/50/60 for singles/doubles/triples. Breakfast is not included. The cafe serves smoothies, sandwiches, cakes and cheap steaks and kebabs.

One of the cheapest and cleanest budget options is *Valentine Parker's* (☎ /fax 22158), PO Box 395, south of the main market on Fugalei St. Single/double rooms cost ST20/30 with access to communal toilets and cold-water showers. Dorm beds cost ST15. Tax is included. Breakfast is available on request and guests can use the family kitchen if they ask in advance. A shop on the premises sells groceries and beer.

South of the centre and tucked away amongst village houses is *Seipepa* (☎ /fax 25447; seipepa@samoa.net), PO Box 1465 Lalovaea, Apia, a delightful 'Samoan Travel Home' run by Mats Loefkvist, from Sweden, and his Samoan wife Sia. Mats was so impressed with the hospitality and warmth of the Samoan people he wanted to share the experience with other visitors, hence Seipepa. Guests have the choice of sleeping in one of the two small fales (one with a double mattress and one larger fale with two single mattresses) or in a double or twin room inside the house. There are spotless communal showers (cold) and toilets. Seipepa is a great place to sample traditional food (eaten sitting on the floor), especially on Sunday when a midday umu is prepared. Guests are given the opportunity to see how traditional food is prepared, how to open coconuts, weave a basket and make Samoan coconut oil. There are no set accommodation rates here – guests simply pay what they feel to be fair. English, German, Swedish and Samoan are spoken. Signposted off Vaitele St, Seipepa is about a 15 minute walk from the centre of town. If you go by taxi, ask for Filipo's Tyre Repair.

Fiasili's Guesthouse & Backpackers Centre (☎ 22336; fax 23929), opposite the Mormon temple, offers a range of room prices. Formerly called the Travellers' Inn, the guesthouse is a 25 minute walk or five minute bus ride west of town. It's mostly used by visiting church dignitaries. Rooms with fan and communal facilities cost

ST37/50/60. Add air-conditioning, a fridge, toilet and shower and the price jumps to ST73/85/97. Prices include tax. Credit cards are not accepted. There's a good Chinese restaurant, The Oriental, downstairs.

Places to Stay – middle

Some of Apia's mid-range hotels cater for budget-conscious travellers as well as those wanting a little more in the way of creature comforts. Middle and upper-range hotels often quote prices in US dollars. Most mid-range hotels accept credit cards. The best option in this category is the *Pasefika Inn* (☎ 20971; fax 23303; pinn@samoa.net), PO Box 4213, just off Beach Rd on Mata'utu St. The inn offers comfortable, air-conditioned balcony rooms, featuring spa baths, for ST120/140 and smaller, but equally comfortable, air-conditioned rooms with shower and toilet for ST100/120. You can choose to go without the air-conditioning and pay just ST50/60 (with the luxury of hot water, this is possibly the best deal in town). All rooms have a fridge and telephone. Dormitory beds (one room with four bunks) are also available for ST22 per person. All room prices, unless you're sleeping in the dorm, include breakfast. The inn has a big, fully equipped communal kitchen, a TV and video room, same-day laundry service and fax and internet service. Every Sunday afternoon the Pasefika offers an excellent traditional Sunday dinner, *to'onai*, for around ST30 per person.

Ah Kam's Full Moon Inn (☎ /fax 20782), PO Box 1299, is centrally located just a short walk from the market and the town centre. Comfortable single/double/triple rooms with shower, fan, fridge, and with tea and coffee-making facilities cost ST78/104/130, including tax. Air-conditioned suites cost ST104/130/142. The inn has a bar, restaurant and pleasant courtyard. Guests are offered a free Sunday lunch.

The *Teuila Hotel* (☎ /fax 23000), PO Box 182, on Vaitele St, has plain air-conditioned singles/doubles with shower, toilet and fridge for ST92/107. Family rooms containing two double beds cost ST134. The hotel

has a restaurant and a bar. There's live music in the bar from Wednesday to Saturday night.

The pleasant *Le Godinet Beachfront Hotel* (☎ 25437; fax 25436), PO Box 9490, is out on the quiet Mulinu'u Peninsula. Air-conditioned rooms with private facilities cost ST107/133/160 a single/double/triple. Le Godinet is actually better known for being one of Apia's finest restaurants, serving unforgettable lobster and seafood dishes and a super Polynesian buffet on Friday nights. The *Fesili Motel* (☎ 26476; fax 22517), opposite the National Hospital, is a ramshackle, sprawling place which comes complete with a bar and disco on the roof, a supermarket and bank on the ground floor and a laundrette and chapel of rest in the basement! The large air-conditioned single/double rooms with shower and toilet, fridge, and tea and coffee-making facilities cost ST100/125. The best grocery store in town, Lynn Netzler's, is just around the corner.

Nearby is *Tori's Place* (☎ /fax 23431), PO Box 1604, a super-clean suburban home which caters mainly for Japanese and Germans working in Samoa. Comfortable, carpeted rooms with overhead fans and shared bathroom cost ST95/115/135, including tax and breakfast. Upstairs, there's a large lounge and kitchen. Child care facilities, same-day laundry service, rental cars and secretarial services are offered.

Out of town is the very quiet *South Sea Star Hotel* (☎ /fax 21667), PO Box 800, in Alafua village. The hotel occupies a leafy setting just a two minute walk from the University of the South Pacific campus. Clean rooms with shared facilities cost ST30/40. Newer rooms upstairs with shower (hot), toilet, fridge and tea and coffee making facilities cost ST100/150. A continental breakfast costs an additional ST7 and an English breakfast is ST10. Other meals are available in the attached Cappuccino Club restaurant for ST15 for lunch and ST25 for dinner. To get there, take a taxi (ST4 from the Post Office) or the Alafua bus (60 sene) from the Maketi Fou.

The *Rainforest Ecolodge* (☎ /fax 22144;

INDEPENDENT SAMOA

Aggie Grey's – From Snack Bar to Movie Stars

The daughter of William Swann, a Lincolnshire chemist who'd migrated to Samoa in 1889, and Pele, a Samoan girl from Toamua village, Agnes Genevieve Swann was one of the Pacific's most famous personalities and did more for Samoan tourism than any other individual.

In 1917 she married Gordon Hay-Mackenzie, the recently arrived manager of the Union Steamship Company. They had four children before Gordon died eight years later. Soon afterwards, Aggie married Charlie Grey, who was, unfortunately, a compulsive gambler. Charlie succeeded in losing everything they had and Aggie had to look for some means of supporting the family.

In 1942, American soldiers arrived in Apia carrying 'unimaginable wealth', and Aggie saw an opportunity to earn a little money. With the aid of a loan of US$180, she bought the site of a former hotel and began selling hamburgers and coffee to US servicemen..

Response to her business was overwhelming and although supplies were difficult to come by during WWII, Aggie built up an institution which became famous Pacific-wide as a social gathering place for war-weary soldiers. She even succeeded in getting through the New Zealand-imposed prohibition of alcoholic beverages.

When James Michener published his enormously successful *Tales of the South Pacific*, Aggie Grey was so well known throughout that realm that it was widely assumed she was the prototype for the character of Michener's Tonkinese madam, Bloody Mary. Michener has said that he did visit Aggie's place whenever he could, to get away from 'unutterably dull and militarily stuffy' Pago Pago, where he was frequently stationed. However he denies that anything but the good bits of Bloody Mary were inspired by Aggie Grey. In an interview with Aggie's biographer, Nelson Eustis, Michener said that when he returned to New York to edit the manuscript of his first book and needed to know what Bloody Mary would do or say, he used Aggie as a reference.

Over the next few decades, the snack bar expanded into a hotel where numerous celebrities stayed while filming or travelling in the area. (Many of the *fale* rooms are named after such famous people.)

Aggie said she wanted her hotel to be a place where visitors could feel at home, though these days, the price of rooms in the hotel will prevent most travellers from doing so. However, you can still probably afford to go to Aggie's for drinks at the pleasant bar, to spend Wednesday night at the *fiafia*, or to splurge on a wonderful buffet meal.

If you'd like to read more about Aggie Grey, who died in June 1988 at the age of 91, pick up a copy of her biography, *Aggie Grey of Samoa*, by Nelson Eustis, on sale at the gift shop in Aggie Grey's Hotel and at several shops around Apia. ■

ecotour@samoa.net), PO Box 4609 Matautu-uta, is a quiet and peaceful colonial homestead situated on the Tanumapua Tropical Plantation in the cool foothills to the west of Apia. The lodge offers three large rooms which open onto a wooden balcony that overlooks a lush tropical garden. Singles/doubles/triples cost ST170/219/268, including breakfast and afternoon tea. There's a shared, open-to-the-sky, shower. There is no hot water, but there are plans to install solar panels. The first night is free. The lodge is run by Steve Brown and Lumaava Sooaemalelagi, who also offer excellent environmental and cultural tours in Steve's unmissable Eco-Tour bus (Eco-Tour Samoa won the 1997 South Pacific Ecotourism Award). See Organised Tours in the regional Getting Around chapter.

Places to Stay – top end

A very pleasant upmarket option, which actually straddles the middle and upper price ranges, is *Vaiala Beach Cottages* (☎ 22202; fax 22008), PO Box 2025, Apia, close to Vaiala Beach east of Apia. Family-sized cottages, with bathroom, ceiling fans and cooking facilities (gas stove), will cost you ST158/183/207/244. The cottages, set in spacious gardens overlooking the sea, can sleep up to three adults and two children. Vaiala offers a laundry service and traditional *fofo* massage on request.

The three-storey *Hotel Insel Fehmarn* (☎ 23301; fax 22204), PO Box 3272, Apia, at Moto'otua on Falealili St, is named after the German Baltic Sea island where the grandfather of the present owner was cast adrift on a roof beam during a storm in 1872.

After 27 hours at sea, the 12-year-old was rescued by a French brig. With large air-conditioned rooms, balconies, TV and private facilities, it is a quiet but rather stark alternative to the hotels nearer the shore. Single/double rooms, with air-conditioning, bathroom and kitchen facilities cost ST158/183; the 3rd floor rooms are the nicest, affording views across Apia and out to sea. The hotel also has a swimming pool, tennis court, laundrette, restaurant and live music every Saturday.

The busiest upmarket hotel in Apia is *Aggie Grey's Hotel* (☎ 22880; fax 23626; aggiegreys@samoa.net), PO Box 67, on Beach Rd. The building can expanded enormously over the years and can now cater for more than 300 people. Well-appointed rooms and cute individual fales (named after movie stars) are gathered around a pleasant tropical garden and swimming pool. The standard rooms are gradually being refurbished, with the red carpet and wood panelling giving way to rattan furniture and cool colours. A standard single room costs ST219, doubles are ST231 and triples cost ST256, with discounts for children under 12. For fale accommodation, add ST50 per night to the above prices. Rooms in the new wing at the front (no children under 16 permitted) cost ST329/341/353. To all these rates, add 10% GST. Meal plans cost an additional ST109 per person per day.

The hotel's pleasant fale bar, which is open from 8 am to 11 pm daily, offers nightly Polynesian musical entertainment. On Wednesday, don't miss the famous *fiafia* with spectacular dancing, drumming and singing. The show, with buffet dinner, costs ST44; tickets for the show only are ST11.

For a slightly more elegant bar scene, go to Le Kionasina at the front of the hotel, which is open from 3 to 11 pm Monday to Saturday.

Apia's other big hotel, the *Hotel Kitano Tusitala* (☎ 21122; fax 23652), PO Box 101, is a bit less of a tourist venue and more of a business traveller's hotel. Situated on the Mulinu'u Peninsula, the Tusitala feels quieter and more spacious than Aggie's.

Standard air-conditioned single/double/triple rooms cost ST178/202/226. 'Deluxe' rooms with TV cost ST257/280/304. Children under 12 can stay for free. The hotel has a swimming pool, tennis courts, bar and two restaurants featuring traditional Samoan and Japanese food. The Tusitala's fiafia is on Thursday night and costs ST45 per person with the buffet, ST10 without.

Places to Eat

Snacks & Cheap Meals One of the best places for a cheap meal, particularly breakfast, is the *Maketi Fou* or the food stalls behind the *Flea Market*. Try a few Samoan pancakes (more like small doughnuts) washed down with a cup of fresh koko Samoa (locally grown cocoa served hot and black with lots of sugar). If you're really hungry, you can order a plate of fish or chicken and vegetables (usually cooked banana and breadfruit) for just a few tala. Look out for delicious palusami (coconut cream wrapped in taro leaves and cooked in banana leaves) and drinking coconuts.

The *Black Coffee Cafe* (☎ 26528), on Convent St, is one of the cheapest and most pleasant sit-down places in town. The food is fresh, well made and served in Samoan-sized portions. A breakfast of pancakes with papaya and banana and two large mugs of coffee costs around ST7. A few tala more will get you a special 'hangover breakfast' of steak and the works served on a platter. The cafe also does excellent fruit shakes and a range of cakes. Lunch and dinner menus (daily specials from ST7) feature authentic curries, spicy food, fresh pasta, seafood, steaks and chicken dishes. Vegetarians can be catered for. The cafe has a BYO licence and is open for breakfast, lunch and dinner from 6 am Monday to Friday and for breakfast and lunch on Saturday.

Another of Apia's favourite restaurants is *Gourmet Seafood & Grill* (☎ 24625) on the corner of Convent St and Post Office St, open from 7 am to 9.30 pm, Monday to Saturday. It has a pleasant, relaxed feel and offers a good range of simple dishes such as ham and eggs, burgers, veggie burgers, fish and chips, steak teriyaki and Samoan specialities. For dinner, there's a great seafood platter with salad for ST10.50.

Giordano's Pizzeria (☎ 25985), opposite the Insel Fehmarn Hotel, offers excellent pizzas in a pleasant courtyard setting. For a pizza large enough for two people, you'll pay around ST15. It's open from 3 to 10 pm Monday to Saturday and from 5 to 9 pm on Sunday.

There are plenty of cheap takeaway places around town, including a drive-through McDonald's on the corner of Convent St and Mt Vaea St. *Betty's Place* and *Pinati's*, both opposite McDonald's on Convent St, offer cheap Samoan and Chinese dishes. Pinati's does a filling meat and vegetable soup for ST2. *Cam's Food Bar*, just up the road, is also recommended for cheap eats.

The snack bar next to Magrey Ta's Beer Garden on Beach Rd is good for takeaway fish and chips and sometimes does roast beef. *Skippy's Restaurant*, upstairs in an arcade near the Pacific Commercial Bank on Beach Rd, is a popular place with students. For fish and chips or chicken and chips with salad, you'll pay around ST4.50. For good cheap burgers and steaks, try the *Steak House* (☎ 22962) in the ACE Hardware building on Mt Vaea St. Burgers cost ST1.80, steak sandwiches cost ST2 and blade steak, chips and salad will set you back ST7.50. It's open from 8 am to 4 pm and from 6 to 10 pm Tuesday to Friday and from 6 to 10 pm on Saturday and Sunday. *Jean's Blue Marlin* (☎ 24065), on Beach Rd, offers cooked breakfasts, cheap fast-food lunches and dinner specialities such as barbecue kebabs for ST16 and vegetable stir-fry with rice for ST14. Apia's welcoming *Yacht Club* (☎ 21313), at the top of the Mulinu'u Peninsula, offers cheap meals (fish and chips and salad for ST7) from 4.30 pm Tuesday to Sunday.

Chinese Restaurants There are quite a number of Chinese restaurants around town. The *Oriental Restaurant* (☎ 25171), below Fiasili's Guesthouse & Backpackers Centre opposite the Mormon temple, is the most popular and probably the best value, offering lunch specials from just ST5. A full meal at dinner will cost between ST20 and ST25. It's open for lunch from noon to 2 pm Monday to Friday, and for dinner from 6 to 10 pm every evening.

Wong Kee's, in the alley behind Otto's Reef on Beach Rd, and the related *Canton*, next door to Betty Moor's Guest House, are great for minimal decor and big portions (from about ST10 for a meal). Locals' recommend the Canton's crab with black bean sauce.

The recently refurbished *Treasure Garden*, on Fugalei St, (closed at the time of writing) may be worth investigating. The shiny red and gold *Hua Mei Restaurant*, above the Lotemau Centre, has a lunch buffet, Monday to Friday for ST20; normal main courses start at ST15.

More Expensive Restaurants A recommended option at the cheaper end of this price range is the *Rainforest Cafe & Restaurant* (☎ 25030), on Beach Rd opposite the harbour. Breakfast items include fresh blended fruit juices, cappuccino, French toast and pancakes (from ST5). Lunch specials – excellent salads, curries, fish and chicken dishes and huge sandwiches – range from ST9 to ST15. Main courses at dinner start at ST18. The restaurant is closed on Saturday and Sunday. The owners of the restaurant, Christian Duürst and Barbara Schmal, offer reasonably priced customised tours around Upolu. They also have bicycles to rent from ST15 per day.

Le Moana, inside the Lotemau Centre, caters for expats and people working in the central business area. It's open seven days a week. Breakfast dishes (yoghurt and fruit, pancakes etc) start at ST6.50; lunches (curry and rice, fish and chips) cost around ST10; main courses at dinner (local fish, New Zealand lamb, Samoan dishes) start at ST25. On Sunday you can have English roast dinner for ST20. Le Moana also sells Australian and New Zealand wine, international magazines and weekend Australian and New Zealand newspapers.

Lesina's Lounge (☎ 20836), in a great location overlooking Apia, specialises in a mixture of Japanese, Samoan and continental dishes. Starters (palolo on toast, oysters) range from ST10 to ST15; main courses start at around ST25. There's an adjoining bar with a large deck area and pool table, and live music every Friday and Saturday evening. The restaurant is open from 4.30 to 11.30 pm Monday to Saturday (lunchtime opening is on the cards).

Back on Beach Rd is the upmarket *Sails Restaurant & Bar* (☎ 20628), housed upstairs in an old colonial building overlooking the harbour. Lunch offerings include sashimi (ST14), oysters (ST16.50) and imported steak (ST26.50); the dinner menu is more extensive with starters from ST10 and mains going up to ST45. It's open for lunch and dinner Monday to Saturday and for dinner only on Sunday.

The elegant *Le Godinet's* (☎ 23690), on the Mulinu'u Peninsula, is best known for its seafood and Friday night Polynesian buffet. Seafood dishes with deliciously prepared vegetables cost from ST26; lobster thermidor is ST32. Book ahead, if possible in the early afternoon.

The *Belle Ile Restaurant* (☎ 21010), on Beach Rd not far from Aggie's, specialises in French dishes, though Samoan meals are on offer, too. Special three-course European meals cost ST35; a Samoan gourmet meal costs ST28. A la carte main courses start at around ST25. It's open for lunch and dinner Monday to Friday and for dinner only on Saturday.

The *Fale Restaurant* at Aggie Grey's Hotel offers an excellent weekly dinner buffet (ST44 plus drinks), following the Wednesday evening fiafia. On Friday night the speciality is steak and pasta, while Sunday is barbecue night. The restaurant, in a pleasant garden setting by the pool, is open daily for breakfast and lunch also, but prices are high by Samoan standards. You'll pay ST22.50 for a cooked breakfast, ST14 for Aggie's Hamburger Deluxe. Aggie's other restaurant, *Le Tamarina*, offers lunch and dinner for around ST40. Aggie's coffee lounge, just inside the hotel entrance, serves excellent coffee (ST3 including a refill). It's open from 7 am to 5 pm daily.

The main restaurant at the Hotel Kitano Tusitala, *Stevensons*, puts on an elaborate buffet dinner (ST45) to accompany its fiafia night every Thursday. Dinner here is served before the show, which cuts down a little on eating time! The hotel's *Apaula Terrace* serves snacks and Japanese food on Friday evenings. Prices are on a par with Aggie's.

Sunday Lunch On Sunday mornings you'll find the islands shrouded in smoke as villagers everywhere light fires to warm the stones needed for the umus – the ground ovens used to bake Sunday lunch (to'ona'i), and for other festive occasions. Visitors sometimes complain that nothing happens in Samoa on Sundays, but it's hardly true – after a small breakfast (on account of the looming lunch) Samoans go to church and sing their lungs out, at noon they eat an enormous roast dinner and in the afternoon they sleep. You may be lucky enough to be invited to a family to'ona'i, if not, there are quite a few options for a traditional Sunday lunch. One of the best is at the *Pasefika Inn* (☎ 20971), on Mata'utu St. A typical spread includes baked fish and other seafoods (freshwater prawns, crabs, octupus cooked in coconut milk), suckling pig, baked breadfruit, bananas, tamu, palusami, salads, curry dishes and more. For ST30 per person, it's excellent value.

Dave Parker's Silver Streams (☎ 24426), up in the hills above Apia, puts on Sunday lunch in the rainforest. *O Le Satapuala Beach Resort* (☎ 42212), 25 minutes west of Apia, also stages a well-attended to'ona'i for ST30 per person.

On the south coast, the upmarket *Sinalei Reef Resort* offers traditional Sunday lunch for ST33 per person (ST17 for children under 12).

Self-Catering For fresh produce, the best place to head for is the main market, the *Maketi Fou*, off Fugalei St, or the *Fish Market*, just north-east of the Flea Market, which also has a few fruit and vegetable stalls. Bargaining isn't part of Samoan culture; marked prices are what you pay. You'll find a reasonable selection of groceries at *Chan Mow's*, near the clock tower, the *Molesi Store*, further west on Beach Rd, and also at *Greg's Store*, next to the Belle Ile Restaurant up near Aggie Grey's.

For the best bread in town, a good selection of imported foods and wines, and the weekend Australian and New Zealand newspapers, go to *Lynn Netzler's Store* (☎ 20272), on Salenesa Rd, around the corner from the Fesili Motel. *CJ's Deli*, in the Lotemau Centre, also stocks imported foods such as cheese, olives, maple syrup and crumpets.

Entertainment

Bars & Nightclubs Most of the bars around town are to be found in the middle and top-end hotels. *Don't Drink the Water*, on Beach Rd opposite the harbour, is an air-conditioned, no-smoking cocktail bar which serves huge cocktails for very reasonable prices. Prices start at ST8 (jugs for ST20) and you can order anything from a margarita to an orgasm (screaming or Celtic). Snacks such as chocolate cake, sashimi and smoked deep-sea fish are also available. Go early to get a table outside. *Otto's Reef* and *Magrey Ta's*, both on Beach Rd, are beer gardens which sometimes feature bands on the weekends.

Otto's Reef has pool tables and darts. Don't miss Cindy's excellent and hilarious fa'afafine show at Magrey Ta's every Thursday evening at about 9 pm. Tickets cost just ST7. The small, down-to-earth bar at the *Seaside Inn* is a good place to meet other travellers. The *Fale Bar* at Aggie Grey's Hotel has live Polynesian-style music nightly and a pleasant, if slightly restrained, atmosphere. It's a good spot to meet well-heeled locals. Aggie's *Le Kionasina* bar is open from 3 to 11 pm Monday to Saturday.

The *Ocean Terrace Bar* at the Hotel Kitano Tusitala stages live music and dancing until midnight nightly, Monday to Saturday. On the south coast, the upmarket Sinalei Reef Resort and Coconuts Beach Club have bars open to nonguests. Traditional Samoan music is played in the beach bar at Coconuts every Tuesday to Friday evening and on Saturday and Sunday afternoons.

For a small place, Apia has an extraordinary number of nightclubs, almost all featuring their own live band playing pretty much the same mixture of popular Polynesian/rock/reggae music. There's usually a cover charge of a couple of tala. All close down at the stroke of midnight.

The most pleasant of them all is the *Penisula Nightclub*, built on the edge of the mangrove forest on the Mulinu'u Peninsula, next to the petrol storage tanks. The large open dance floor is nicely lit, there's a good mixture of ages (20s to 50s) and beyond the dance floor and bar, there are tables and chairs gathered beneath enormous pulu trees. The *Beach Club Bar*, just down the road, also has live music.

In the evenings the *RSA Club*, on Beach Rd near the clock tower, turns from a big rattling pool hall and bar into a popular nightclub – thanks mainly to an excellent band and some serious ultraviolet lighting. There's a younger crowd and more serious beer drinking here. The *Mt Vaea Nightclub*, on Vaitele St, is similar to the RSA and just as popular. *Crystal's* and *William's Bay*, both off Fugalei St, are variations on the established theme, with Crystal's appearing to be housed in a shed. William's Bay does a great barbecue plate for ST6 from around 11 pm. *Evening Shades*, near the corner of Beach Rd and Mata'utu St, is a disco playing current dance music. Other places to investigate for live music and night life include the *Teuila Hotel, Lesina's Lounge, Jean's Blue Marlin* and *Dave Parker's Silver Streams*. The Visitors Bureau also has a list of what's on.

Fiafias Spectacular Samoan dance performances, called fiafias, are staged regularly at various hotel venues. They're all equally good; choose a venue that appeals and book ahead to get decent seats. A buffet dinner usually accompanies the performance, though you can choose to see the show only.

The fiafia at *Aggie Grey's Hotel* is staged on Wednesday evening. Dinner and show cost ST44; the show only costs ST11. The *Tusitala's* fiafia is on Thursday. The fiafia and buffet cost ST45; the show only is ST10. *Sinalei Reef Resort* stages a fiafia on Friday evening (ST40) and *Coconuts Beach Club* puts on its show on Saturday.

Around the Island

Venturing into Apia's hinterland will reveal Upolu as the archetypal tropical island, with beaches, reefs, rainforests, mountains and quiet villages. Those who've always dreamed of sliding down a jungle waterfall into a crystalline pool will not be disappointed, either, and unlike those constructed at tourist resorts in Hawaii, it's all natural!

Robert Louis Stevenson Museum & Mt Vaea Scenic Reserve

Just 4km inland from Beach Rd, off The Cross Island Rd, is the beautifully restored home (☎ 20798; fax 25428) of Robert Louis Stevenson, who spent the last four years of his life in Samoa. Stevenson and his wife, Fanny, are buried on nearby Mt Vaea, which overlooks Apia and the surrounding mountains. When Stevenson died in 1894, the Vailima estate was purchased by a wealthy German retiree and philanthropist, Gustav Kunst, who added extensions to each end of Stevenson's house. During the New Zealand administration, the estate was occupied by the government administrator and after Independence it became the official residence of the head of state.

To commemorate the centenary of Stevenson's death, the directors of the RLS Museum/Preservation Foundation in the USA set about looking for funds to restore the estate. They duly raised the necessary US$2.5 million and after much painstaking work, the museum opened in 1994.

With its distinctive red corrugated-iron roof, enormous verandas, polished wooden floors and fascinating artefacts, Vailima provides a real thrill for Stevenson lovers. The 'Smoking Room', papered in a beautiful siapo wallpaper copied from the original, contains the fireplace Stevenson installed to remind him of home and, among other things, an original tobacco crate with the words 'Always in Perfect Condition' stamped on it. Stevenson's library and bedroom, where some of his favourite books and his own original editions are displayed, opens onto Fanny's bedroom, which is lined entirely with polished redwood from Califorinia.

The museum is open from 9 am to 3.30 pm Monday to Friday and from 8 am to noon Saturday. Tickets cost ST15 for adults and ST5 for children under 12. Visitors are obliged to take a guided tour around the house; there's plenty to look at so don't let the guide rush you through (this may happen on the last tour of the day). Downstairs is a gift shop offering a good selection of RLS titles and books about Samoa as well as some overpriced souvenirs.

If you'd like to walk up to the Stevensons' tombs (a relatively short but very steep climb), or spend some time wandering around the botanical gardens and rainforest trails, in addition to seeing the museum, allow a good half day or more. Wear sturdy shoes, bring water, perhaps a picnic lunch and mosquito repellent. The reserve is an excellent area for bird and bat watching. There's no charge to enter the reserve or walk up to the tombs. If you'd like a guide to accompany you, contact the park ranger.

To get to Mt Vaea, follow the trail down to the Vailima Stream, cross the stream and turn left (the trail to the right leads to a waterfall). After a few minutes you'll come to a fork where a sign announces that the short trail to the top will take 35 minutes and the left fork, the long route, will require 55 minutes. If you're reasonably fit, take 10 minutes off those times. The trails can be very muddy and slippery after heavy rain. The tombs, on a plateau just below the summit, look down onto Vailima and out to the surrounding mountains. It's a tranquil and silent spot and it's not difficult to under-

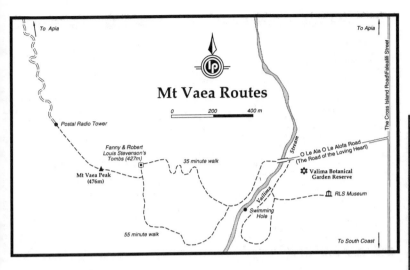

stand why Stevenson wanted to be here forever.

An alternative route down is via the postal radio tower on the next hill back towards town, but it will require a bit of jungle-bashing, especially after prolonged rainy periods. The route branches off about 20m down the long trail from the Mt Vaea summit. Look for a bare spot on your right less than a metre above the trail. This is the beginning of a route along the ridge to the tower, a walk of several hundred metres through heavy bush that could take up to 30 minutes. However, the ridge is narrow and fairly easily followed; from the tower, return to Apia via the winding road down the hill.

Getting There & Away A taxi from Apia to Vailima should cost around ST6. To go by bus, take the Mulivai or Salani bus from the Maketi Fou or wave it down on Falealili St around the Hotel Insel Fehmarn.

Island Styles & Talofa Winery
Just south of Vailima, on The Cross Island Rd, is the Island Styles outlet (☎ 21436), where you can buy reasonably priced hand-printed T-shirts and lavalavas. The winery produces fruit wines made from banana, passionfruit and papaya (ST8.50 a bottle) and the delicious Stevenson's Coconut Cream Liqueur (ST35 a bottle), which is made from coconut cream, coffee, vanilla and Fijian rum.

Baha'i Temple
From near the highest point of The Cross Island Rd, the 28m Niue limestone dome of the Baha'i House of Worship (☎ 24192) points skyward. Designed by Iranian Husain Amanat and dedicated in 1984, this imposing and very beautiful structure is one of seven Baha'i houses of worship in the world. According to church literature, it is a 'place of spiritual gathering and of the manifestation of divine mysteries'.

The Baha'i faith, which has no professional clergy or priesthood, originated in Persia in 1844. It recognises the basic unity of all religions and the oneness of mankind. Its services are simple, consisting of prayers, meditations and readings from the scriptures of the faith as well as from other religions of the world.

Here he Lies Where he Longs to Be

In December 1889, the already famous Scottish author and poet Robert Louis Balfour Stevenson and his wife Fanny Osborne arrived in Apia aboard the schooner *Equator*. Stevenson had left Europe in search of relief from worsening tuberculosis and the general sickliness that had plagued him all his life. He was enchanted by Samoa and in 1890 he paid £200 for 126 hectares of land in the hills above Apia.

Stevenson's health improved and, with his family, he set sail for Australia. However, he became ill again in Sydney and it was decided that the climate of Samoa would be much better for him. The Stevenson family returned to Apia in September 1890 and constructed Vailima, the grandest home ever seen on the island. They imported furniture from Stevenson's native Scotland and dressed their Samoan employees in lavalavas patterned with the Stuart tartan.

In the 1890s, during the period of strife in Samoa between Britain, the USA and Germany, Stevenson became an activist for Samoan rights, maintaining that the people should be left to govern themselves and to determine their own destiny in accordance with their customs. Most Europeans there would have liked to see him deported at the time but this would have been very unpopular indeed; Stevenson came to be loved by the Samoans for his friendliness towards them and his ability to entertain with stories. They respectfully and affectionately referred to him as Tusitala (teller of tales).

Stevenson spent only four years in Samoa. On 3 December 1894 he died of a stroke at Vailima. When the Samoan chief Tu'imaleali'ifano spoke of Stevenson's death he echoed the sentiments of many Samoans: 'Talofa e i lo matou Tusitala. Ua tagi le fatu ma le 'ele'ele,' he said. ('Our beloved Tusitala. The stones and the earth weep').

Stevenson had stipulated that he wished to be buried at the top of Mt Vaea, part of the Vailima estate. Just two months before his death, in gratitude for his kindness to them, a delegation of Samoan chiefs had arranged for a hand-dug road to be made between Apia and Vailima, which they called O Le Ala O Le Alofa, the Road of the Loving Heart.

Stevenson had to be buried as quickly as possible because of the tropical heat and these same chiefs worked through the night to clear sections of bush to make a path up the mountain for the funeral procession. After the Christian burial service the coffin was laid on a base of coral and volcanic pebbles and the grave lined with black stones – a practice normally reserved for Samoan royalty.

No discussion of Stevenson in Samoa would be complete without citing his epitaph, two of the most beautifully poignant verses he ever composed.

> Under the wide and starry sky,
> Dig the grave and let me lie.
> Glad did I live and gladly die,
> And I laid me down with a will.

> This be the verse you grave for me:
> Here he lies where he longed to be;
> Home is the sailor, home from the sea,
> And the hunter home from the hill.

Fanny, who was known as Aolele by the Samoans, stayed on for a while in Samoa but died in California in 1914. In her will, however, she requested that her ashes be taken also to Mt Vaea and buried beside her husband's. Her epitaph, which was also composed by Stevenson, reads:

> Teacher, tender comrade, wife,
> A fellow farer, true through life,
> Heart whole and soul free,
> The august father gave to me. ∎

Visitors are welcome. There is an adjoining information centre, where attendants will happily answer your questions. The well-groomed lawns and gardens are worth a visit, too. Services are held on Sundays at 10 am.

Tiapapata Art Centre

To the south-west of the Baha'i temple, signposted off the main road, is the Tiapapata Art Centre (☎ 23524). Run by Galumalemana Steven Percival and his wife Wendy,

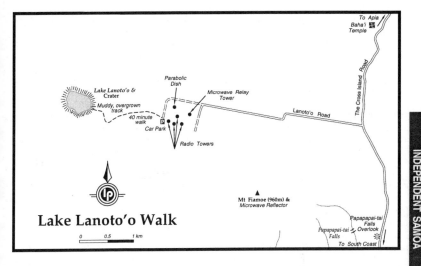

Lake Lanoto'o Walk

both accomplished artists, the centre offers workshops and demonstrations in traditional arts. There's also a small gallery selling beautiful traditional and contemporary arts and crafts including carvings, prints and pottery. The centre is open from 9.30 am to 4 pm Tuesday to Saturday. A taxi from Apia (the only way to get there if you don't have your own transport) will cost between ST12 and ST15.

Lake Lanoto'o

Known also as Goldfish Lake, Lake Lanoto'o is an eerie, pea-green crater lake in the central highlands of Upolu. Anyone keen on the unusual should make a point of visiting this little-known spot. The lake just missed out on becoming an easily accessible tourist attraction in 1919. During the German occupation it had become quite a resort and the Germans built two huts and provided a rowing boat for those who ventured in there. In 1919 local traders suggested that a road be built to the lake to allow easy access to holiday-makers, but proponents of 'controlled tourism' saw to it that the idea remained only a suggestion.

To get there, take The Cross Island Rd beyond the Baha'i temple until you see a microwave relay tower on a low hill to your right. Ask the driver to drop you at the Lanoto'o Rd turn-off. Walk west on this road for about 3km, at which point it will narrow into a track at a turn-off to the left. Don't turn, however. Continue straight ahead for about another kilometre to where the track makes a 90° turn to the left. Follow it until the array of radio towers and a satellite dish are visible on your left.

If you have your own car, you can drive to this point. From here, look to the right and you should be able to make out a badly overgrown track leading away across a muddy bog-like area. This is the route. After several hundred metres the trail improves considerably, becoming slippery red clay. Follow it for about 40 minutes until it climbs a hill. The murky green lake is in the volcanic crater ahead. Lake Lanoto'o is full of wild goldfish that congregate around the shore. Locals used to collect them for pets until the government banned it. It's a great place for a swim too, but a little spooky because of alternating warm and cold currents and the fact that the bottom of the lake has never been found.

Very few visitors ever see this lovely and unusual spot. In order to avoid the multiple unpleasantries of ankle deep mud, thorn bushes, sleeping grass (which stings like nettle) and leeches, hikers should wear long pants and sturdy, covered shoes. Carry food, water and insect repellent.

Papapapai-tai Falls

About 3km south of the Baha'i temple, look out for a small parking area on your right. This is the overlook for the spectacular 100m Papapapai-tai Waterfall which plunges into a dramatic, forested gorge.

Papasee'a Sliding Rock

A trip to the Papasee'a Sliding Rock is obligatory for every visitor to Samoa, although once there, many can't seem to muster the nerve to enjoy the star attraction, a 5m slide down a waterfall into a jungle pool. It's better than Disneyland. If the big one puts you off, though, there are three other smaller ones to choose from. Don't miss this place! Take the Se'ese'e bus from the Maketi Fou and ask to be dropped off at the intersection for Papasee'a. It's a good idea to remember the route the bus takes to get to this point because drivers divert from their standard route to drop visitors close to the park and you'll probably have to walk out to the paved road to catch a bus back to town. Walk 2km up the hill to the entrance. Admission to the park is ST2, but pay only the women at the entrance and not the children who hound you as you approach. They have no authority to collect and you'll just have to pay again as you enter.

Tanumapua Plantation

The Tanumapua Tropical Plantation (☎ 27037), a few kilometres inland from Vaitele, just west of Apia, is a pleasant rural outing from town. You can spend an afternoon strolling around the planted areas and tropical flower gardens and seeing examples of such tropical crops as coffee, bananas, papaya, pineapples, kava and cacao. You can also see the plantation on horseback.

If you've always wanted to see a cacao pod, here's your opportunity. The whimsical trees are short and mouldy-looking affairs with cacao pods sprouting from the trunk and branches. If you can manage to find a ripe one (ask a plantation worker), open it and chew on the white cushioning material between the beans. It's delicious and the Samoans consider it quite a treat.

If you'd like to stay in these lush surroundings, bed and breakfast is available at the Rainforest Ecolodge (☎ 22144), an original plantation house located in Tanumapua. From town, the plantation is about 8km along Alafa'alava Rd on the right hand side. To get to Alafa'alava Rd, take the first left turning west of the Mormon Temple. A taxi from Apia costs about ST18.

Vailima Brewery

Samoa Breweries (☎ 20200), which is halfway between the airport and Apia, produces the award-winning national beer, Vailima. Managed by the German firm Haase Braurei, of Hamburg, the brewery opened in 1978 and has grown into Samoa's biggest industry, producing three million litres of beer annually. The latest in a line of professional brewers is Swiss brewmaster Marcel Rappo. There are no formal tours of the brewery, but if you turn up with three or four people (no more, however) and display an interest, you'll probably be able to arrange a friendly, informal tour around the plant and, of course, a sampling of the product.

Leulumoega Church

On the stretch of road between Apia and Faleolo airport, there are more than 60 multi-coloured churches representing numerous denominations. One of the most interesting of these is the Congregational Christian (London Missionary Society) church at Leulumoega, 5km east of the airport, the design of which is unique on the island. While you're in Leulumoega, visit the School of Fine Arts, beside the Maloa Theological College, where you can appreciate some wonderful woodcarvings and other artwork done by students.

South Coast Beaches

Along with the Aleipata Islands area and Manono Island, the south coast of Upolu offers plenty of beautiful palm-fringed beaches where it wouldn't be difficult to pass a week or two. Custom fees may vary slightly but, in general, access to beaches costs ST10 for buses; ST5 for cars; ST3 for motocycles and bicycles; and ST2 for pedestrians. Some beaches offer basic fale accommodation.

In the Lefaga district is the idyllic Return to Paradise Beach, made famous in the 1951 Gary Cooper film, based on the James Michener novel, *Return to Paradise*. The setting lives up to its name, but while the beach is picturesque, it is not ideal for swimming due to the shallow reefs, volcanic boulders and heavy surf pounding on it all. It's a popular weekend spot for barbecues. To get there by public transport, look for the brightly painted Return to Paradise Beach bus at the Maketi Fou in Apia.

The next beach east of Return to Paradise is Matareva, a series of delightful coves with safe, shallow snorkelling and lots of rock pools to explore. There are a couple of basic overnight fales, showers and a shop which is sometimes open for snacks and drinks. Access from the main road is down a 2.5km dirt track. The seclusion of Matareva is being threatened, however, with plans to build a 300-room luxury hotel nearby.

A couple of kilometres east is another good spot, Salamumu Beach, about 5km off the main road. About 15km further east is Aganoa Black Sand Beach. Unlike most of the beaches around Upolu, the water here is deep enough for swimming (it's sheltered and safe) and there's some good snorkelling at the far end of the bay. There's also a popular surf break here, called Boulders, just off Cape Niuato'i. East of O Le Pupu-Pu'e National Park is Vaiula Beach, which has a good surf break and cheap accommodation. It's also possible to hike to nearby Vaiula Cave from here. There are several more beaches worth investigating on the way to Aleipata. Beyond Lotofaga, there are countless beachside fales which can offer cheap

accommodation – see the following Places to Stay section.

Sataoa & Sa'anapu Conservation Area

In an effort to preserve one of Upolu's most important coastal wetland areas, the mangrove forests around the villages of Sataoa and Sa'anapu on the south coast have been declared a conservation area. Mangroves provide a vital habitat for the breeding of fish and crabs; they help to keep erosion in check; the bark is used to make natural dyes; and the leaves and bark are used in traditional medicine. The local conservation committee maintains the nature trail which winds through the mangroves for a couple of kilometres and offers excellent outrigger canoe tours for ST20. Guided trips to nearby Anaseao Cave can be arranged and there are good opportunities for birdwatching, too. The villages provide basic fale accommodation. Sataoa and Sa'anapu are signposted off the Main Coast Rd about 12km to the west of The Cross Island Rd.

O Le Pupu-Pu'e National Park

O Le Pupu-Pu'e is Independent Samoa's only fully fledged-national park. The name means 'from the coast to the mountain top', which is a fair description of its 29sq km. The park was created in 1978 to protect a sample of the island's natural environment and the scientific, recreational and educational interests of its people. The northern boundary is formed by a ridge between volcanic 840m Mt Le Pu'e and 1158m Mt Fito. In the south is the rugged O Le Pupu Lava Coast. There are plans to rebuild the visitors' centre, destroyed by the cyclones of the early 1990s. The park entrance is near Togitogiga Scenic Reserve, which lies just outside the park to the east. There are three hiking trails in the park and two basic campsites. Campers need to bring all their own supplies, including food and water. The park ranger can provide guides up to the cave for ST10; ST20 for the day. Hikers are expected to provide food for the guide.

The main inland trail, which begins to the south-west of the car park and leads past the

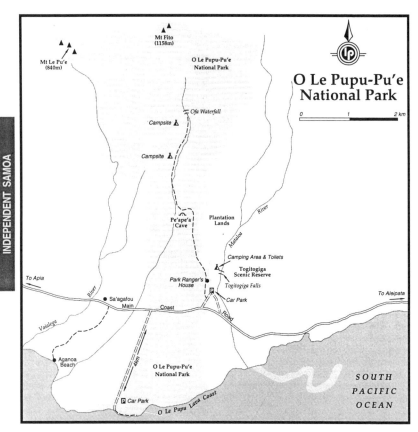

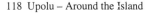

ranger's house, will take you up through thick rainforest to the lava tube, Pe'ape'a Cave. The return walk will require a minimum of three hours. The large pit-like cave – actually a lava tube – is full of circling swallows, or *pe'ape'a*. It's possible to explore the cave with a torch but be careful climbing down into the pit on the mossy, slippery rocks. From the cave, the new Kalati's Trail heads north for another 4km to Ofa Waterfall. This is an overnight trek; campsites are located halfway along the trail and by the waterfall. The trail crisscrosses a stream at several points.

At the far western boundary of the park a 4km track leads south from the road to the magnificently rugged O Le Pupu Lava Coast. It's possible to drive most of the way down. There's a car park to the left of the track just before the trail hits the coast. A coastal trail leads eastwards for about 25 minutes.

Togitogiga Falls

The falls and reserve with the tongue-twisting name, Togitogiga, lie just outside O Le Pupu-Pu'e National Park, up a dirt track from the park entrance. Several levels of falls are separated by pools, all great for swimming, and you can jump from the cliffs into the churning water below the largest one. There's a basic campsite here.

Sopo'aga Falls
On Le Mafa Pass Rd, just south of the turnoff to the southern Main Coast Rd, is a lovely garden, picnic site and overlook to the 50m Sopo'aga Falls and its immense gorge. The custom fee is ST3 per car; ST1 if you're on foot. Just west of the falls lookout, along the road, an unassuming concrete bridge crosses the uppermost reaches of the Sopo'aga Falls gorge and the view down is quite impressive.

Fuipisia Falls
Three kilometres north of Sopo'aga Falls is the trail to Fuipisia Falls, a 55m plunge off the Mulivaifagatola River. Follow the track west for 400m to the lookout. The custom fee should be between ST3 and ST5 per car.

Aleipata District
The reefs in the Aleipata district at the easternmost end of the island are 50m or so offshore and the water is a remarkable turquoise blue, making for the loveliest beaches and the best swimming on Upolu. The snorkelling is excellent, but beware of the numerous cone shells found here. Some are mildly poisonous, but the most beautiful ones can be deadly.

The offshore islands of Nu'utele and Nu'ulua also offer good snorkelling. Part of the Aleipata Islands Conservation Area, the islands are important sea bird nesting grounds. Nu'utele served as a leper colony from 1916 to 1918 when the lepers were relocated to Fiji.

The village of Ulutogia, the first village north of Lalomanu, is also part of the conservation area and it has committed itself to becoming fully sustainable by the year 2000. Sagapolotele Uitime of Ulutogia can organise tours around the area and trips across to the islands. Vaitoa Amituanar of Lalomanu can also organise sightseeing and snorkelling trips to the islands. Ask for him at the house opposite the church. A half-day tour

---

A Tiny Space on the World Wide Web
The Samoan moss spider, *Patu marplesi*, is the tiniest spider in the world. Measuring about 0.5mm fully grown, the weeny creature lives in the rainforests of Upolu Island. ■

---

will cost from ST10 per person. The first bus leaves the Maketi Fou for Lalomanu around 5 am.

Uafato Conservation Area
The north-eastern coastal region of Upolu is the wildest and least visited part of the island, containing some of the best scenery. Most of the population of the area is centred on Fagaloa Bay, the most prominent inlet on the Upolu coastline. A 4WD track follows the rugged coastline as far as the picturesque village of Uafato, where 14 sq km of the surrounding rainforest and coastal waters have been declared a conservation area. This is believed to be one of the few areas left in Samoa where there is an intact band of rainforest stretching from the sea to the interior uplands. The area also contains one of the largest remaining stands of *ifilele*, the tree used for carving kava bowls, as well as a range of bat and bird species, including the rare *manumea* or tooth-billed pigeon.

A number of traditionl carvers live in Uafato and are more than happy to demonstrate their art to visitors. There are several sites on the western side of the bay associated with the ancestral god Moso, who was said to have caused a whole flock of chickens to turn to stone. Villagers will point out the stone chickens as well as Moso's chair, kava bowl and taro. From Uafato, a coastal walking track (about four hours) continues eastward to Ti'avea, which is connected by road to the Richardson Rd which is just above Aleipata. Although there is no formal accommodation in Uafato, it is possible to stay overnight. Ask to speak to the mayor, the pulenu'u, when you arrive.

Officially, the conservation committee is

responsible for hosting visitors (see Society & Conduct in the Facts about the Region chapter and Staying in Villages in the regional Facts for the Visitor chapter). To drive to Uafato, take the 4WD track that leads eastward off Le Mafa Pass Rd at Falefa Falls; heading from Apia, look out for a sharp left over a precarious-looking bridge. The track meanders above the coastline with numerous beautiful views through the rainforest and down to the sea. A shorter 4WD track (about 10km) leads over the mountain from Le Mafa Pass to the village of Taelefaga. If you have plenty of time, this makes an excellent walk. The track isn't signposted; look for a sharp turning by a small roadside fale. From Apia, this route is occasionally served by buses marked Fagaloa.

Piula College & Fatumea Pool

Usually known simply as 'Piula Cave Pool', Fatumea Pool lies beneath Piula Methodist Theological College 18km east of Apia. It's a wonderful spot to spend a few hours picnicking, swimming in the clean, clear springs and exploring the water-filled caves. Just metres from the sea, the freshwater pool is separated from salt water by black lava rock. At the rear of the first cave you'll be able to see light through the wall under the water. A 3m swim through the opening will take you to the second cave pool. If you don't fancy a James Bond-type swim, follow the path leading to the opening on the seaward side of the second cave. There's a ST1 custom fee to use the pool.

Be sure also to have a look at the church above the pool, a unique and photogenic old structure surrounded by flower gardens and lush vegetation. Not far from Piula, near the village of Falefa, are the powerful Falefa Falls. The best vantage point for a photograph is on an old concrete platform just coastward from the overlook. It's also possible to scramble down onto the rocks just above the falls.

Places to Stay & Eat

An increasing number of places to stay are springing up around Upolu Island. There are countless beachside fales to choose from and several upmarket resorts, including Coconuts Beach Club and the Sinalei Reef Resort on the south coast, a short drive from Apia on The Cross Island Rd. When looking for

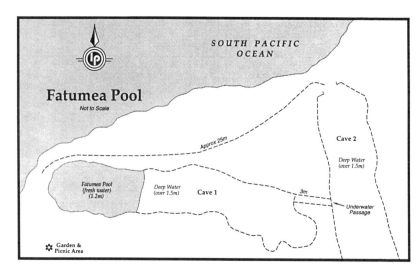

SOUTH PACIFIC OCEAN

Fatumea Pool

Not to Scale

Approx 25m

Cave 2

Deep Water (over 1.5m)

Fatumea Pool (fresh water) (1.2m)

Deep Water (over 1.5m)

Cave 1

3m

Underwater Passage

Garden & Picnic Area

accommodation, it's worth bearing in mind that 'resort' can refer to any accommodation anywhere near the sea. Almost all the fales can provide cheap home-cooked meals and the resorts have good, but expensive, restaurants. There are plenty of small grocery shops selling fresh bread, eggs, biscuits, tinned fish and cold beer.

North Coast At Cape Fatuosofia on the western tip of Upolu is the *Samoan Village Resort* (☎ 46028; fax 46098), PO Box 3495, which offers 10 deluxe self-contained fales all with excellent sea views. The beach is very picturesque, but not great for snorkelling or swimming; the beaches on nearby Manono Island are better. The fales are very large with full kitchen, separate living room, bedroom, bathroom and verandah. The living rooms have hideaway queen-sized beds so the fales can sleep up to four adults. Prices range from ST220 to ST366 for single or double occupancy; plus ST20 for each additional person. The resort has a small restaurant and bar, swimming pool and Jacuzzi. A taxi from the airport will cost about ST20.

A couple of kilometres east along the coast is the new *Airport Lodge* (☎ 45583; fax 45584; airportl@samoa.net) which has eight small double or twin units containing bathroom, fridge, table and chairs and small fan. There is a well-equipped separate kitchen. Singles/doubles cost ST122/134. Fishing charters and boat tours can be arranged.

Just 1km east of Faleolo airport is *O Le Satapuala Beach Resort* (☎ 42212; fax 42386), PO Box 1539, Apia. Enclosed beach fales with fans, kitchens and private facilities cost ST59/79 for single/double occupancy. Basic open-sided fales *(faleo'o)* cost ST20 per person. Camping on the site costs ST5 per person and a meal plan is available for ST50 per person per day. If you'd prefer a cultural experience, home stays may be arranged for around ST50 per person, including bed, transport and meals. The attached bar and restaurant are quite popular with locals and expats, especially on Satur-

day nights when there's live music. On Fridays, there's a ST5 barbecue and on Sundays, the resort prepares a well-attended Samoan umu lunch for ST30 per person.

Apart from the options in town (see the previous section), the next accommodation along the north coast of Upolu is down by the shore at the village of Saluafata, 25 minutes east of Apia. *Saluafata Beach Fales* (☎ 40216) offers accommodation in three beach fales and four rooms in the family house (which is not on the beach) for ST15 per person. Meals are available for about ST5. Day access to the beach, which offers good snorkelling around the offshore islet, costs ST2 per person. Book into the fales at the shop on the northern Main Coast Rd.

Aleipata Area Travellers will find a concentration of basic beach fales around the eastern end of Upolu, mainly in the Aleipata area. Locals have seen a money-spinning opportunity in these easily-constructed shelters – they consist of little more than a raised wooden floor sheltered by a roof – so expect many more such places to spring up in the near future. Shower and toilet facilities are usually very basic; cold water is the norm and it's worth bringing your own supply of toilet paper.

There are a number of places to choose from at Lalomanu village in the Aleipata district. In one cluster, which is strung out along one of the finest beaches in Samoa, you'll find *Litia Sini's Beach Fales*; *Tafua Beach Fales*, run by helpful Ben and Faasega Tapelu and with a small store and snorkelling gear for hire; *Sieni & Robert's Beach Fales*; *Romeo's Beach Fales* and the welcoming *Malo Beach Fales*. There are at least half a dozen more places around Lalomanu and there's not a great deal of difference between them. All charge ST20 per person and between ST20 and ST25 for three meals, depending on what you have. In all cases, sleeping mats and mosquito nets are supplied. Some fales have electric lights, others provide oil lamps. Make sure owners can provide a secure storage area for valuables – theft from open fales can be a problem.

There's a store at Cape Tapaga, just beyound Lalomanu, which sells basic supplies and petrol. Up the road, by the shore in the village of Satitoa, is *Joseph's Coffee Shop*. Sit on the ocean-view patio while the friendly ladies here rustle up burgers, fish and chips or very tasty tuna sandwiches. The coffee's good, too.

West of Lalomanu, near the villages of Saleapaga and Lepa, are several more bunches of fales. Granted, they're situated on a lesser beach, but the accommodation is identical to those at Lalomanu. Prices are a bit cheaper than at Lalomanu. *Boomerang Creek*, built on the hillside at Saleapaga, has four enclosed fales which cost ST50/80 for singles/doubles, including meals. The owners, Ana and Steve Harrison, plan to open a restaurant serving light meals and drinks for passing motorists. Visitors to this area should be aware that beer is not permitted in Saleapaga (although the rule is relaxed for foreigners). Noncompliance is punished with a fine of 10 pigs. Anyone who can't pay the fine is banished from the village until they can pay, so think twice before you offer someone a beer!

South Coast Travelling west along the south coast from the Aleipata area, visitors may notice more beach fales marked on the tourist map at Vava'u and A'ufaga. The fales here, however, are now part of an apparently successful, high-security rehabilitation programme involving delinquent US teenagers who are sent out to Samoa by their wealthy parents to learn a little Samoan island-style discipline.

About 10km east of the O Le Pupu-pu'e National Park, on a decent beach at Tafatafa, are the *Vaiula Beach Fales* (☎ 22808; fax 20886), PO Box 6600, Apia, owned by the Peterson family. There are five beach fales which cost ST15 per person. Meals can be provided. Camping in your own tent, including use of facilities, costs ST5 per tent and picnickers are charged ST5 per car. If you just want to swim or lie on the beach, you'll pay ST5 per car. There are two basic campsites in the *O Le Pupu-pu'e National Park*,

for those who are interested in hiking up to the Pe'ape'a Cave and the Ofa Waterfall. Facilities are minimal and campers will need to bring all their own food and water.

Just a kilometre or so west of the national park is a dirt track which leads 2.5km south to *Aganoa Black Sand Beach*, a spot often visited by surfers. There's one large fale here (which sleeps six) run by Tua Vaa, who'll charge around ST20 per person. Meals can be provided. Things are fairly basic down here and visitors would be advised to bring their own water and food. The Tautua family also has a beach fale they sometimes rent out.

Next up on the south coast is the luxurious *Sinalei Reef Resort* (☎ 25191; fax 20285; sinalei@talofa.net), PO Box 1510, Apia, which opened in 1996. Set in 13 hectares of landscaped grounds, Sinalei offers 20 very comfortable self-contained units, many of which overlook Sinalei's picturesque stretch of beach. It is possible to snorkel here but the waters are very shallow and subject to strong currents. All the units have a private porch, air-conditioning, tea and coffee-making facilities, fridge, TV, telephone, and a partially open-air bathroom. Garden-view fales cost ST390 for single or double occupancy; partial ocean-view fales cost ST439; ocean-view fales are ST463; and fale suits cost ST634. Meal plans cost ST109 for half board, ST146 for full board. The resort features a huge traditionally built dining fale, swimming pool, bar and gift shop. The restaurant and bar are open to nonguests. Light lunch dishes start at around ST16; main courses at dinner start at ST32. Menus feature lots of seafood and a mixture of international dishes.

Sinalei hosts a Friday night fiafia followed by a buffet barbecue dinner (ST40 for dinner and the show) and a Sunday to'ona'i (traditional lunch cooked in an umu) which costs ST33 for adults and ST17 for children under 12. The resort also offers various tours and activities including canoe tours through the mangroves, glass-bottom boat tours, diving and deep-sea fishing.

Next to Sinalei at Maninoa village is the more established *Coconuts Beach Club*

Resort (☎ 24849; fax 20071), PO Box 3684, Apia, which was set up by Barry and Jenny Rose, a couple of escaped Los Angeles lawyers who did a computer search for paradise and came up with Samoa. The main complex is reminiscent of a jungle treehouse. The magical upper level rooms, all with large private balconies, air-conditioning and double bathtubs, cost ST340/365 a single/double, while rooms on the lower floor are ST217/241. If you prefer the sand at your front door, individual beachfront fales start at ST583/607 for singles/doubles. The enormous beach villa, with two bedrooms, two bathrooms, sitting room, kitchen and private terrace costs ST680/705. Built out on a jetty, the new over-the-water fales, with their very own glass bottoms, cost ST705/729. All rates include a full American breakfast and use of snorkelling gear.

Even if Coconuts is beyond your accommodation budget, it's well worth visiting Sieni's 3-Stool beach bar and Mika's excellent American Bistro restaurant, where you'll find a variety of US and European dishes, including the best lobster you'll ever taste (we promise). Lunch prices start at around ST16; main courses at dinner start at ST30. There are set-price barbecues at lunchtime on Wednesday and Sunday. Traditional Samoan music is played in the beach bar every Tuesday to Friday evening and on Saturday and Sunday afternoons. Coconuts' fiafia is held on Saturday night. The swimming pool, complete with swim-up bar, is open to non guests (provided you buy a drink at least).

The resort has its own diving and snorkelling shop and tour company, Coconuts Watersports, operated by Roger and Gayle. Tours include a jungle boat cruise aboard the *African Queen* through the beautiful mangrove-lined waterways around the village of Mulivai, and self-guided kayak trips through the mangroves or along the south coast. For further information on their offerings, see under Organised Tours in the regional Getting Around chapter.

About 12km west from Coconuts, signposted off the main road, is the Sataoa

and Sa'anapu Conservation Area, where visitors have the chance to stay in a traditional village. The villagers of Sataoa and Sa'anapu are making a concerted effort to preserve their mangrove forests, which, among other things, provide a vital habitat for the breeding of fish and crabs. Revenue raised through village accommodation and various activities, such as guided walks, canoe tours and fishing trips, will help to maintain and protect the mangroves.

Lanu's Beach Fales, just beyond Sataoa village, are situated right by the seashore and next to the village cricket pitch. There are three basic fales big enough to sleep six or more. Charges are ST20 per person and ST25 for three meals. There are two toilet and shower blocks and night security is provided. The mangrove canoe tour costs ST20; the nature trail just behind the fales costs ST1. To book ahead, call the local women's committee on ☎ 24300 and ask for Lanu.

The village of Sa'anapu is on the other side of the estuary, accessible from the main road down a 1km paved road. When you arrive in the village ask to speak to a member of the conservation committee and they'll organise accommodation for you. There are two large fales built to accommodate visitors (prices as above), or you can arrange to stay in a village fale (see Staying in Villages in the regional Facts for the Visitor chapter). Sa'anapu also offers access to the nature trail (ST1) and canoe tours through the mangroves (ST20).

A short walk along the beach from Sa'anapu is the *Manuia Wetland Holiday Retreat* (☎ 26225), PO Box 900, Apia, which has seven beachside fales (ST20 per person) and three self-contained bungalows with singles/doubles/triples for ST80/120/150. The homely bungalows have a double and single bed, dining table, fridge, small electric stove and cold-water shower. You'll need to bring your own food, though you can buy fresh fish from the locals. There are three barbecue areas and if you're staying in a fale you may be able to use the cooking facilities in one of the bungalows. The retreat has a small beach bar.

Lagoon Lodge (☎ 20196; fax 22714), right next to Manuia, has five bungalows, each containing cold-water shower, gas cooker and fridge; one sleeps up to six, the others sleep a maximum of three. Singles/ doubles cost ST30/80 on weekends; ST30/50 from Monday to Thursday. Meals can be provided.

Further around the coast and accessible by dirt road is *Anapu Beach Fales* (☎ 70152) at Nu'uavasa Beach. There are two bungalows, with shower (cold) and gas cooking facilities. The bungalows sleep up to three and cost ST50 to rent. Visitors must provide their own food; tank water is available. There's a shop at the top of the road. There are five picnic fales on the beach; the fee to use the beach is ST5 per car.

A couple of kilometres further west and 2km or so down a rough dirt track is *Matareva Beach Fales*. Here you'll find several basic fales (ST10 per person) set in well-kept gardens beside a lovely beach. You'll need to provide your own food; tank water is sometimes available. The area is popular with locals on the weekend. Beach fees cost ST5 per car, ST3 per motorcycle or bicycle and ST2 if you're on foot. At the time of writing, a New Zealand company was negotiating the lease of 120 hectares of land at Matareva for the establishment of a 300 room luxury hotel.

MANONO ISLAND

The tiny, traditional island of Manono harks back to an earlier Polynesia. With no vehicles, no roads, no dogs, no noise and little evidence of the 20th century anywhere, it's a magical and extremely relaxing spot to spend a few days. Although it's the third-largest island of Independent Samoa, Manono has an area of only 3 sq km, four villages and a population of less than 1500. You can walk all the way around it in 1½ hours. People live almost exclusively in thatched fales and enjoy a semi-subsistence lifestyle. The villagers of Manono have recently pledged to work towards creating a totally sustainable island by the year 2000 and are looking at ways to protect their

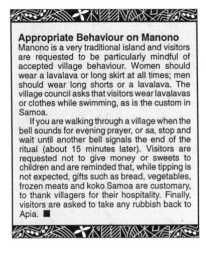

Appropriate Behaviour on Manono
Manono is a very traditional island and visitors are requested to be particularly mindful of accepted village behaviour. Women should wear a lavalava or long skirt at all times; men should wear long shorts or a lavalava. The village council asks that visitors wear lavalavas or clothes while swimming, as is the custom in Samoa.

If you are walking through a village when the bell sounds for evening prayer, or *sa*, stop and wait until another bell signals the end of the ritual (about 15 minutes later). Visitors are requested not to give money or sweets to children and are reminded that, while tipping is not expected, gifts such as bread, vegetables, frozen meats and koko Samoa are customary, to thank villagers for their hospitality. Finally, visitors are asked to take any rubbish back to Apia. ■

fragile island ecosystem. Tourism is community based with activities designed to contribute to the conservation of the environment and the traditional way of life on Manono.

Things to See & Do

At around 6.30 am the sound of a conch shell signals that it's time for the island's fishers to set off for work, trawling by outrigger canoe around the limpid waters of Manono. Early in the morning is the best time to **stroll around the island**. Wending its way between the sea and the bottom of people's gardens, the track is less a road and more a garden path, edged with distinctive yellow *lautalotalo*, banana palms and hibiscus.

At Lepuia'i village is the **Grave of 99 Stones**, which dates back to the late 19th century. The story goes that high chief Vaovasa, who reportedly had 99 wives, was killed by villagers as he tried to escape from Upolu with this 100th wife. His body was brought back to Manono in his raiding longboat, or *fautasi*, for burial. A grave was to be built with 100 stones, but remains unfinished. You can see a large gap where the final stone was to be placed. At Faleu village near Matasiva Point, there's a monument com-

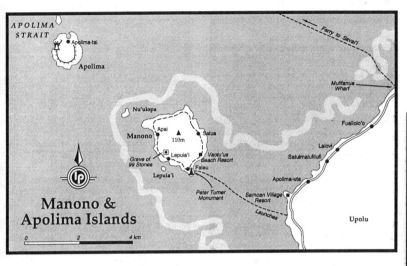

APOLIMA
STRAIT

Apolima-tai

Apolima

Ferry to Savai'i

Mulifanua
Wharf

Nu'ulopa

Apai
Manono   Salua
110m

Lepuia'i   Vaotu'ua
Beach Resort

Grave of   Faleu
99 Stones

Lepuia'i

Peter Turner
Monument

Fuailolo'o

Lalovi

Satuimalufilufi

Apolima-uta

Samoan Village
Resort

Launches

Upolu

**Manono &
Apolima Islands**

0   2   4 km

memorating the landing of the Methodist missionary Reverend Peter Turner on Manono in 1835.

On top of Mt Tulimanuiva (110m) is a large, 12 pointed **star mound**, thought to have been used in the ancient competitive sport of pigeon-snaring (see the Star Mound aside later in the book). Nearby is the grave of Afutiti, who was buried standing up, to keep watch over the island.

You can take a **guided tour** around the island, including a visit to the star mound, for ST30 per person including lunch. It costs less without lunch or for groups. Outrigger canoe **fishing trips and canoe tours** to uninhabited Nu'ulopa Island can be arranged from ST40 per person. For ST10 you can join village women in traditional **weaving, cooking and craft making**. For any of the above activities, contact Willie or Tauvela at the Vaotu'ua Beach Resort on ☎ 46077. Eco-Tour Samoa (☎ 22144) offers **sea kayaking trips** to Manono. A portion of the income from all of these activities goes into an environmental conservation fund for Manono Island. The island is well protected by coral reef and all around are lovely beaches and excellent snorkelling opportunities. Each of

the four villages has declared its waters to be marine reserves. If you'd like to explore the reefs, don't forget to bring your own snorkelling gear.

Places to Stay & Eat

Not far from the launch landing is the laid-back *Vaotu'ua Beach Resort* (☎ 46077), run by Willie and Tauvela Vaotu'ua. Three open-sided fales, shaded by enormous talie trees, sit by the water's edge. One large fale sleeps groups and has a rustic dining room attached. The other two fales sleep one or two people. Rates are ST45 per person including dinner and breakfast. Tauvela's excellent dishes include turkey noodle soup, deep fried eggplant and fresh fried fish.

There are no shops on Manono, so if you're thinking of staying for a few days you may want to bring supplies from Apia.

Getting There & Away

To visit Manono, take the Falelatai bus from Apia and get off just south of the Samoan Village Resort at the western end of Upolu (ST1.70). From there, small launches leave for Manono as often as there is passenger interest. You'll pay about ST1 each way if

How Shame Made a Name

In ancient times, according to legend, an old man called Vaotua found a young brown noddy bird, or *gogo* (pronouned nong-o), on the shore of Manono. He cared for the bird until it was old enough to fly. But when the noddy was ready to fly away, it was ashamed *(ma)* because it didn't have a gift for Vaotuua to show appreciation of his kindness. As the ashamed bird *(ma-gogo)* disappeared, Vaotuua decided to call the island Magogo (now spelt Manono). ■

there are more than several people waiting or a bit more if there are only a couple of passengers. If you miss the regular morning runs, special charters will cost as much as ST20 for the entire boat.

APOLIMA ISLAND

Samoa's fourth island, Apolima, lies in the Apolima Strait, outside the reef that encircles Upolu and Manono. The remnant of a volcanic crater, it meets the sea in high, steep cliffs, and there's only a tiny and difficult entrance from the sea through to the single, hardly touched village of 150 people. The soil of the island is poor, and therefore fish and coconuts are the primary sustenance of the people. The name of the island is said to be derived from Apo i le Lima, meaning 'poised in the hand', in reference to the spear used by a prince to kill his brother. The wound the spear caused is the small and easily defended entrance to the island's crater, which shelters the village and its harbour. Visitors should make a point of climbing the concrete steps to the lighthouse for a good view. There are also sea bird rookeries on the cliffs of the island.

Getting There & Away

Arranging a visit to Apolima Island will be tricky, but it can be done. The best possible situation would be to receive an invitation from a resident of the island, thereby assuring the islanders that your visit won't be too disruptive. If you're keen, seek out Mr Sa'u Samoa at the village of Apolima-uta on Upolu, who can arrange permission for you to visit and transport over there.

Savai'i Island

Much of the island of Savai'i – the largest in Polynesia outside New Zealand and Hawaii – remains uninhabited and pristine. This is a large part of the island's appeal, along with the fact that Savai'i has retained its traditional ways even more thoroughly than has Upolu. Its sense of Polynesian history is strong, too. Scattered across the island are numerous archaeological sites – fortifications, star mounds and ancient platforms – many of which have been swallowed up by the nearly impenetrable jungle. Though unknown to present-day Samoans, these ancient structures and monuments still figure strongly in Samoan myth and legend.

Savai'i also has its share of sandy beaches but because the island has less reef area than Upolu, the coastline is wilder. There's good surfing and snorkelling in several places, however, and there's world-class diving off the east coast at Lalomalava. If you do make the effort to visit Savai'i, you won't be disappointed, but to see the island properly and to make the most of it, you'll need time and patience. Even more than on Upolu, transport is infrequent and unreliable, so allow time if you plan to travel by bus.

History

All Polynesians who migrated around the Pacific carried with them legends of the ancient homeland, 'the largest island of the leeward group', from which all the islanders had been dispersed. The Hawaiians called that island Hawai'i, the Maoris called it Hawaiki, the Tahitians called it Havaiki, the Cook Islanders called it Avaiki and the Samoans said the island was Savai'i.

The largest island of the Hawaiian group, which was settled relatively late in the scheme of things, was named after it. No one knows for certain which island it was, but many researchers believe it was the largest island of the leeward group of Tahiti – Raiatea; in his book *Hawaii*, James Michener takes this opinion. Others, though,

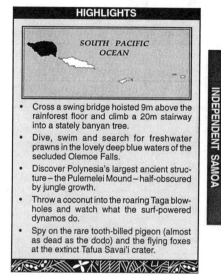

HIGHLIGHTS

SOUTH PACIFIC OCEAN

- Cross a swing bridge hoisted 9m above the rainforest floor and climb a 20m stairway into a stately banyan tree.

- Dive, swim and search for freshwater prawns in the lovely deep blue waters of the secluded Olemoe Falls.

- Discover Polynesia's largest ancient structure – the Pulemelei Mound – half-obscured by jungle growth.

- Throw a coconut into the roaring Taga blowholes and watch what the surf-powered dynamos do.

- Spy on the rare tooth-billed pigeon (almost as dead as the dodo) and the flying foxes at the extinct Tafua Savai'i crater.

subscribe to the claims of Rarotonga or Manu'a. Most Samoans, however, have no doubt that their own 'big island of the leeward group', Savai'i, is the 'cradle of Polynesia'.

It was on Savai'i, in the village of Safotulafai, that the Mau Movement was formed by Namulau'ulu Lauaki Mamoe.

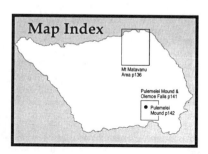

Map Index

Mt Matavanu
Area p136

Pulemelei Mound &
Olemoe Falls p141

● Pulemelei
Mound p142

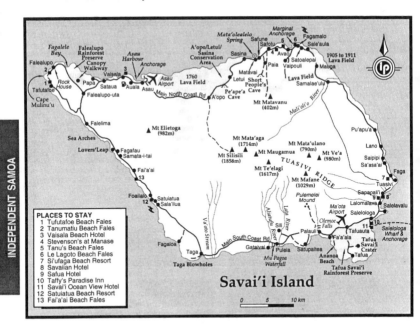

PLACES TO STAY
1 Tufutafoe Beach Fales
2 Tanumatiu Beach Fales
3 Vaisala Beach Hotel
4 Stevenson's at Manase
5 Tanu's Beach Fales
6 Le Lagoto Beach Fales
7 Si'ufaga Beach Resort
8 Savaiian Hotel
9 Safua Hotel
10 Taffy's Paradise Inn
11 Savai'i Ocean View Hotel
12 Satuiatua Beach Resort
13 Fai'a'ai Beach Fales

Savai'i Island

0   5   10 km

The group's original objective was to replace the German administration, which it thought lacked interest in Samoan concerns, with a British one set up in much the same way as the loosely defined one in the British protectorate in Tonga. This stand was later softened to merely advocate an administration which would be more sensitive to local interests and show more respect for the Samoan king, Mata'afa.

As a result of his political activism, Namulau'ulu was exiled to the Mariana Islands, never to return to Samoa. He died at sea in 1915 on the ship sent by the New Zealand administration to retrieve him. The Mau Movement, however, carried on through the New Zealand years, which were so fraught with strife that there were times when the Samoans probably wished for the return of the Germans.

During the past century, Savai'i has fallen victim to several natural disasters. The first was the eruption of Mt Matavanu between 1905 and 1911, destroying property and villages. A song composed during the eruptions reflects the people's reaction to the disaster:

Alas, how fearful! The fire burning over there
The fire below which is swallowing Savai'i,
Reminding us to repent of our stubborn ways.
We cannot know God's will, but the slow...lava
May indicate His Mercy
Because it allows...escape
It may be a warning concerning our sins
As a result of which Savai'i has been turned to stone.

As if that wasn't enough, Savai'i was the epicentre of devastation by the cyclones, Ofa and Val, which struck in February 1990 and December 1991, respectively. Many of the villages in the north-western corner of the island, including Falealupo, Tafutafoe, Papa, Sataua, Vaisala and Asau, were either utterly destroyed or damaged beyond recognition. For more information, see under History in the Facts about Independent Samoa chapter.

DEANNA SWANEY

DEANNA SWANEY

DORINDA TALBOT

DEANNA SWANEY

Top: Waiting for God – Falealupo-tai church on Savai'i, before the cyclone
Middle: Act of God – Falealupo-tai church after the cyclone
Bottom: Church at Leone, Tutuila, American Samoa
Right: Catholic church on Beach Road, Apia

DORINDA TALBOT

DORINDA TALBOT

PADDY RYAN

Left: Lalomanu – one of the loveliest beaches on Upolu
Right: Lush rainforest of Uafato on Upolu's north-east coast
(an important conservation area)
Bottom: Late afternoon at Taga Blowholes area, Savai'i, Western Samoa

Orientation & Information

The Samoas' largest island is also its wildest. Its 50,000 inhabitants are concentrated in a string of villages along the east and southeast coasts; there are only a scattering of villages elsewhere. The vast, trackless interior of the island lies empty and distorted by recent bouts of vulcanism. A string of craters, some active, extend all along the central ridge of the island from the east coast at Tuasivi to within 5km of Samoa's westernmost tip at Cape Mulinu'u. At 1858m, Mt Silisili is the highest point in the Samoan islands. The north coast of Savai'i is punctuated by lava fields; the western one between Asau and Sasina flowed from Mt Afi in 1760, and the eastern one came from the eruptions between 1905 and 1911.

There isn't much of a service centre on Savai'i, and even the main populated area between Salelologa and Lano is just a cluster of 30 or so rural villages. There are basic hospitals at Tuasivi, Safotu, Sataua and Foailalo.

Getting There & Away

Air Flying between Upolu and Savai'i is highly recommended – the flight isn't expensive and the bird's-eye view of the islands is wonderful. From Fagali'i airport just east of Apia, Polynesian Airlines flies to Ma'ota airport on the south coast of Savai'i three times a day, at 7.35 am, 12.15 pm and 4.15 pm, returning to Fagali'i 35 minutes later. The fare is ST34 one way or ST60.50 return. Polynesian flies from Apia to Asau airport on the north coast of Savai'i once a day at 9.25 am, returning at 10.15 am. Tickets cost ST55 one way and ST90 return. For bookings, ring Polynesian Airlines (☎ 22737) in Apia. Samoa Air (☎ 51387 in Apia) flies between Pago Pago in American Samoa and Ma'ota airport every Friday and Sunday morning.

Boat The Samoa Shipping Corporation (☎ 51477 in Salelologa; ☎ 45518 in Mulifanua) operates a vehicle and passenger ferry between Mulifanua Wharf on the western end of Upolu and Salelologa, Savai'i. In theory, it runs two or three times daily. Monday to Saturday it sails from Salelologa at 6 am, 10 am and 2 pm and from Mulifanua at 8 am, noon and 4 pm. On Sunday, it sails from Savai'i at 10 am and 2 pm and from Mulifanua at noon and 4 pm. However, it frequently misses a run so passengers often face long waits on the dock. If you can, avoid travelling on Saturday or Sunday, as the ferry will be crammed to the gills. You can buy tickets from the Shipping Corporation office on the corner of Mt Vaea St and Convent St in Apia, or at the dock. Those travelling with vehicles should be at the wharf one hour before departure. The fare is ST6 each way for foot passengers; ST30 each way for jeeps and taxis; and ST65 for trucks and buses. The 22km crossing takes one to 1½ hours.

Getting Around

The Airports The majority of flights from Apia arrive at Ma'ota airport in the southeast of the island, 5km west of Salelologa. Whenever a plane arrives, nearly every taxi on Savai'i is waiting for it, so there'll be no problem finding transport. The taxis, however, are expensive. To Salelologa, the fare is ST7; to Safua, ST15; and to Tuasivi, ST22. From Asau airport in the north-west to Tanu Beach the taxi fare is ST55; to Falealupo, ST25; and to Satuiatua, ST60.

All Savai'i hotels offer airport transfers, provided you book in advance. The public buses are very convenient for getting to Salelologa from the airport but if you're travelling to Safua, Tuasivi or further north, you'll have to change buses at Salelologa.

Bus The buses of Savai'i, which rarely have glass in their window frames or doors in their doorways, are crowded, vibrantly coloured affairs that blare reggae music and awaken all the senses. The market near the wharf is the main terminal for regular buses to Lalomalava, Tuasivi, Palauli and Gataivai. The Lava Fields Express (you can't miss it) trundles regularly between Salelologa and Fagamalo. Less frequently, buses go to Safotu or Sasina on the north coast and Asau in the north-west.

INDEPENDENT SAMOA

Last Bus to Paradise (and back if you're lucky)

On the big island of Savai'i, public transport is limited and buses seem to operate on a schedule known only to their drivers. For example, in Asau I visited the owner/driver of one vehicle to find out what time the following morning the first bus to Salelologa would leave. He told me that passengers should be waiting at the petrol station at 3 am

I turned up at 2.30 am, however, because the previous day I'd missed the '6 am bus', which for some reason had departed at 5.40 am. Of course there was no-one else waiting when I arrived at the petrol station and when the 3 am bus finally turned up at 4.30 am there was still no-one else waiting. I soon learned why. Instead of departing for Salelologa, the bus set off in the opposite direction.

We pulled up in front of a house. The driver got out, knocked on the door, and the lights came on. There was evidence of people bustling around inside and then, 15 minutes later, two girls emerged with baskets and luggage and boarded the bus. We proceeded to another house and the same thing happened. Then another house and another ... The first and only bus of the day from Asau to Salelologa was providing a wake-up and pick-up service for its passengers! At 5.45 am we finally set out for Salelologa.

The bus was scheduled to return to Asau at noon (leaving me only three hours in Salelologa), so at precisely 12 I was waiting beside the road. Two hours passed, then three. The ferries between Savai'i and Upolu had been undergoing repairs so there was no way of knowing if there might be a bus to meet a ferry. Everyone I asked about the matter had a different answer. Since traffic is thin on Savai'i after about 2 pm, I realised it was time to begin hitching. After several short rides and many kilometres of walking, I arrived back in Asau, well after dark.

There is a seating hierachy on Samoan buses

Later, I learned from a friend that the driver of the Asau bus had decided to stay in Salelologa to play pool and drink with his buddies that night and that no afternoon ferry had ever called there.

The moral of the story is that you shouldn't set out between any two points without leaving your options open. If you have a plane to catch in Apia the following day, don't count on the bus getting you to the wharf or the airport, and for that matter, don't depend on the plane or the ferry getting you back to Upolu in any reasonable amount of time either. Go back a day early – or even two days early – if you'd rather not risk missing an international flight.

Welcome to paradise!

Deanna Swaney

There is no public transport across the lava field between Asau and Safotu so travelling between the two by bus will require passing through Salelologa.

Way out on the north-western end, buses run regularly between Asau and Falelima. There's even a rumour of a once-daily bus out to Falealupo from Asau at 6 am.

Ferry passengers will have the most luck connecting with buses to out-of-the-way destinations – that is, beyond the cluster of villages along the south-east coast. Buses bound for the north and west coasts depart as soon as the ferry comes in and then aren't

seen again until the ferry returns. When the ferry is late or cancelled, the buses are, too, so anyone awaiting a bus away from the wharf area will have no idea when or if a bus is likely to pass. The fare from Salelologa to Palauli and Lalomalava is only 50 sene. To either end of the main road – Asau or Safotu/Sasina – it's ST5. The trip to the blowholes at Taga costs ST2.

Car It's a joy to motor along the quiet roads of Savai'i but, as in Upolu, keep an eye out for kids, stray pigs – and *kirikiti* games. The Main Coast Rd is paved all the way. There are dirt tracks on the far side of the Falealupo Peninsula and down to Ananoa Beach. Petrol is available at Salelologa, at Avao in the north-east and at Vaisala in the north-west. The Savai'i Travel Centre (☎ 51206) and the West End Co (☎ 51415), both just up the road from the wharf in Salelologa, have Suzuki jeeps to rent from about ST100 per day. You can also bring hire cars on the ferry from Upolu (see the earlier Getting There & Away section in this chapter for ferry details). The Upolu chapter has a list of car rental agencies in Apia.

Bicycle The Savaiian Hotel (☎ 51206) at Lalomalava has mountain bikes to rent from ST20 per day. For general information on cycling around the islands, see Activities in the Facts for the Visitor – Independent Samoa chapter.

Hitching Travellers relying on public transport will probably have to resort to hitching at one time or another. Most of your rides will only take you from one village to the next, but it will get you around eventually. Hitching is relatively easy prior to mid-afternoon, when the daily kirikiti and volleyball matches begin in the villages. Be prepared to pay a tala or two (not per person – this will suffice for a group of two or three) for a ride of a longer distance. Payment should be proportional to the length of time you're aboard and a good rule of thumb (pun unintentional) is to offer the equivalent of the bus fare for that distance travelled.

Some stretches of the coast road, especially the 28km stretch across the lava field between Asau and Sasina and the stretches between Taga and Sala'ilua or Falelima and Samata'i'tai, see very little traffic. At times, hitching will seem more like walking; you may find yourself hoofing it for long stretches before someone comes by.

Boat There are no ferries travelling between ports on Savai'i, so if you want to cruise around Savai'i, you'll need a private yacht. Yachties wanting to travel around Savai'i must first obtain a cruising permit from the immigration office in Apia. If you're planning to leave Samoa from Savai'i, you must check out of the country in Apia before leaving Upolu. In Savai'i, there are anchorages at Fagamalo, Salelologa Wharf and Asau Harbour.

Organised Tours For organised sightseeing and cultural tours around the island, you can't beat Safua Tours at the Safua Hotel. Warren Jopling, the tour organiser, guide and resident geologist, has spent many years on Savai'i and knows the island like the back of his hand. Half-day tours cost ST60 per person and full-day trips are ST90, including light lunch and custom fees. The tours focus on natural history, hands-on cultural experiences and soft adventure. Particularly interesting is the *siapo* tour, visiting the home of a local woman who will demonstrate siapo-making from start to finish, but any sort of cultural interests can be accommodated, including such things as Samoan dancing, woodcarving, weaving, language courses or even kirikiti.

There are four basic day tours, but these are flexible and can be altered according to individual interests. One takes in the 1905 to 1911 Lava Field, several of the villages along the north coast, the Pe'ape'a Cave as well as a swim and snorkel at Tanu Beach. For those who are reasonably fit, there's a half-day tour to the Pulemelei Mound, Polynesia's largest ancient structure. The third possibility takes you on an excellent cliff-top walk along the rugged Tafua Peninsula and also includes a visit to the Mu Pagoa Waterfall. The fourth tour is a more sedentary option which takes you round the island and includes stops at the Taga Blowholes, the lava fields and lunch at Cape Mulinu'u on the far north-western tip of the island.

Around the Island

SOUTH-EASTERN SAVAI'I
The south-east coast of Savai'i is the centre of population, government and commerce

INDEPENDENT SAMOA

for the island. It is also the arrival and departure point for most flights and all inter-island ferries.

Information

You can change money in the air-conditioned Bank of Samoa in Salelologa; it's open Monday to Friday until 3 pm. The post and telephone office is a bit out of the way, about 500m outside Salelologa village, towards the airport. The post office is open from 9 am to noon and from 1 to 4.30 pm Monday to Friday. The telephone office is open from 8 am to noon and from 1 to 4.30 pm daily. Beside the Big Island CCK, the largest store on the island, you'll find the new OK Laundromat. The main police station, immigration office and other government offices are in Tuasivi. For travel arrangements to and from Upolu or transport around the island, try the Savai'i Travel Centre (☎ 51206; fax 51291) in Salelologa, a private agency operated by the Savaiian Hotel.

Salelologa

Apart from the comings and goings of the ferry, not much happens in Salelologa. Beside the market, the only real points of interest in the Salelologa area are the blowholes on the lava coast south of the wharf. Most people see them as they arrive on the ferry from Upolu. Naturally, they're at their best in high winds and surf, so on calm days, you won't have as grand a show. The route is fairly straightforward; just follow the coast south from the wharf. There are two ancient star mounds just north of the Main Coast Rd, about 200m west of its intersection with the wharf road, and across the street there are two platform mounds. They're overgrown and difficult to find, so you may need directions from locals. If the first person you ask looks blank, keep trying. Eventually, you'll find someone familiar with them.

In 1997, the Samoan government announced plans to convert Salelolga village into a town. At the time of writing, more that 800 hectares of rainforest in the eastern section of the Tafua Peninsula was slated for clearing. The move has been strongly opposed by local conservation groups as well a the village of Tafua. See Tafua Rainforest Preserve below.

John Williams Monument

In front of the Congregational church at Sapapali'i is the stone monument commemorating the landing of the former British ironmonger turned missionary, Reverend John Williams who arrived on his makeshift vessel, the *Messenger of Peace* in 1830. At that time, Malietoa Vainu'upo, one of the most powerful chiefs on Savai'i, and the chiefs of A'ana district were embroiled in a war.

Williams left behind eight missionary teachers who were successful at converting the victorious Malietoa. It is believed that he accepted the Christian message as the fulfilment of an ancient prophecy of a new religion by the goddess Nafanua. Following a civil war, Nafanua had been given the task of dividing up the power between the districts. Regarding government, she had determined that only a 'tail' of the true spiritual government existed and that the people would have to wait for the 'head' to come from heaven. Thanks to the Malietoa's example and influence, many Savai'ians were encouraged to convert.

Tuasivi Ridge

The Tuasivi ridge begins near the village of Tuasivi and rises in a series of craters that form the spine of Savai'i, ending just inland of the village of Falealupo. As you approach on the ferry, the barricade, or *olo*, formed by it will be obvious, looking very much like a series of artificial mounds climbing skyward. The craters visible from the sea are Asi, Misimala, Vaiala, Vaiolo, Afutina and Masa.

In Samoan, the word *tuasivi* means 'ridge', so to say 'Tuasivi ridge' is actually a bit repetitive. The Samoans called it the enchanted ridge because they believed it possessed supernatural powers to harm and kill those who dealt with it improperly: pregnant women had to walk up to it three times before proceeding across it or the child would die.

The crater of Mt Asi, the one nearest the sea, is said to be the mark left when an inland mountain wandered towards the sea to fetch some water to make *palusami*. Asi didn't want to be second from the sea so he threw a breadfruit in the other mountain's face as it approached; where it fell, a crater was formed. There are two ancient terraces and a platform atop Mt Asi, as well as a good view out to sea.

Beaches

All along the east coast between Salelologa and Pu'apu'a, there are nice beaches and good snorkelling. Most of the villages will charge custom fees of about ST5 per car or ST2 per person to use their beaches. The best are at Faga and Lano. The area also has numerous freshwater pools and springs for either bathing or rinsing.

Pu'apu'a

In the village of Pu'apu'a are two freshwater bathing pools maintained by the local women's committee. The pool on the eastern side of the road is for women and the one on the western side, for men. If you'd like to have a swim there, the locals will be flattered that you chose their pool, but it's still best to ask villagers' permission before jumping in. Just south of Pu'apu'a are several other springs, including Vaimanuia, whose name means 'healthy waters'.

Tafua Rainforest Preserve

The Tafua Rainforest Preserve occupies much of the Tafua Peninsula, Savai'i's south-easternmost extremity. In addition to one of Samoa's most accessible and beautiful stands of rainforest, it contains beautifully rugged stretches of lava coast, which are studded with cliffs, sea arches, lava tubes and blowholes. On the western coast of the peninsula is a track leading south to the lovely Ananoa dark sand beach, where there are several picnic fales. There are strong currents here, however, so ask locals about conditions and swim with care.

Custom fees are ST10 per bus; ST5 per car and ST2 for cyclists and pedestrians. The beach is open from 8 am to 6 pm.

The village of Fa'a'ala, at the top of the track, shares responsibility for the conservation area along with Salelologa and Tafua and can offer visitors village accommodation and local guides.

Another highlight of the preserve is the extinct Tafua Savai'i crater, which rises above the village of Tafua. This forest-choked crater harbours a colony of flying foxes; from the crater rim, they may be seen circling above the treetops in the morning and late afternoon. The Tafua preserve is also one of the only remaining habitats of the *manume'a*, or Samoan tooth-billed pigeon, believed by some zoologists to be the closest living relative of the dodo (it does bear a vague resemblance!). To reach the crater, take the 5km paved road off the Main South Coast Rd to the village of Tafua on the coast. From there, a 20-minute track will take you up the steep southern slope of the crater. This worthwhile walk ends at a rest fale on the southern rim, which affords a far-ranging view of the island's southern coastline and up to the crater-studded highlands.

In Tafua, chief Ulu Taufa'asisina and his wife Anita (☎ 50041) can organise guided walks and local accommodation for visitors. The Tafua village council is building a rainforest information centre which will house a library with ecological information to teach village children and visitors about rainforest conservation issues. Donations are welcome.

Places to Stay & Eat

There are a couple of accommodation options in Salelologa. Convenient to the wharf and the market is *Taffy's Paradise Inn* (☎ 51544; 51534), a small and slightly shabby nine-room guesthouse. Rooms cost ST33 per person, but discounts can be negotiated if they're not busy. Breakfast costs ST12, set-menu lunches are ST15 and dinners are ST25.

Closer to the wharf is the *Savai'i Ocean View Hotel* (☎ 51258; fax 51377), where reasonable single/double rooms with facilities cost ST77/99. The adjoining Le La Oso Nightclub has live music on Friday and Saturday nights.

The *Salafai Inn* (☎ 51245; fax 51250), beside the market in Salelologa, was still closed at the time of writing, but it plans to have rooms for budget travellers in the near future.

The general store opposite the Ocean View serves good fish and chips, Chinese buns, curry and rice and other basic dishes. It's open Monday to Friday. *OK's Takeaway Food Bar* in the CCK store serves similar meals and is also closed on the weekend. Inside the market are a number of food stalls serving very passable local dishes for rock-bottom prices. Behind the market is a whole bank of little general stores where you'll find inexpensive staple items.

The *Safua Hotel* (☎ 51271; fax 51272), just 5km north-east of Salelologa at Lalomalava, is one of the most pleasant places to stay on Savai'i. The proprietor, Moelagi Jackson, is as interesting as any of the sites on the island and visitors to Savai'i should make a point of meeting her.

You'll rarely find such an excellent chance to gain the insights into Samoan ways and history that she can provide and you'd be hard-pressed to find a more knowledgeable, vivacious and charismatic individual. Single/double/triple fale-style bungalows with shower (cold water) and toilet cost ST77/88/99. There are two family rooms which can sleep up to six for ST110. With the three-meal plan, the single/double rate is ST165/215. This includes three *immense* and incredible Samoan-style meals. Tent space costs ST11 per person. If you stay more than four days, there's a 15% discount and if you settle in for more than 15 days, the discount increases to 25%. If you'd prefer to stay in a village, Moelagi will arrange accommodation in private homes for ST30 per person. In addition to its typically fabulous meals, the hotel stages a *fiafia* on Friday and Saturday nights and an *umu* feast at midday on Sunday.

Across the road and about 200m south of the Safua Hotel is the mid-range *Savaiian Hotel* (☎ 51206; fax 51291), PO Box 5082, Lalomalava, Salelologa. Single/double rooms with air-conditioning, cooking facilities and hot showers cost ST105/125. Fales with shower and toilet cost ST35/50. Prices include complimentary transfers to and from the wharf or airport. Breakfast costs from ST5.50 to ST15 and dinner between ST25 and ST35. On Friday and Saturday nights, there's live music and dancing in the restaurant/bar.

Another favourite travellers' haunt is the friendly *Si'ufaga Beach Resort* (☎ 53518; fax 53535), PO Box 8002, Tuasivi, which is in the village of Faga immediately north of Tuasivi. It's run by Italian Dr Peter Cafarelli and his wife Alauni (and their 11 children). The hotel consists of six self-contained fales, each with shower (one has hot water), toilet and cooking facilities. The fales, which are set in a large grassy lawn, can sleep up to three or four. Camping is also permitted. The real draw card, however, is the white and sandy Si'ufaga Beach across the road, which is safe for swimming and snorkelling. Single/double/triple fales cost ST100/110/122; campers pay ST15 per person. If you book in advance, complimentary pick-up service is available from the wharf or airport. A restaurant and bar were being built at the time of writing. For staples, there's a small shop at the hotel; the family can also provide transport to the supermarket in Salelologa upon request.

NORTH-EASTERN SAVAI'I

Between Pu'apu'a and Samalae'ulu, fast-growing eucalypts are being planted as part of a reforestation project. As you travel along this stretch of road, notice the great views of far-off craters and the volcanic landscapes of the island's interior.

Lava Field

The Mt Matavanu eruptions of 1905 to 1911 created a moonscape on the north-eastern corner of Savai'i as the flow of hot lava 10 to 150m thick rolled across plantations and villages destroying everything in its path.

Between Samalae'ulu and Sale'aula, the Main Coast Rd crosses the lava field and passes a couple of interesting sites. Just east of the road is the village of Mauga, which means 'mountain'. It is built in a circular pattern around a nearly perfect crater. After the eruptions, the intense heat and the porous rock caused a scarcity of fresh water in the area. The priest in the village felt inspired to instruct the villagers to dig in the bottom of the crater to find water. After many days of exhausting labour, they reached the water table and the village well has been located in the crater ever since.

Just north of Mauga, about 100m east of the road, in a large hole in the lava, is the partially built Methodist church that 'miraculously' survived the lava flow while the Mormon and Catholic church buildings were destroyed. Many people attribute its survival to the fact that it was constructed of cement. Look out for the imprint of the corrugated tin roof in the lava.

A short walk north-west of the church is another 'divinely protected' site, the Virgin's Grave. Legend states that a novice Catholic nun from the convent in the village of Lealatele had been buried there in the usual manner beneath a raised concrete headstone. When the lava ploughed through, the church adjoining the site was destroyed, but as it approached the girl's grave, the stream of molten rock parted and flowed around it.

Geologists, however, take the view that the so-called miracle can be scientifically explained by the fact that there was a steam vent which was so placed that it interrupted the lava flow.

The grave can still be seen in a pit 2m below the surface of the lava field. It has been left alone completely since the eruptions and today there are beautiful plants and wildflowers growing around it.

Members of the local women's committee look after the sites and are generally on hand to guide people around. There's a custom fee of ST2 per person. The sites are signposted just north of Mauga. To get up this way by bus, take the Lava Fields Express which runs regularly between Salelologa and Fagamalo.

Satoalepai Wetlands

The village of Satoalepai, 5km north-west of the lava fields, is one of a growing number of Samoan villages committed to the sustainable development of their local resources and to this end offers visitors village accommodation, local guides and canoe tours through the wetlands (ST3 per person). Look out for a signpost to the turtle wetlands where you'll find picnic fales and a large pond inhabited by several enormous (and in one case amorous) sea turtles. If you'd like to arrange accommodation, ask to speak to the *pulenu'u* or one of the local conservation officers.

Fagamalo

Immediately west of Satoalepai is Fagamalo, which is known as an excellent spot for surfing and windsurfing. There's a marginal anchorage here, too. You'll find comfortable bungalow accommodation on the beach just west of the village; see under Places to Stay & Eat later in this section. At nearby Avao, 3km west of Fagamalo, is the site where early missionaries began translating the Bible into Samoan in 1834. The task took 11 years. The pulpit of the Congregational Christian church is carved from the stump of the tree which shaded the translators as they worked. There's also a monument to them at the site where the tree actually grew.

Safotu

The long, strung-out village of Safotu is interesting in that it has three large and prominent churches in a row near the centre. The large and sparkling white one is a landmark to sailors. To the west of the churches, near the sea, are a series of freshwater pools for bathing or swimming. Some are for men and some for women, so be sure to ask rather than make assumptions. Just to the east of Safotu are pleasant beaches, a new upmarket resort and the most popular budget accommodation on the island (see Places to Stay & Eat).

Mt Matavanu Crater Walk

One of the most easily accessible and dramatic natural features of Savai'i is Mt

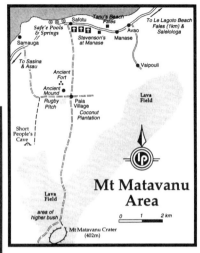

Mt Matavanu, a great spot for a picnic lunch. If you continue to follow the track around the crater to the left, it will swing downhill and turn into a route down the lava field to the village of Vaipouli. If you'd rather not risk getting lost – a real possibility – it's probably best to go back the way you came. Access to the crater up this route from Vaipouli is also possible, but don't go without a guide from the village. Take insect repellent, picnic food and plenty of water with you.

Short People's Cave

Legend has it that the cave above Paia was a secret hide-out inhabited by a tribe of dwarfs with magical abilities. One man who stumbled upon them found that he was able to make food appear by simply wishing for it. When his wife questioned the source of this extraordinary ability, the man revealed the secret of the dwarfs' hide-out and instantly fell dead.

A trip to this cave will take all day. The custom fee, which is payable to the pulenu'u of Paia, is ST20 per group. This fee includes a guide, who will be essential because the cave is difficult to find. If you don't have a torch, you'll need to hire kerosene lamps before heading up; the pastor, the pulenu'u and the family living in the highest fale in town all charge around ST5 per day.

To reach the cave, walk south along the dirt track west of the rugby pitch for about 2.2km. Upon entering, you'll come to a room that appears to be furnished with stone tables. From there, one cave leads off to the left and another to the right. The left cave goes the furthest – more than 1km – and involves swimming across five small pools and down underground waterfalls. The right cave goes only about 50m.

Mata'olealelo Spring

This ample freshwater spring in the village of Safune bubbles up through a pool into the sea – perfect for a refreshing jet-bath type of swim. Be sure to ask permission before plunging in.

Matavanu, the errant crater that sent a flow of destruction from the heart of the earth to the north-east coast of the island. From Safotu, it's a pleasant day walk but can be done in about five hours if you can catch a lift as far as Paia village. Once you get to Paia, you may want to stop to have a look at the ancient fort and mound atop the hill there. The mound is about 4m high and has several fales on top. The fort, which is surrounded by a ditch, is just to the north of the mound. It's not terribly dramatic but may be of interest to archaeology buffs. Expect to pay a custom fee of ST2 to pass through Paia en route to the crater, but be sure to pay only the pulenu'u. You can also ask the pulenu'u for a guide.

From Paia, follow the plantation road south. After a little more than an hour of walking you should enter the lava field. Nearly another hour on, the lava field gives way to heavier bush and clumps of acacias. At the point where the road begins to dip for the first time, you'll see a trail to the left leading uphill through a forest (if you reach the end of the road, you've gone too far). Several hundred metres up the trail (keep to the left) is the rim of the immense crater of

Sasina & Letui Conservation Area

The villages of Sasina and Letui are part of a large coastal rainforest conservation area which extends from the coast up to the inland village of A'opo. Just outside Sasina is a pleasant rainforest walk. Take the signposted track which leads past the village and after about 1km you'll see a well-maintained path leading off to the right. Ask the village pulenu'u for access and a guide. Fiu Sefau of Letui can take people to visit the nearby Pe'ape'a Cave (ST3 per person). Both Sasina and Letui offer basic village accommodation for around ST20 per person. See Staying in Villages in the regional Facts for the Visitor chapter and Society & Conduct in the Facts about the Region chapter.

Places to Stay & Eat

Apart from the conservation villages of Satoalepai, Sasina and Letui, there are three accommodation options in North-East Savai'i. Situated on a beautiful beach immediately west of Fagamalo village is *Le Lagoto Beach Fales* (☎ 58189; fax 58249), PO Box 34, Fagamalo, which offers four bungalows and a large beach house. The bungalows, with shower (hot water), toilet, kitchenette, TV and standing fan, cost ST134/161/187/214. The beach house, which sleeps up to seven, costs ST150 per night. Upstairs is a four-poster bed and a balcony overlooking the bay. Le Lagoto also has a restaurant, bar and shop. Breakfast costs ST12, lunch from ST10 and dinner between ST25 and ST35.

Just west of Manase is *Tanu's Beach Fales* (☎ 54050), one of the most popular spots for budget travellers in all of Samoa. Muese Tanu and his vast family have created a particularly relaxing and welcoming environment. The 16 basic fales – six scattered along the white sandy beach – cost ST50 per person, including lunch and dinner. Meals are eaten communally at a huge table in an open-sided fale. Bananas and purified water are provided free. Showers (cold) and toilets are communal. There are outrigger canoes for guests to use, a couple of jeeps for rent, a small shop on the premises and fiafias

every Friday and Monday night. Tanu's Beach Fale Bus meets the noon ferry at Salelologa, arriving back at Tanu's at around 2 pm.

Just up the road from Tanu's is the more upmarket *Stevenson's at Manase* (☎ 58219; fax 54100), PO Box 210 Apia, which offers 20 air-conditioned rooms with private shower from ST146 for single or double occupancy – somewhat overpriced for what you get. Across the road is a large and very comfortable air-conditioned beachfront villa which sleeps two adults and up to three children for ST305. Also on the beach are several basic fales for ST25 per person. The hotel has a pleasant restaurant and bar, paddle boats and outrigger canoes for guests and fiafia nights on Friday and Saturday. Airport and ferry transfers cost ST43 per person.

NORTH-WESTERN SAVAI'I
A'opo Conservation Area & Mt Silisili

With some planning it is possible to climb Mt Silisili (1858m), the Samoas' highest point. The peak itself is nondescript – really little more than a volcanic knob, much like scores of other little volcanic knobs in the area – but the three-day trip up takes you through some stunning and rarely visited rainforest. Those interested in the trip should speak to the pulenu'u of A'opo (the mayor's house is by the big mango tree in the centre of the village) who will arrange a guide for the trek. The charge is ST30 per person per day. You'll need to carry food and water for three days and provide supplies for the guide. Temperatures on the mountain can get quite cold at night so you'll also need to bring one change of warm clothing, a sleeping bag and a tent. Sturdy walking boots are essential. You might also want to get hold of topographical sheets for the area from the Department of Lands, Surveys & Environment in Apia.

Asau & Vaisala

Asau, 9km west of A'opo, is the main anchorage on Savai'i and service centre for the western end of the island. Asau airport,

INDEPENDENT SAMOA

which was completely destroyed by Cyclone Ofa in 1990, has only recently been rebuilt. There's a store here selling groceries and crafts and a post office. At Vaisala, 5km further up the road, there's a petrol station, a branch of the Pacific Commercial Bank and the established Vaisala Hotel (see Places to Stay & Eat). In the village of Auala, in between Asau and Vaisala, the local women's committee looks after a large pond full of protected sea turtles.

Falealupo Peninsula

At the far north-western end of Savai'i is the wild and beautiful Falealupo Peninsula where you'll find rock pools, caves, ancient star mounds, a handful of romantic beachside fales (see Places to Stay & Eat) and any number of spectacular sunsets. Take great care swimming around Cape Mulinu'u, though, or you could end up in the Solomons. There's a good swimming beach at Papa on the north-eastern side of the peninsula, not far off the Main Coast Rd. Beach fees on the peninsula are ST5 per car, ST20 per bus and ST2 for those on foot. If you're not driving, you'll have to walk or take a taxi the 7km from the main road at Falealupo-uta to the end of the peninsula.

In 1990 and 1991, cyclones Ofa and Val struck the peninsula with a particular vengeance, completely destroying the village of

---

Gateway to the Underworld

The Falealupo Peninsula figures prominently in local legend. The natural beauty of the area belies the dark significance it holds for Samoans, who believe that the gateway to the underworld of the *aitu* (spirits) is found at the place where the sun sets in the sea. According to tradition, there are two entrances to the underworld, one for chiefs and another for commoners. One entrance is through a cave near Cape Mulinu'u and the other is on the trail made by the setting sun over the sea. During the night, these spirits wander abroad, but at daybreak they must return to their hellish home or suffer the unpleasant consequences of being caught out by daylight. ∎

Falealupo on the western tip (villagers have rebuilt slightly inland). The ruins of the old Catholic church have been left standing as a monument to the power of the cyclones.

Falealupo Rainforest Preserve Considered sacred by the villagers of Falealupo, the 12,000 hectare area of lowland rainforest on the northern side of the peninsula became the first customary owned conservation area in Samoa in 1989. The development of the preserve was achieved thanks to the assistance of Dr Paul Alan Cox, an American ethnobotanist and founder of the conservation foundation Seacology. Dr Cox was working with indigenous healers in Falealupo when he discovered that the *matais* of the area had reluctantly signed a contract with a Japanese logging firm in order to pay for the construction of a primary school in the village.

After watching the whole village weeping over the loss of their rainforest, Dr Cox decided to personally guarantee the money for the school. On learning of this, chief Fuiono Senio grabbed his machete and ran 9km through the forest to stop the bulldozers toppling another tree. Unfortunately, the reserve suffered serious damage during the 1990 and 1991 cyclones (60% of the trees were destroyed and bird and bat numbers dropped significantly), but it is slowly and surely recovering.

Canopy Walkway The Falealupo Canopy Walkway not only provides the opportunity to climb to the top of a stately banyan tree, but if you feel so inclined you can sleep up there, too. The Seacology Foundation raised funds to build the walkway, which opened in May 1997, as an 'ecotourism' project designed to help support Falealupo village and its rainforest.

The walkway consists of a 24m-long swing bridge hoisted 9m above the rainforest floor and a 20m stairway that ends in the uppermost reaches of an old banyan tree. It took carpenter Tapuotaota Aeau, who lives in the house nearby, six weeks to build the stairway and platforms (with holes for the

Top-end accommodation – spend a night
in a banyan tree

banyans roots) around the tree. His wife Lesina provides meals for treehouse guests. It costs ST50 per person to sleep in the tree (the platform can hold a maximum of six people, but facilities are minimal), including breakfast and dinner, and ST20 to just visit the walkway (the entrance fee may have decreased since writing). You can book tree accommodation in advance through the Vaisala Hotel (see Places to Stay & Eat). The walkway is signposted off the Falealupo Rd, just by the village primary school.

Rock House About 300m inland from the village of Falealupo are the two closely associated lava tubes known as the Rock House. Inside is a very crude stone armchair and there are stone benches around the sides. Legend says that the Rock House is the result of a competition between the men and the women of Falealupo. They staged a house-building contest to find out which sex was more adept at it. At the end of the first day of construction, the men were winning so the women decided to stay up and work through the night while the men were asleep. The women won, of course, and the men were so angry about it that they never finished their house, leaving the hole in the ceiling that is

still in evidence. There's a custom fee of ST5 per group to visit the Rock House.

Moso's Footprint The ancient 1m by 3m rock enclosure called Moso's Footprint (a steep ST5 for a look) is found in the uncharacteristic scrubby bush along the road that winds north and then east from Falealupo back towards the Main Coast Rd. The footprint was said to have been made by the giant Moso when he stepped from Fiji to Samoa. There is said to be another 'footprint' on the Fijian island of Viti Levu which marks his point of departure. The scientific explanation is a bit more complicated. When lava cools and contracts, it breaks into blocks. These blocks are often lifted and moved by tree roots growing down into the joints. Once they're on the surface, a cyclone could easily clear them away, leaving regularly-shaped indentations in the crust. Hence, Moso's Footprint.

Sea Arches
Near the village of Falelima, the coastal lava flows have been sculpted by rolling surf into dramatic shapes and terraces. If you're mesmerised by rolling surf, this area is great for a few hours of maritime contemplation. A couple of kilometres south-east of Falelima are two impressive natural sea arches, caused by the pounding waves. About 300m east of the large arch at Falelima is an odd blowhole which shoots blasts of warm air. It's known as – you guessed it – Moso's Fart.

Lovers' Leap
The sheer cliff called Lovers' Leap is just north-west of the village of Fagafau. It's a nice view down to the sea but don't go too far out of your way to see it. The story goes that a woman from Tutuila married a man from this corner of Savai'i. When he died, the broken-hearted woman and her daughter were so badly treated by the villagers that they leapt into the sea and were turned into a turtle and a shark. For the slightly mangled sequel to this story, see under Turtle & Shark Point in the Tutuila chapter.

INDEPENDENT SAMOA

Beaches

There are pleasant beaches at Fai'a'ai, about 16km south-east of the Falealupo Peninsula, and nearby at Foailalo and Satuiatua. Fai'a'ai and Satuiatua both offer basic beachside accommodation; Foailalo has several picnic fales. Satuiatua, which is about one hour by bus (ST2.30) from Salelologa, has some of the best surf in Samoa. The custom fee for day use of any of the above beaches is ST2 per person.

Places to Stay & Eat

The *Vaisala Beach Hotel* (☎ 58016; fax 58017), at Vaisala on the north-west coast, clings to a slope right above a lovely white sand beach. Often used as a base for surfers, basic rooms with shower (some rooms have hot water!) cost ST73/89/100, including tax. The hotel also has the north-west's only formal bar/restaurant. Breakfast is available from ST9, toasted sandwiches cost ST5 and set-menu dinners are ST27.50.

The Canopy Walkway in the Falealupo Rainforest Preserve offers accommodation in the top of a banyan tree (see Canopy Walkway above). A space on the 20m-high platform (there is room for six people) plus two meals costs ST50 per person. You can book through the Vaisala Hotel, or just turn up at the tree.

A couple of kilometres north of Cape Mulinu'u on the edge of the Falealupo Peninsula is *Tanumatiu Beach Fales*, run by Gisa Seumanutafa Tiitii and his wife Sisa. The four traditional beach fales are situated on one of the most idyllic beaches in Samoa; there's nothing here but wild ocean, magnificent sunsets and lots of coconut palms. The fales are supplied with comfortable mattresses, bedding, mosquito nets and oil lamps. There's a toilet on the site and guests can use the outside shower (keep your lava-lava on) at the family house just up the road. Beyond the family house is an ancient star mound. The fales cost ST40 per person, including two meals. The custom fee for beach use is ST5 per car.

There are a couple of fales on the beach next to Tanumatiu for around the same price

and two more on the other side of Cape Mulinu'u at Tufutafoe, home of all the ghosts in Samoa! It costs ST15 to stay overnight at Tufutafoe and another ST15 for two meals. If you plan to stay down on the peninsula for a few days it may be an idea to stock up on supplies in Asau or Vaisala.

The *Fai'a'ai Beach Fales* (☎ 56023) are about 16km south-east of the Falealupo Peninsula, perched on the cliff-top just off the Main Coast Rd. A well-maintained path leads down the escarpment to a pleasant palm-fringed beach. The two large fales sleep up to about six people; the overnight charge is ST15 per person plus ST15 for two meals.

About 7km further down the coast is *Satuiatua Beach Resort* (☎/fax 56026), PO Box 5623 Salailua, Savai'i, another spot travellers (the surfing variety in particular) return to time and again. Run by Mate Teuila Schuster and situated on a lovely shady beach, Satuiatua has four large beachside fales which sleep six to eight people, and three small fales. The beach is good for snorkelling and has some of the best surf on the island. Mate can organise fishing trips with the locals as well as treks to a nearby cave. Fales cost ST20 per person, ST50 including two meals. If you stay for a week or more the rate drops to ST44 and children pay half price. There's a small restaurant here and a shop selling basic supplies and beer. Satuiatua is about one hour by bus (ST2.30) from Salelologa.

SOUTHERN SAVAI'I

Olemoe Falls

On the Letolo Plantation, once the biggest plantation on Savai'i, is idyllic and secluded Olemoe Falls (marked Afu Aau on the Hema map). This lovely jungle waterfall plunges into the crystalline waters of a deep blue pool which is marvellous for swimming and diving.

To reach it, take the bus from Salelologa west to just past the bridge across the Falealila River near Palauli. About 200m west of the bridge, a small plantation track leads inland. Follow it past the plantation house and continue 300m up the hill until you reach the second break in the stone wall. Take a sharp right here and head through a gentle valley of friendly cows and horses. On the far side of the pasture there's a steep 20m walk down to the river bed. Just upstream are the falls and pool. The track leads around to the western side of the pool, where you can dive from the cliffs into 3m or more of water. Be sure to ascertain the depth, however, before plunging in! Dry weather can lower the water level and make for disastrous diving. With snorkelling gear, you can look for the freshwater prawns which inhabit the pool; there are also pools further downstream where you can observe them without a mask.

Remember that you're on private property here. Don't leave rubbish lying around or disturb any of the crops or animals. There are no custom fees for the falls.

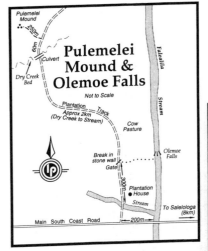

Pulemelei Mound

Polynesia's largest ancient structure is Pulemelei Mound (marked on the Hema map as Tia Seu Ancient Mound), to be found not far from Olemoe Falls, also on the Letolo Plantation. This large pyramid measures 61m by 50m at the base and rises in two tiers to a height of more than 12m. It is almost squarely oriented with the compass directions. The main approaches to the summit are up ramps on the eastern and western slopes. Smaller mounds and platforms are found in four directions away from the main structure. There is a relatively large platform about 40m north of the main pyramid and this is connected to it by a stone walkway.

Unfortunately, this impressive monument is naturally obscured by jungle growth, so unless it has been cleared recently, it is extremely difficult to locate. However, the fact that relatively few travellers have actually found it seems to make it all the more intriguing. Move over, Indiana Jones!

Allow about 45 minutes each way, wear sturdy shoes and don't forget to carry water and insect repellent. After visiting Olemoe Falls, keep following the main plantation road inland until you cross a culvert perpendicular to the road. Standing on the culvert and looking ahead along the road, you're looking straight at the pyramid, although it won't be obvious at the time. About 60m beyond the culvert, a very muddy, narrow, overgrown track leads off to the left. Follow it for about 250m to the top of a hill. You'll be on the summit of Pulemelei Mound.

Given its similarity to religious structures in Meso-America and the midwestern USA, archaeologists have difficulty believing that Pulemelei was used for pigeon-snaring, as oral tradition seems to imply all the ancient Polynesian monuments were. The complexity of its design and the effort expended in its construction leads them to believe that it may have had religious or other significance. Another theory postulates that it was used for strategic purposes since, when cleared, it affords a view right down to the coast.

Satupaitea

The long narrow village of Satupaitea lies on a loop road about 2km south of the Main South Coast Rd. There's nothing of overwhelming interest here but it is an unusual village. It lies beside a foul-smelling inlet which at low tide becomes a mucky paddock

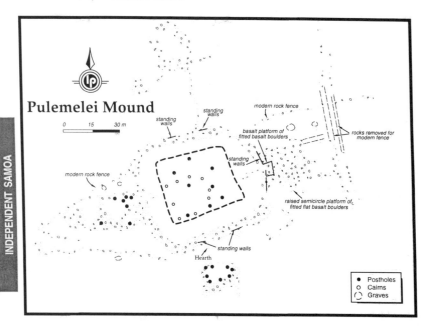

Pulemelei Mound

0   15   30 m

standing walls

standing walls

modern rock fence

basalt platform of fitted basalt boulders

rocks removed for modern fence

standing walls

modern rock fence

raised semicircle platform of fitted flat basalt boulders

standing walls

Hearth

● Postholes
○ Cairns
〇 Graves

for oyster-foraging pigs. Locals maintain that these 'aquatic pigs' produce some of the best-tasting pork in Samoa.

While you're here, take a look at the Peter Turner monument in front of the colourful Methodist church. Several springs bubble up in the middle of streams beside the road.

Gataivai
The beautifully situated village of Gataivai sits beside a veritable water garden of cascades. Here, the waters of Samoa's greatest river rush down to their climax at Mu Pagoa Waterfall, where they plunge 5m into the sea. The approach to the falls is from the subvillage of Gautavai, beside the Main South Coast Rd on the opposite bank of the river.

Taga Blowholes
This is not just another set of blowholes. There's little to equal them anywhere else in the world. It's one of the most impressive natural features in Samoa. At the village of

Taga, pay the custom fee (ST5 per car; ST2 for those on foot) and walk down the hill and west along the coast for about 10 minutes. You'll emerge from the coconut plantation with a clear view across the black lava coast and before the blowholes. They'll entertain you for hours. Locals often demonstrate the incredible power of the surf by tossing in a coconut at just the right moment to send it flying up to 90m into the air.

It's possible to walk a further 5km or so around this spectacular stretch of coast to the village of Fagaloa; to be sure of the way take a guide from the village. About 5km northwest of Taga, just north of the road, is a large jungle-covered Polynesian mound thought to date back at least 1000 years, possibly to the period of Tongan domination. Fashioned of coral and lava blocks it is divided by a low wall. Its use is unknown but it is thought to have served a religious purpose. Alternatively, it may simply have been a platform supporting the home of a noble.

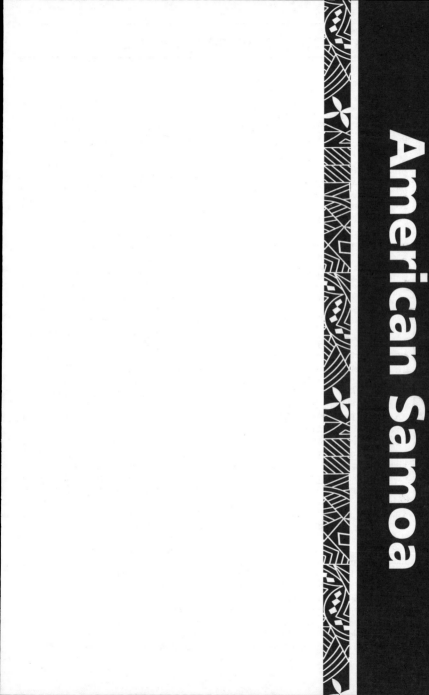

American Samoa

Facts about American Samoa

HISTORY

For a discussion of the history of Western Samoa prior to 1900, see the Facts about the Region chapter at the beginning of the book.

Annexation

The formal annexation of eastern Samoa by the USA took place on 17 April 1900, when a deed of cession was signed by all the chiefs of all the islands involved.

The island of Tutuila of the Samoan group, and all other islands of the group east of longitude one hundred and seventy one degrees west of Greenwich, are hereby placed under the control of the Department of the Navy, for a naval station.

The Secretary of the Navy will take such steps as may be necessary to establish the authority of the United States, and to give the islands the necessary protection.

US Military Rule

Thus, under the jurisdiction of the US Department of the Navy, the territory became a naval station headed by Commander Benjamin F Tilley of the USS *Abarenda*. The United States agreed to protect the traditional rights of the indigenous Samoans in exchange for the military base and coaling station. The territory's inhabitants acquired the status of US nationals but were denied a vote or representation in Washington.

In 1905, the military commander of Tutuila was given the title of governor and the territory officially became known as American Samoa.

The original deed of cession included only the islands of Tutuila and Aunu'u, leaving the Manu'a Islands under the control of the Tu'i Manu'a, the hereditary chief of that eastern group and the holder of perhaps the most revered title in Polynesia. In 1904, however, he also signed a deed of cession. When he died on 2 April 1909, the chief stipulated in his will that the title should die

with him so no other Tu'i Manu'a should ever be subservient to a foreign power.

Swains Island, an atoll more than 300km north of Tutuila in the Tokelau Islands, was acquired in 1876 by a US citizen, Eli Jennings. It was added to American Samoa by joint congressional resolution on 4 March 1925. The two later cessions were formally recognised by the US Congress on 20 February 1929.

The Kennedy Influence

Until the 1960s, American Samoa still retained its very traditional social structure and subsistence economy and the governor at the time recommended that Americans exercise restraint so as not to drag the territory too quickly into the North American version of the 20th century.

In the early part of the decade, however, an influential North American magazine published an article entitled 'America's Shame in the South Seas', which examined the simple subsistence lifestyle enjoyed by the American Samoans and determined it to be poverty by US standards. Americans became outraged and demanded something be done.

In response, President Kennedy appointed H Rex Lee, a Mormon, to the governorship and instructed him to oversee the modernisation of the territory. Funds were appropriated by Congress and, almost overnight, American Samoa became a US construction project, overtaken by haphazard and insensitive development.

Roads were built and European-style homes replaced traditional fales, electrification and sewage treatment projects were implemented and harbour facilities, schools and a tourist hotel were constructed. In addition, an international airport, a public auditorium, a hospital, the tuna canneries and TV transmission from the mainland were laid down. Suddenly, all the problems experienced on the US mainland – alcoholism, crime and juvenile delinquency, to name a few – began to surface in American Samoa. By the time Governor Lee left office in 1967, Samoan leaders were already lamenting the downfall of their society and the creation of a directionless welfare state.

Moves for More Democracy

Between 1967 and 1975, lack of sufficient funds from Washington to maintain all the new amenities caused the whole system to fall into disrepair or go awry for one reason or another. In a series of referenda, the American Samoans voted to continue under the direction of appointed governors. However, under a bit of coercion from Washington, a subsequent referendum determined that the American Samoans were ready for democratically elected leadership and some measure of autonomy.

GOVERNMENT & POLITICS

American Samoa is an unincorporated and unorganised territory of the United States. It is unincorporated because not all provisions of the US Constitution apply to the territory. It is the only territory whose residents are nationals of the United States rather than citizens of the United States and who are not governed (as all other US territories are) by an organic act of the US Congress defining its legal relationship to the US.

Instead, American Samoa has remained an 'unorganised' territory, that is, with its own constitution but under direct US federal government supervision, delegated by the president to the Department of the Interior.

This unique status is not accidental. It is the result of decisions consciously taken by the American Samoan leaders – not to obtain citizenship nor acquire an organic act – in order to keep their traditional land tenure system, because that system's racial preferences would make it unconstitutional under US federal law.

The territory's 1960 Constitution established three branches of government: executive, legislative, and judicial. The executive branch is now headed by a popularly elected governor and lieutenant-governor but, between 1951 and 1977, all of the territorial governors and lieutenant-governors were appointed by the US Department of the Interior.

In late 1956, the US Secretary of the Interior appointed a native Samoan to the Territory's top office. Governor Peter Tali Coleman took office on 15 October, 1956 and served until 24 May, 1961.

Western Samoa's leaders were then able to point out that if the United States of America could trust a native to run the government then there was no reason for New Zealand not to grant Western Samoa its independence. This eventually happened in 1962.

In November 1977, American Samoans were, for the first time in their history, allowed to elect their own governor and lieutenant-governor for four-year terms. Governor Coleman won the first election.

Though the Constitution forbids a governor serving more than two consecutive terms, an incumbent may sit out a term and then run again for the office.

In January 1997, Tavese Pita Sunic was elected Governor and Togiola Talalelei Tulafono Lieutenant Governor.

In 1980, American Samoans were also allowed, for the first time, to elect a non-voting delegate to serve a two-year term, from 1981, in the US House of Representatives. In 1996, Congressman Faleomavaega Eni Hunkin won an unprecedented fifth two-year term. He first won in 1988, and is expected to win a sixth term in 1998.

Known in the vernacular as the Fono, the legislative branch of the government is bicameral, composed of a Senate and House of Representatives, and meets for 45-day sessions twice a year. The Senate consists of 18 high chiefs who serve four-year terms. In a bow to Samoan tradition and custom, the Constitution of American Samoa calls for the election of only high-ranking chiefs to the Senate by the County Councils, which are made up of village councils. Though recent popular opinion favours the public and general election of senators, it isn't yet strong enough to back a constitutional amendment.

The House of Representatives consists of 20 voting members from the 17 districts of American Samoa and one non-voting member who represents Swains Island. The House is popularly elected every two years.

The judicial branch of the government functions independently of the other two branches. Judicial power is vested in a High Court of American Samoa, a district court and a village court in each village. The Chief Justice and the Associate Chief Justice of the High Court are appointed by the United States Secretary of the Interior. The district court judge and associate judges, who are Samoan chiefs, are appointed by the Governor of American Samoa and the appointments are subject to confirmation by the Senate.

Though American Samoans are not automatically granted US citizenship, they may freely apply for it. They are classified as US nationals and have freedom of entry into the continental United States. The US government has readily acknowledged the many Samoans who have served with distinction in its armed forces.

ECONOMY

About one-third of the territory's workforce is employed by the government. The two tuna canneries on Tutuila – StarKist Samoa and COS Samoa Packing – employ another third of the workforce with the remaining one third employed in retail and service enterprises. Many of these firms provide goods and services to the canneries.

American Samoa's territorial status allows all businesses based there, such as the tuna canneries and textile manufacturers, to export their goods duty-free to the US. This is an important consideration, as American Samoa does not have to adhere to Federal minimum-wage standards.

The tuna canneries benefit particularly from the islands' status as a US territory. Being exempt from the Nicholson Act, which prohibits foreign-flag bearing vessels from bringing fish into US ports, means foreign vessels can deposit their catch directly on the cannery docks in American Samoa.

The canneries (and any other American Samoa-based US company) also benefit from being outside the customs territory of the United States. Cannery products can enter the US duty-free provided they do not contain more than 50% of foreign components – a provision easily met by canned tuna.

The annual volume of shipments fluctuates, though it has usually been around one third of total US production.

In 1996, 104 million kg of canned tuna, valued at US$322.5 million, was shipped from American Samoa to the US mainland.

US Financial Aid

The US Department of Interior provides operating and capital improvement projects (CIP) grants to the American Samoa Government. In 1988, the operations grant was US$20.7 million and the CIP grant was US$4.4 million. In 1992, the operations grant was raised slightly to US$23.4 million, and the CIP grant dropped to US$3.8 million.

In 1997-8, the American Samoa Government was allocated an operations grant of US$23.1 million, a CIP grant of US$10.1 million and a technical assistance grant of about $1 million for education-related programs, such as the Junior Statesman program that allows promising island high school students to travel to the US mainland to study at major US universities during the summer.

Facts for the Visitor

TOURIST OFFICE

The well-staffed American Samoa Office of Tourism (☎ 633 1091/2/3; fax 633 1094), PO Box 1147, Pago Pago, American Samoa 96799, is housed in a white weatherboard building next to the yacht club in Utulei, Pago Pago. The office can provide a rudimentary map of Tutuila and the harbour area and several brochures. The tourist office runs an official home-stay program which is known as Fale, Fala ma Ti, (meaning 'House, Mat and Tea'), which provides the option of staying with Samoan host families for US$25 to US$35 per night. Accommodation varies from Western style homes to traditional thatched roofed guesthouses, or *fale talimalo*. Some places also offer space for campers. Contact the tourist office for the most current listings of participants.

VISAS & DOCUMENTS

No visas are required of visitors to American Samoa but US citizens need proof of citizenship and everyone else must have a valid passport. Everyone, including US citizens, must have an onward ticket. Crew arriving on yachts must either hold an onward ticket or have the captain's guarantee of responsibility for all crew members' departures. Citizens of Independent Samoa, who were once permitted to pass freely between the two Samoas, are now required to hold a permit to enter and may no longer remain indefinitely in American Samoa. Normally, stays of 30 days, extendible to 90 days, are initially granted to tourists and business travellers. Anyone wishing to remain longer or to work in American Samoa must secure permission to stay.

Visa Extensions

Applications for length of stay extensions, work permits and long-stay permits must be organised through the immigration office in the Executive Office building in Utulei. Advance inquiries should be directed to the Chief Immigration Officer, American Samoa Government, Pago Pago, American Samoa 96799.

EMBASSIES

All American Samoan diplomatic affairs are handled by the USA. There are no consulates or embassies in American Samoa and there is currently no place in American Samoa that will issue visas for the USA.

CUSTOMS

Customs and immigration are handled at the airport or at the port facility in Fagatogo. Be prepared for fairly thorough customs searches. If you're arriving by yacht, raise the quarantine flag upon entering Pago Pago Harbor and anchor. If customs officials don't turn up in an hour or two, radio the harbour authorities for instructions. Customs fees vary according to the length of the vessel. Visitors can bring in one gallon of liquor and up to 200 cigarettes duty free.

MONEY

Costs

As might be expected, costs in American Samoa are quite a bit higher than in Independent Samoa. There's little choice of accommodation and what is available is relatively expensive: at the cheaper end of the scale, there's B&B or village accommodation from US$35 per person per night; hotel rooms with shared facilities start at US$50 for single or double occupancy. Expect to pay from around US$5 for a cheap breakfast or lunch, from US$15 for dinner. To eat in an upmarket restaurant such as Sadie's, you're looking at a minimum of US$30 per person. You can buy inexpensive fresh produce at the market in Fagatogo. Imported foods and alcohol can be quite pricey. As in Independent Samoa, public transport is cheap and you're unlikely to pay more than US$1.50 for a bus fare on Tutuila Island. Rental cars cost from US$50 per day. A return air fare to the Manu'a Islands – a must for anyone visiting American Samoa – costs US$86.

Credit Cards

Visa, American Express and MasterCard are all accepted at the Rainmaker Hotel, at the Motu-o-Fiafiaga Hotel as well as by tourist-oriented shops and restaurants on Tutuila. Both banks give credit card cash advance.

Currency

The US dollar is the currency used in American Samoa. Notes come in denominations of 1, 2 (rare), 5, 10, 20, 50 and 100 dollars and coins in circulation in denominations of 1 (a penny), 5 (a nickel), 10 (a dime), 25 (a quarter) and 50 cents (somewhat rare). There is also a one dollar coin, but it's not in common usage outside Nevada and other casino areas.

Currency Exchange

Australia	A$1	=	US$0.66
Canada	$1	=	US$0.69
Fiji	F$1	=	US$0.52
France	1FF	=	US$0.16
Germany	DM1	=	US$0.54
Independent Samoa	ST$1	=	US$0.36
Japanese Yen	¥100	=	US$0.78
New Zealand	NZ$1	=	US$0.57
Tonga	T$1	=	US$0.74
UK	£1	=	US$1.64

Changing Money

There are two banks near the town square in central Pago Pago, the Bank of Hawaii and the Amerika Samoa Bank; the latter charges a US$5 commission on travellers' cheques. Both have ATMs and can give cash advances on major credit cards. There's also an ATM and branch of the bank of Hawaii in Pava'ia'i, towards the western end of the island. Banks are open from 9 am to 3 pm Monday to Friday, with a service window open until 4.30 pm on Fridays. The Tafuna branch of the Amerika Samoa Bank is open from 9 am to noon on Saturdays.

There is no exchange office at the airport, so if you arrive at night or weekends, have some US currency or travellers' cheques. US

dollar travellers' cheques are accepted at most shops, restaurants and hotels.

Tipping & Bargaining

In Pago Pago some tipping is acceptable for exceptional service at finer restaurants, but otherwise, it's not the custom. Bargaining isn't the norm either – the price listed is the price you're expected to pay.

Consumer Taxes

There is a 2% territorial sales tax on consumer goods but it's not worked into the posted prices. Take this into consideration when you're down to your last few cents and want to pay in exact change.

POST & COMMUNICATIONS
Sending Mail

The main post office is near the *malae* in Fagatogo on the ground floor of the Lumana'i building, the same building the Bank of Hawaii occupies. It is open from 8 am to 4 pm Monday to Friday and from 8.30 am to noon Saturday.

Postal Rates

Because US stamps are used and US postal rates apply, travellers from the USA will find it particularly inexpensive to post parcels home from American Samoa. The zip (postal) code for all of American Samoa is 96799.

Receiving Mail

Visitors who wish to receive correspondence here should have mail addressed to themselves care of General Delivery, Pago Pago, American Samoa 96799. Those arriving on a yacht should have the name of the vessel included somewhere in the address. Mail is normally filed under the name of the vessel if it is available.

Telephone, Telex & Fax

The communications office is to the west of the malae in Fagatogo and is open 24 hours a day for both local and international calls. Telex and fax services are also available. Station-to-station calls to the US mainland

and Hawaii cost US$6.60 for the first three minutes and 90 cents for each minute thereafter. To Australia, the charge is US$6.50 for the first three minutes and US$1.80 thereafter; to New Zealand, the charge is US$5.70 and then US$1.60 per minute; to Europe, calls cost US$8 for the first three minutes and US$2.65 thereafter. On weekends and evenings, there are discounts on calls to the US. The telephone code for American Samoa is ☎ 684. Local calls cost 10 cents. Fax charges are the same as above plus another US$2 per page.

NEWSPAPERS & MAGAZINES

The *Samoa News* (☎ 633 5599) is published daily Monday to Friday and the *Samoa Journal* is published weekly on Friday. Both contain minimal news of international interest but they do cover local and sports news in detail. There are no magazines specifically about American Samoa. Those concerned with the Pacific in general include *Le Pasefika*, a new travel and lifestyle magazine; *Pacfic Magazine*; and *Pacific Islands Monthly*.

RADIO & TV

Radio WVUV (AM 1640) plays a variety of music 24 hours a day, with brief news programmes hourly. Broadcasts are in Samoan and English. Radio KSBS (FM 92.1) plays a similar selection of popular music from 6 am to midnight. The government-owned TV station, KVZK, broadcasts on two channels from a transmitter atop Mt Alava above Pago Pago Harbor. Channel 2, which operates from 6 am to midnight, shows local and noncommercial programmes from the USA. Channel 4 broadcasts commercial US programmes from noon to midnight on a week-delay basis. Cable TV arrived in American Samoa in 1996. Cablevision provides 20 channels, the majority from the USA, to subscribers who pay US$32 per month. A second cable TV company, Nuanua, offers fewer channels.

ELECTRICITY

Power is supplied mainly from the Tafuna and Satala power plants on Tutuila. The current in the outlets is 110V, so US plugs and appliances may be used.

LAUNDRY

In American Samoa there are numerous good old western-style laundrettes, which are open from Monday to Saturday and occasionally even on Sunday. For specifics, see under Information in the Pago Pago section.

HEALTH

The LBJ Tropical Medical Center in Faga'alu can provide basic medical services but anyone suffering serious medical problems is advised to go to Hawai'i or New Zealand. Emergency doctors are on duty at all hours and the LBJ clinic is open from 8 am to 4 pm weekdays. Patients are charged a small fee. The emergency telephone number is ☎ 911, as it is throughout the USA. There is a good pharmacy closer to the harbour area in the Samoa Sports building in Fagatogo.

ACTIVITIES
Snorkelling & Swimming

Some of the best snorkelling in all of the Samoas is to be found in the National Park of American Samoa on the rugged little island of Ofu (see the Manu'a Islands chapter). The best spots for swimming and snorkelling on Tutuila (none as good as Ofu) are along the south coast near the western and eastern ends of the island and along the north coast. Always ask permission from local villagers before using their beach. It's worth remembering, too, that shallow reefs, pounding surf and the swift movement of water through breaks in the reefs (*'avas*), make much of the coastline of American Samoa treacherous. Always seek local advice on the best places to swim and never swim or snorkel alone. Visitors are best advised to bring their own snorkelling gear. In Pago Pago itself, there is a beach at Utulei, not far from the Rainmaker Hotel, where the locals swim. Though pollution levels have dropped in recent years, the harbour probably isn't the cleanest spot on the island.

Coral Reef – A Beautiful Animal

Many of the coastlines in the Samoas are fringed by coral reefs – fragile environments of calcareous deposits secreted by tiny marine animals known as coral polyps. The glorious white-sand beaches of the Pacific Ocean are often composed of dead coral, shells and marine algae.

Without the reefs, many of the beaches would eventually erode and disappear. The reefs also provide shelter and habitat for a variety of fish, shellfish, crustaceans, sea urchins and other marine life which in turn provide a food source for larger fish and, both directly and indirectly, for humans.

Coral is usually stationary and often looks decidedly flowery and was generally considered to be a plant up until around 250 years ago. In fact, it's an animal – a hungry carnivorous one.

Corals belong to the coelenterate class of animal which also includes sea anemones and jellyfish. The true reef-building coral, or *Scleractinia*, is distinguished by its lime skeletons, which are relatively indestructible and actually form the coral reef. As new coral continually builds on old, dead coral, the reef gradually builds up.

Coral takes a number of forms but all are distinguished by polyps, the tiny tube-like fleshy cylinders which resemble their close relation, the anemone. The top of the cylinder is open and ringed by waving tentacles which sting any passing prey and draw it into the polyp's stomach, the open space within the cylinder. Each polyp is an individual creature but it can reproduce by splitting to form a coral colony of separate but closely related polyps. Although each polyp catches and digests its own food, the nutrition passes between the polyps to the whole colony. Most coral polyps only feed at night; during the daytime they withdraw into their hard, limestone skeleton, so it is only at night that a coral reef can be seen in its full, colourful glory.

Hard coral may take many forms. One of the most common and easiest to recognise is the staghorn coral, which grows by budding off new branches from the tips. Brain coral is huge and round with a surface that looks very much like a human brain. It grows by adding new base levels of skeletal matter and expanding outwards. Flat or sheet coral, like plate coral, expands out at its outer edges. Many corals can take different shapes depending on their environment. Staghorn coral can branch out in all directions in deeper water or form flat tables when it grows in shallow water.

Like its reef-building relative, soft coral is made up of individual polyps, but they do not form a hard limestone skeleton. Lacking hard coral's protective skeleton, soft coral might be expected to fall prey to fish, but in fact it seems to remain relatively immune, either due to toxic substances in its tissues or to the presence of sharp limestone needles that protect the polyps. Soft coral can move around and will sometimes engulf and kill off hard coral.

Coral catches its prey by means of stinging nematocysts. Some corals can give humans a painful sting: the fern-like stinging hydroid, for example, should be given a wide berth. ■

Diving

There's plenty of good diving in American Samoa; on the northern and western ends of the island, corals are prolific and visibility is excellent. Many places have walls of coral which are 18m or more deep. Certified divers can organise dives through John Harrison (Divemaster), who runs the Tutuila Dive Shop (☎ 699 2842; Tutuiladiveshop @samoatelco.com), PO Box 5137, Pago Pago, American Samoa 96799-5137, at Vaitogi, south of the airport. Single tank dives cost US$30; if you have your own equipment, you need only pay for the air and a gratuity. All dives are from the beach, mostly at spots around the south-western end of the island. John, who has lived on Tutuila for 12 years, is happy to provide tips and advice on local surf spots, too.

Surfing & Windsurfing

According to those in the know, the surf in American Samoa is (was) one of the best-kept secrets of the South Pacific. Powerful

2m waves breaking in very shallow water over very sharp coral, however, make it an activity for the advanced only. Tutuila is one of the few Pacific islands outside Hawaii that has a high concentration of surf spots. Some of the best surfing is found just beyond the reef near Faganeanea, but if the trade winds are blowing and the tides aren't right, surfing will be impossible. The rest of the time, it is still very risky.

Other breaks worth investigating include those at Poloa, Amanave, Sliding Rock, Nu'uuli, Lauli'ituai, Alofau and Tula. For more detailed local information, contact John Harrison of the Tutuila Dive Shop (☎ 699 2842), in Vaitogi. Thanks to the strong winds funnelled up the harbour, especially during the winter months, conditions in Pago Pago Harbor are favourable for windsurfing but the hazards are obvious. Watch out for cargo ships, longliners and yachts (between August and October they're everywhere!). At the time of writing, there were no agencies renting sailboards.

Hiking

At the moment there are limited opportunities for hiking in American Samoa, but the US National Parks Service does plan to establish a series of walking trails in the Tutuila and Ta'u sections of the park. It's worth checking developments with the National Park Visitor Information Center in Pago Pago (☎ 633 7082; fax 633 7085; NPSA.Administration@nps.gov). Anyone intending to hike in the national park should contact the superintendent anyway.

The well-established 5km trail to the top of Mt Alava (built for access to the TV transmitter) above Pago Pago Harbor is easily accessible and offers excellent views of the harbour and the rugged north-west coast. For those willing to leave all tourist comforts behind them, the remote island of Ta'u offers some very wild and untouched scenery. Sections of the coast are accessible and inland walks to Judds Crater (six hours) and Mt Lata (overnight trek) are possible. You'll need to take a local guide and carry camping equipment plus food and water.

Golf

The 'Ili'ili Golf Course, south of Pago Pago airport, may qualify as one of the most scenic as well as one of the cheapest golf courses in the world. Established 25 years ago, the 'very forgiving' 70 par course has dramatic mountain peaks overlooking it to the north and a view of the South Pacific to the east. It costs US$10 to hire clubs; green fees are US$7 on weekdays and US$15 on the weekend. The 'Ili'ili Country Club has a dining room and pleasant sports bar which are both open seven days a week.

WORK

For employment purposes, American Samoans will always be considered before foreigners, although teachers and medical personnel are often in demand. Foreigners, including US citizens, may not purchase land or controlling percentages of businesses in American Samoa. However, land may be leased to outsiders for up to 55 years. Work permit applications are best handled from abroad; enquiries should be directed to the Chief Immigration Officer, American Samoa Government, Pago Pago, American Samoa 96799.

ACCOMMODATION

Accommodation options are extremely limited throughout American Samoa. At the 'top end', the large government-owned and unfortunately titled Rainmaker Hotel in Pago Pago not only monopolises the market but represents very poor value for money. There's not much at all in the way of formal budget accommodation, though local villagers living close to the National Park are being encouraged to provide inexpensive lodging for visitors. At the time of writing, there were no basic beachside *fales* to rent anywhere in the islands.

For those who would like to experience village life in American Samoa, the tourist office runs a home-stay programme called Fale, Fala ma Ti (meaning 'House, Mat and Tea'). Accommodation may be in western-style homes (as the vast majority are in American Samoa) or in traditional open-sided guesthouses. Space for campers is also offered. Prices start at US$25 per person per night. Contact the American Samoa Office of Tourism (see Tourist Office in the earlier Information section for the address) for a full list of participants.

THINGS TO BUY

The Senior Citizens' Handicraft Fales, at the far south-western end of the harbour, are probably the best place to head for if you're looking for locally produced handicrafts such as *siapo*, woven mats, wooden carvings and coconut and shell jewellery. The artists are always happy to chat and discuss their work with visitors. The fales are open from 8 am to 3.30 pm Monday to Friday. The Jean P Haydon Museum, opposite the town square, sells a small but interesting selection of locally made items. There are a couple of places selling handicrafts within the large Laufou Shopping Center in Nu'uuli. J-Len T's, in the Laufou Center and at Malaloa near Sadie's Restaurant, sells a good selection of crafts as well as locally designed T-shirts and lava-lavas.

Polynesian Pics, at the airport and the Rainmaker Hotel, sells a pricier selection of local handicrafts. For a rundown of the sorts of arts and crafts produced in the Samoas, see Things to Buy in the regional Facts for the Visitor chapter. For inexpensive US-made clothing (and US sports shoes) you can't beat Spencer's in Pago Pago. For household goods and imported groceries (should you need plastic mops and American cookies) go to the enormous bulk store, Cost-U-Less, just by the airport.

Tutuila Island

Like a sinuous green dragon slinking through the sea, the island of Tutuila, 30km long and never more than 6km wide, has numerous bays and indentations where deep and fertile valleys plunge into the sea. The most prominent of these is Pago Pago Harbor, the safest and most renowned harbor in the South Pacific, which nearly divides the island in two.

Tutuila is by far the largest of the seven islands of American Samoa, comprising 145 of the territory's 197sq km and with more than 95% of its 55,000 inhabitants. The dramatic landscape of Tutuila is characterised by steep, rugged and lush forested mountains which branch out from the central ridge and dominate the wild topography, confining most of the development to a narrow strip along the south coast and the level area between the airport and the village of Leone. This is the only flat land in the entire territory. The north coast is so wildly eroded that only a few tributary roads connect it with the island-long highway that snakes around the south coast.

Matafao Peak, just west of Pago Pago Harbor and above Fagatogo, is the highest point, at 653m. Immediately to the east of the harbor is 523m Mt Pioa, more commonly known as the Rainmaker Mountain for its habit of capturing precipitation in large quantities and dumping it unsparingly onto harbour-area settlements.

Tutuila's most important feature these days is Pago Pago Harbor, which is all that remains of the volcanic crater that created Tutuila in the first place. Sometime in the dim geological past, one wall of the crater collapsed and the sea came rushing in, creating a nearly perfect shelter from the wrath of the ocean at large. During the days of the big sailing ships, however, it was of little value. Without motors, the ships were unable to turn around in such a confined area and the most common anchorage in those days was Leone Bay near the western end of the island.

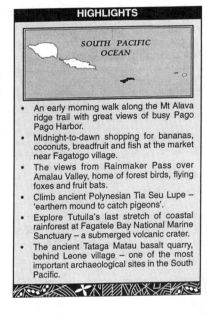
The first missionaries landed at Leone (now American Samoa's second-largest village) and built the most ornate church in the territory.

On 1 November 1988, Ronald Reagan signed a bill creating the National Park of

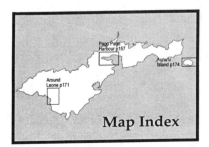

Map Index

AMERICAN SAMOA

AMERICAN SAMOA

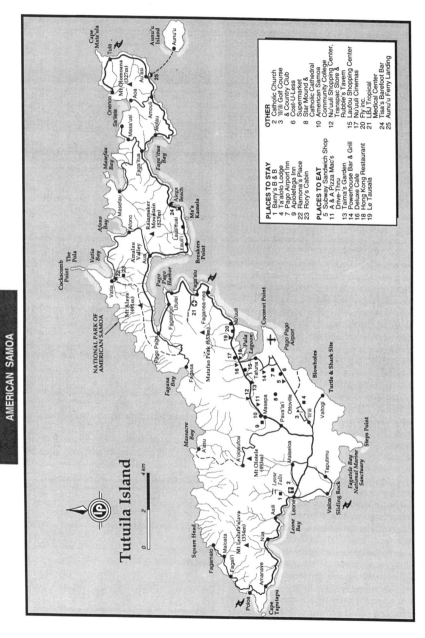

Tutuila Island

0   2   4 km

PLACES TO STAY
1 Barry's B & B
4 Ta'alolo Lodge
9 Pago Airport Inn
22 Ramona's Place
23 Rory's Cabin

PLACES TO EAT
5 Subway Sandwich Shop
11 A & A Pizza Mac's Drive-Thru
13 Taima's Garden
14 Powerhouse Bar & Grill
16 Deluxe Cafe
18 Hong Kong Restaurant
19 Le Tausala

OTHER
2 Catholic Church
3 'Ili'ili Golf Course & Country Club
6 Cost-U-Less
8 Supermarket
 Star Mound &
 Catholic Cathedral
10 American Samoa Community College
12 Nu'uuli Shopping Center, Transpac Store & Rubble's Tavern
15 Laufou Shopping Center
17 Nu'uuli Cinemas
20 Fly inc.
21 L&J Tropical Medical Center
24 Tisa's Barefoot Bar
25 Aunu'u Ferry Landing

American Samoa, which includes much of the island of Ta'u, part of Ofu in the Manu'a group and a sizable portion of the northern slopes of Tutuila. The park, which protects areas of coral reef as well as significant areas of mixed species old-world rainforest, offers spectacular snorkelling and some good hiking possibilities. Ambitious future plans for the park include the resurrection of the cable car which once ran across Pago Pago Harbor to the top of 491m Mt Alava.

Apart from the park, Tutuila has the usual gamut of palm-fringed white beaches, jungle waterfalls, colourful reefs and quiet villages that the world has come to expect of South Pacific places. Visitors will also find archaeological sites, pleasant bushwalks, sites made famous by history and legend (or a bit of both) and an ancient culture in transition, careering headlong into the modern world.

History

The Samoans believe that Tutuila was the last island of the archipelago to be created by Tagaloa, and once it came into existence, he asked Tutu and Ila to set about peopling it. Archaeological finds near the villages of Tulaand Aoa on the far eastern tip of Tutuila, and at To'aga on the island of Ofu, reveal that the islands have been inhabited for more than 3000 years. It is believed that early Samoan authorities used Tutuila as a place of exile for wrongdoers banished from Upolu. Studies made following the discovery of several large ancient stone quarries on Tutuila suggest that up until the time of European contact the island was the centre of a vast trade network which stretched as far as the Solomons.

Getting Around

Bus Riding the squat, colourful aiga buses (small, individually owned pick-up trucks modified for public transport and equipped with ear-busting sound systems) of Tutuila is a real highlight of a visit to American Samoa. The buses do unscheduled runs around Pago Pago Harbor and the more remote areas of the island from the main terminal at Fagatogo market.

Aiga buses leave every couple of minutes between early morning and about 6 pm eastbound for Tula (US$1), and westbound for Tafuna and the airport (50 cents), and Leone (75 cents). Less frequently, buses go to Fagasa (50 cents), A'oloaufou on the central ridge (75 cents), Amanave (US$1), and Fagamalo in the far north-west (US$1.25). Any trip between the tuna canneries and the hospital in Faga'alu costs 25 cents. The most expensive fare is the US$1.50 trip over the Rainmaker Pass to Vatia.

Try to have as near to the exact change as possible. To stop a bus, wave your hand and arm, palm down, as the bus approaches. To signal that you'd like to get off the bus, either knock on the ceiling or clap loudly. Pay the fare to the driver or leave the money on the dash board as you hop off. If you're travelling to the outskirts of the island, be at the market first thing in the morning and start heading back to town by 4 pm at the very latest. You'll be lucky to catch a bus after 2 pm on Saturday, and on Sunday the only buses running will be those taking people to church.

Car Tutuila's one main road (signposted Route 1) follows the twisty coastline from Fagamalo in the north-west of the island to Onenoa in the far north-east, a distance of around 50km. There are several smaller paved roads connecting outlying villages. If you would like to have a good look around Tutuila it may be worth hiring a car for a day or two. The five rental agencies listed below all charge about US$50 per day plus insurance. Petrol costs about US$1.45 per gallon.

Avis Car Rental
    Airport (☎ 699 2746; fax 699 4305)
KS Car Rental
    (☎ 633 2737; fax 633 2738)
Pavitt's U-Drive
    Airport (☎ 699 1456)
Royal Samoan Rent-a-Car
    Rainmaker Hotel (☎ 633 4545; fax 633 2197)
Thrifty Car Rental
    Rainmaker Hotel (☎ 633 7482; fax 633 2953)

AMERICAN SAMOA

Taxi In American Samoa, expect to pay about 16 times the bus fare, or just over US$1 per mile, for a taxi to a particular destination on Tutuila. This works out to US$10 from the harbour area to Pago Pago airport at Tafuna, US$15 to Leone, US$4 to the tuna canneries and US$16 to Au'asi. The fare from the Rainmaker Hotel to the airport is also US$10. There are taxi stands at the airport and local taxi companies have booths beside the market in Fagatogo. The government issues strong directives against overcharging by taxi drivers, but foreigners still have problems. Your only recourse is to take down the number plate of the taxi and report the incident to the American Samoa Commerce Commission (☎ 633 5155/6).

Pago Pago

Much written about and much maligned, Pago Pago (pronounced 'pango pango') is an alluring mixture of the seedy and the dramatically beautiful. The picturesque harbour is surrounded by high, almost wicked-looking mountains which plunge straight into the sea. A more breathtaking view would be hard to find. Unfortunately, on a 'bad tuna day' the smell from the massive tuna canneries on the northern side of the bay will also take your breath away.

Pago's unfavourable reputation has been mainly due to the belching tuna canneries, a heavily polluted and muddy harbour, high levels of rainfall and the fact that many writers have happened to visit during the wet season! The truth is that levels of pollution have dropped in recent years and filters have considerably reduced the smells from the tuna canneries. It still rains in the wet season, people continue to toss coke cans out of the windows of their pick-up trucks and the Rainmaker Hotel remains a pretty dreadful hotel. But anyone interested in characterful places and urban realities will love Pago.

The capital of the territory is actually the village of Fagatogo on the southern side of the harbour. The several small villages

around the harbour area that contain the territorial government, and most of the industry and commerce in American Samoa are known collectively as Pago Pago, after the small settlement at the head of the harbour. The Rainmaker Hotel itself is in Utulei and the canneries are in Anua, both of which are other villages of 'metro' Pago Pago. The banks, post office, museum, central market and bus station are all close to the grassy town square in Fagatogo.

The harbour area is relatively compact, so it's not difficult to walk between the major points of interest. If you don't want to walk, aiga buses are constantly zipping around the harbour and any trip within the bay area will cost 25 cents. The Pago Pago area is a duty-free port, so prices on imported goods are cheaper here than in other parts of the South Pacific.

Information
Tourist Office The tourist office in Pago Pago (☎ 633 1091/2/3; fax 633 1094) is next to the yacht club at Utulei, a short walk south of the Rainmaker Hotel. It offers brochures and a basic map of Tutuila and the harbour area. The office is open from 7.30 am to 4 pm Monday to Friday. It's closed on weekends and holidays.

National Park Visitor Information Center The National Park Visitor Information Center (☎ 633 7082; fax 633 7085; NPSA.Administration@nps.gov), in Pago Plaza at the south-western end of the harbour, has an informative brochure about the national park, which includes good maps of Tutuila and the Manu'a Islands. Visitors can also watch a short video covering all three units of the park. There are some excellent landscape and historical photographs in the centre as well as displays of local shells and traditional artefacts.

The centre is open from 8 am to 4.30 pm Monday to Friday and from 8 am until noon on Saturday. There are plans to build a new visitor centre in Utulei. For more information about the national park and what it has to offer, see Mt Alava in this section, the

AMERICAN SAMOA

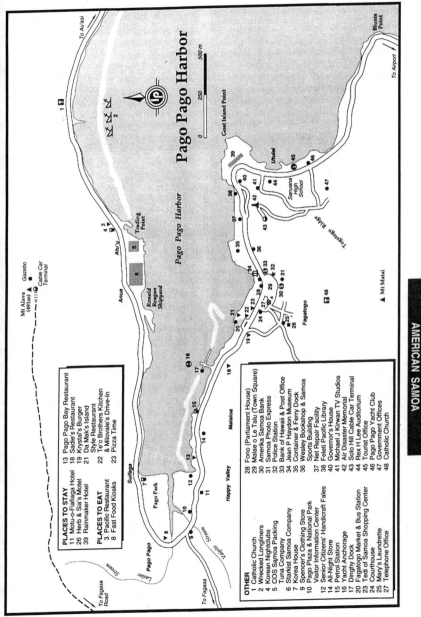

Pago Pago Harbor

Pago Pago Harbor

PLACES TO STAY
11 Motu-o-Fiafiaga Hotel
26 Herb & Sia's Motel
39 Rainmaker Hotel

PLACES TO EAT
3 Pacific Restaurant
8 Fast Food Kiosks
13 Pago Pago Bay Restaurant
18 Sadie's Restaurant
19 Krystal's Burger
21 Da Mak's Island
   Style Restaurant
22 Te'o Brothers Kitchen
   & Milovale's Drive-In
23 Pizza Time

OTHER
1 Catholic Church
2 Wrecked Longliners
4 Korean Nightclubs
5 COS Samoa Packing
6 Tuna Company
7 Starkist Samoa Company
9 Korea House
10 Spencer's Clothing Store
12 Pago Plaza & National Park
   Visitor Information Center
14 Senior Citizens' Handicraft Fales
15 All-Night Store
16 Petrol Station
17 Yacht Anchorage
18 Dinghy Dock
20 Fagatogo Market & Bus Station
23 Tedi of Samoa Shopping Center
24 Courthouse
25 Mary's Laundrette
27 Telephone Office
28 Fono (Parliament House)
29 Malae o Le Talu (Town Square)
30 Amerika Samoa Bank
31 Samoa Photo Express
32 Police Station
33 Bank of Hawaii & Post Office
34 Jean P Haydon Museum
35 Container & Ferry Dock
36 Wesley Bookshop & Samoa
   Sports Building
37 Net Repair Facility
38 Feleti Pacific Library
40 Governor's House
41 Michael J Kirwan TV Studios
42 Air Disaster Memorial
43 Solo Hill Cable Car Terminal
44 Rex H Lee Auditorium
45 Tourist Office
46 Pago Pago Yacht Club
47 Government Offices
48 Catholic Church

AMERICAN SAMOA

Around the Island section further on and the Manu'a Islands chapter.

Money The Bank of Hawaii and the Amerika Samoa Bank, both near the *malae* (town square) in Fagatogo, have exchange facilities; the latter charges a commission on travellers' cheques. The banks are open from 9 am to 3 pm Monday to Friday, with a service window open until 4.30 pm on Fridays. Both banks have ATMs.

Post The post office is by the malae on the ground floor of the Lumana'i building, in the same building as the Bank of Hawaii. It is open from 8 am to 4 pm Monday to Friday and from 8.30 am to noon Saturday. The telephone office is in Fagatogo, on the malae near the courthouse. There is no sign identifying it as such, but anyone will be able to direct you. It is open 24 hours a day, seven days a week, for both local and international calling. Fax services are available too.

Bookshops Bookshops are very sparse on the ground in Pago Pago. The gift shop at the airport, the Wesley Bookshop in Fagatogo, the Rainmaker Hotel gift shop and the Transpac Store at the Nu'uuli Shopping Center all stock a handful of Samoan and Pacific titles. The Transpac Store also has quite a good selection of novels. The yacht club in Utulei keeps a box of reading material dumped by yachties whose boats were filled to overflowing with things they'd already read. This is a good source of nautical and Pacific-related literature, if that is where your interests lie.

Libraries The Feleti Pacific Library in Utulei near the Rainmaker Hotel has a reasonable selection of books, but you'll have to convince staff that you're a resident in order to get a library card. There's no sign on the library, so ask someone to point it out for you. The American Samoa Community College, south-west of Nu'uuli near the Apiolefaga Inn, has an extensive Pacific collection, but research must be done on site. A new public library is being built near the government offices.

Laundry There are dozens of laundrettes in town. Mary's, across the lane from Herb & Sia's Motel, is open 24 hours a day Monday to Saturday and until 10 pm on Sunday. Mary charges 50 cents to wash and 75 cents to dry. JMPL's Laundrette, behind Krystal's Burger, is also open seven days a week. On Sundays during cruising season, the place becomes a yachtie social centre. The laundrette also sells some of the best ice cream on the island.

Mt Alava

Towering above Pago Pago Harbor is 491m Mt Alava. The mountain ridge marks the southern boundary of the Tutuila section of the national park and the National Park Service maintains the 5km trail that follows the ridge to the top of Mt Alava. It's an excellent walk with the summit offering spectacular views of nearly all of Tutuila Island and beyond to Upolu in Independent Samoa and the Manu'a Islands 100km east of Tutuila.

The view down to the busy harbour below is fascinating, too. The trail begins at Fagasa Pass about 1km south-west of the park's visitor centre. For the best and clearest possible view, as well as the most pleasant temperatures, go early in the morning. Wear sturdy shoes, hat, sunscreen and insect repellent and carry plenty of water. Take along binoculars if you have them and maybe a picnic lunch as well. You'll see birds and possibly bats along the way and you may even be lucky enough to see whales out to sea on the north-western side of the island. See the later Around the Island section for information on plans to extend the ridge trail.

If the view appeals, but you don't fancy the walk, be patient. The National Parks Service has ambitious plans to resurrect the cable car that once ran from Solo Hill above Utulei village 1.8km across Pago Pago Harbor to the top of Mt Alava. Constructed in 1965 as a service access to the TV transmission equipment on the mountain, the cable car was one of the world's longest single-span cable-car routes. Operations stopped several years ago and the above-mentioned trail became the access route to the TV antenna.

The terminals are still in place, as is the cable itself, which plunges dramatically into the harbour. During a Flag Day military demonstration in 1980, a US Navy plane hit the cables and crashed into the Rainmaker Hotel below. All six naval personnel aboard were killed, as were two guests of the hotel. A monument near the Solo Hill terminal commemorates those who died in the disaster. To get there, turn right at the first street past the Rainmaker Hotel (heading away from Pago) and follow it around the Rex H Lee Auditorium and some school buildings until another road leads away uphill. Follow it for about 250m to the monument. Just beyond it around the corner, there's a gazebo and a pleasant garden with a view.

Kirwan Studios

The Michael J Kirwan TV Studios are in the village of Utulei, behind the Rex H Lee Auditorium. It was here that the pioneer programme of broadcasting school lessons to elementary and secondary students began during the modernisation rush of the Governor Lee era. With more teachers and schools in the territory these days, the emphasis has shifted to public programming and commercial TV from Hawaii. The studio has been known to offer guided tours to interested groups.

Governor's House

This two-storey wooden colonial mansion atop Mauga o Ali'i (the chief's hill) was built in 1903 and served as the home for all of American Samoa's naval commanders until the Department of the Interior took control of the place in 1951. Since then, all the territorial governors have used it as a residence. You can't go inside the building, but it is possible to stroll around the gardens on the grounds. To get there, climb the road leading uphill across the street from the entrance to the Rainmaker Hotel.

Jean P Haydon Museum

Across the road from the post office in Fagatogo is the Jean P Haydon Museum, named for its founder, the wife of Governor John Haydon, who devotedly saw the project through to completion. The building itself has an interesting history. It was constructed in 1917 to house the original naval commissary, after which it served as the main post office.

The museum houses numerous artefacts of early Samoa, including the va'a and alia (bonito canoes and war canoes) that inspired the old name for Samoa, the Navigator Islands. There are also other items that were in common use in early island life, such as coconut-shell combs, seashell and whales' teeth necklaces, fruit and seed jewellery, pigs' tusk armlets, fly whisks, bamboo pan-pipes (which are strikingly similar to the South American variety), siapo cloth, stone tools and an impressive variety of weapons.

Also fascinating is the display of native pharmacopoeia used by the early Polynesians. The museum is open from 10 am to 3 pm Monday to Friday (if there's a cruise ship in town, the museum will open on the weekend too).

Admission is free. The museum has a small gift counter selling locally made items. Kava ceremonies and weaving and wood carving demonstrations sometimes take place in the fale next to the museum.

The Fono

The large and impressive group of buildings beside the museum is the Fono (legislature), where American Samoan law-makers convene and legislate during the months of January and July. The building was completed in October 1973, at a cost of US$1 million. Those interested can visit the Fono during sittings.

Traditional Samoan architecture and building styles were integrated into the structure, including the fale afolau style, which may be seen as the primary home design in Independent Samoa, and the fale tele (meeting house) design.

AMERICAN SAMOA

Courthouse

The attractive two storey, colonial-style courthouse in Fagatogo was built at the minuscule cost of US$46,000 between 1900 and 1904. Its original purpose was to contain the territorial executive and naval offices but it now houses the judiciary. It was expanded in 1929 and underwent total renovation in 1975. It is listed on the US National Register of Historic Places.

Market

The market and aiga bus terminal is near the western end of Fagatogo village. Here, local growers come to sell their bananas, coconuts, breadfruit and other fresh produce. The big market day is Saturday, but arrive before 7 am if you want to get a decent selection. Better still, turn up at about 11 pm on Friday night for the pick of the produce. Fresh fish is available at the Star of the Sea fish market, near the shore behind the main market. On weekday evenings the market serves as a bingo hall and the turn-out is phenomenal. Proceeds go to charity.

Sadie Thompson's

All American Samoans will assure you that Sadie Thompson is a historical figure, and the account they provide of her antics is far more involved than the Somerset Maugham classic *Rain* ever was.

The tale of Sadie Thompson was written after Maugham paid a visit to Pago Pago and was delayed there in the rain by an outbreak of measles while en route between Honolulu and Papeete on the steamship *Sonoma*. It is assumed that he stayed at the Rainmaker Boarding House with his US lover Gerald Haxton, but there seems to be some dispute over just where that was.

Many sources believe it was on the main street in Fagatogo in the building now occupied by the Reid Company Store. Others (particularly the owners of Sadie's Restaurant) maintain that it was in the same building as Sadie's is today. It would be nice to believe the latter claim, because that building's style and atmosphere certainly reflect the mood in the story better than the

other building does. The building was bought by shopkeeper Max Haleck in the late 1940s and has since changed hands a couple of times.

Samoans say that the historical Sadie Thompson, who lived upstairs in this building, was a laundress by day and practised her trade by night. We may never know her real name, but the woman Maugham called Sadie Thompson had been evicted from the Honolulu red-light district and travelled south in hopes of finding a new market for her goods. However, the ship was detained in Pago Pago and while the passengers were holed up, the Reverend Davidson, a holier-than-thou missionary who also happened to be holed up in the same hotel, took more than a passing concern for Miss Thompson's immortal soul. He set about changing her ways and persuaded her to repent. In the end, however, it was she who changed *his* ways (or at least brought out the human and humane in him).

Maugham's story more or less ends there, but the Samoans go on to say that Sadie stayed on in Pago and continued her chosen profession there until one night she was found drunk in the rain somewhere in Fagatogo. A police officer gathered her up and placed her, unconscious, on an Australia-bound steamer.

Every year, usually around 17 April (Flag Day), there is a well-attended performance of *Rain* at Sadie's Restaurant starring the local red-headed actress Kathleen Kolhoff.

Pago Pago Village

There's really not much to the village itself which has given its name to the entire harbour area. At the head of the harbour (the area the yachties call the 'low rent district') is a large reclaimed area called Pago Pago Park (the tongue-tied use just one 'Pago' and are still understood). In Pago Park are basketball and tennis courts, a football field, a gymnasium, a bowling alley and a series of cheap food kiosks. Korea House, built as a social centre for fishers from that country and at one time an excellent restaurant, was gutted by fire in 1997.

Tuna Canneries

The two tuna canneries are found in the kilometre-long industrial complex on the north coast of the harbour. Nearest to Pago Pago is Starkist, the home of 'Charlie Tuna'. The other – the smaller of the two – is COS Samoa Packing which makes 'Chicken of the Sea'.

Charlie probably wouldn't want to be 'Starkist' if he knew what went on at the cannery. It is estimated that US$250 million worth of tuna per year is caught, killed, cut up and crushed or canned in American Samoa, which amounts to 9.7 million cases (at 48 cans to a case) of tuna per year. Most of the workers relegated to the unpleasant task of cutting and cleaning the fish (yes, it is done by hand) are Independent Samoans and Tongans earn US$3.10 per hour. Though the wage is meagre by American standards, it would be unheard of in the workers' home countries.

To arrange a tour of the canneries, go to the personnel office and ask if they're conducting tours. They may question your motives in order to ascertain that you're not a corporate spy from the other cannery. Chances are you won't be conducted through alone or even in a small group, but if you can muster a group of 10 or more (and your politics check out, of course), your chances of getting in to see all the blood, guts and general carnage involved in the tuna industry are better.

Flowerpot Rocks

The Flowerpot Rocks, or Fatumafuti, are found along the highway, near the village of Faga'alu. The legend says that Fatu and Futi were lovers living on the Manu'a Islands. They wanted to marry but were forbidden to do so because tradition prevents members of the same aiga marrying. Fatu, the woman, built a coconut raft and set off for Tutuila. When Futi learned that she had gone, he was distraught and set out after her. Both their boats were destroyed by a tidal wave as they approached Tutuila and the two lovers were stranded on the reef where they have remained to this day. The area around Fatumafuti is nice for picnics.

Places to Stay

Pago Pago *Herb & Sia's Motel* (☎ 633 5413; fax 699 9557), on the hillside behind Fagatogo, has very basic rooms for US$35/40/60, with shared bathroom (cold water). You can stay in equally basic rooms with private cold shower for US$40/45/65. Not the premium choice.

The *Motu-o-Fiafiaga Hotel* (☎ 633 7777; fax 633 4776), at the south-western end of the harbour in Pago Pago village, is a comfortable mid-range option, which offers air-conditioned rooms with shared (hot) shower for US$60 for single or double occupancy (US$50 if you stay for two or more nights). All rooms have queen-sized beds and TV. Lavalavas are provided for guests and a breakfast of Samoan pancakes (which are more like doughnuts), fruit and coffee is included in the room price. The hotel also has a small workout room and sauna. Adjoining the hotel is a bar and restaurant specialising in Mexican food. After about 10 pm, the restaurant/bar area becomes Evalani's Nightclub with dancing until 2 am six nights a week. The bar is a fair distance away from the rooms so noise isn't a problem. On Sunday, a latest release film is shown with dinner.

The government-run *Rainmaker Hotel* (☎ 633 4241; fax 633 5959), PO Box 996, Pago Pago, named after the famous mountain across the harbour, was built in the early 1960s to give island tourism a kick start. It failed miserably and instead established for itself a reputation as one of the worst hotels in the South Pacific. From all accounts, things have improved in recent years; the hotel underwent renovations for the South Pacific Mini Games in 1997 and when I visited there was little evidence of mould growing on the bedroom carpets (no evidence of carpet either, come to think of it). Even so, the whole place feels like a bit of a relic and standards don't live up to the prices charged.

The rambling fale-style complex, built on

a prime piece of real estate on the harbour in Utulei, has 182 rooms and several self-contained fales. All rooms are air-conditioned and prices are based on double occupancy. Standard (no frills at all) rooms with private bathroom (bath and shower) cost from US$72, VIP Fales cost US$90, and Executive Fales cost US$150. A third bed costs US$15. There's no charge for children under 12, provided they share with their parents and don't require an extra bed! The best rooms are the beachside ones on the 2nd floor.

If you want to book ahead, the hotel asks for a 50% deposit 30 days in advance, with the remainder to be paid before arrival. The hotel has a dining room, a pleasant coffee shop which serves cheaper meals, a bar and a classic oval swimming pool (not open to nonguests) that looks like something out of a Bob Hope and Bing Crosby movie. Guests can also swim at the Rainmaker's private beach, but there are rules: 'No eating or drinking. No horseplay. No swimming after 6 pm'.

Out of Town *Barry's B&B* (☎ 688 2488; fax 633 9111) is a comfortable modern home (all polished wooden floorboards) outside Leone offering four double rooms with shared bathroom for US$35/40. Its only drawback is that it's a long way from the harbour and difficult to reach after 6 pm when the buses stop running. If necessary though, Barry can arrange pick-up from the airport or town. Barry's place is in a quiet and leafy setting a short walk from Leone Falls and an ancient stone quarry site. Barry can provide evening meals for guests, a free laundry service and custom-made island tours which range from gentle outings to strenuous five-hour hikes.

The *Apiolefaga Inn* (☎ 699 9124; fax 699 4892), at Masepa near the American Samoa Community College, has 27 large, air-conditioned rooms with private bathroom (bath and shower), fridge and TV for US$50/60. Breakfast is not included. The inn has a bar, swimming pool and two kitchens that guests can use.

A stone's throw from the airport is the new *Pago Airport Inn* (☎ /fax 699 6333), PO Box 783, Pago Pago, American Samoa 96799, which has 20 air-conditioned rooms with private bathroom, TV, fridge and telephone for US$75/85. There are plans to build a restaurant. The inn is a 20 minute walk or US$3 taxi ride from the airport.

Ta'alolo Lodge (☎ 688 7294; taalolo@ samoetelco.com), opposite the entrance to the 'Ili'ili Golf Course, is an elegant home which has been converted into an upmarket guesthouse. Run by Chande Drabble, the lodge offers bed and breakfast from US$65. Chande will prepare a traditional umu (feast cooked in a ground oven) if guests give her a day's notice. The lodge also has a swimming pool.

Ramona's Place (☎ 644 4976), PO Box 5222, Vatia, American Samoa 96799, is a family home in the quiet, traditional village of Vatia on the north coast of the island. Though only half an hour's drive from Pago Pago, Vatia seems a million miles away from the harbour area. At the time of writing, Ramona's Place offered one guest room for US$45/70 including three meals a day. There's a shared (cold) shower. Another six rooms, kitchenette and hot water are planned.

Tucked away in the family plantation above Vatia is *Rory's Cabin* (☎ 644 1416), PO Box 3412 Pago Pago, American Samoa 96799, where the self-sufficient can reside in rustic splendour for as little as US$10 per night. There's an outside shower and toilet and basic cooking facilities. The garden, which is crammed with exotic fruits and vegetables, is home to dozens of fruit bats. Rory West also runs North Shore Tours, which offers boat and fishing tours around the northern side of the island.

Places to Eat

Most of the restaurants (and shops) on Tutuila are concentrated either in Fagatogo and Pago Pago or along the stretch of highway between Pava'ia'i and Nu'uuli. Foodwise there's not a vast amount of choice and if you particularly want to eat traditional Samoan dishes, you may have to hang a sign around your neck which says: 'I really like taro, breadfruit, *palusami*, suckling pig, baked fish, and fresh tropical fruits'. American Samoans have taken to US-style fast foods with a vengeance, and if you're not careful you can easily end up living on spam and eggs, ham and eggs, bacon and eggs, fried chicken, pizza, Coca-Cola and Cheezeballs.

Snacks & Cheap Meals One place where you can get traditional Samoan dishes, as well as Hawaiian and Chinese dishes, is at *Da Mak's Island Style Restaurant*, behind the market. Run by Gretchen and Mel Makaiwi, the cafe-style restaurant has a very pleasant outdoor section which overlooks the harbour. It's open for breakfast and lunch from 6.30 am to 4 pm Monday to Friday. A cooked breakfast costs US$3.75; lunch, which may include Hawaiian-style palusami with pork or Chinese roast duck, costs from US$3 to US$6. There are a few other places near the market which serve decent cheap meals. *Te'o Brothers Kitchen* and *Milovale's Drive-In*, next to each other on the eastern side of the market, offer fish and chips, curries, barbecue lamb and chicken, hot dogs and sausage, taro and chop suey for about US$4 for a heaping plateful. They're both open from around 5 am to 3 pm Monday to Saturday. Milovale's is open 24 hours on Friday.

Krystal's Burger is a popular chain serving some of the best burgers in the territory as well as a variety of other meals. There's a Krystal's in town opposite the market, one in Nu'uuli, one in Leone and another at the airport. A full cooked breakfast costs US$6.99; burgers, hot dogs and sandwiches cost from US$4; a plate of teriyaki chicken with steamed rice and salad is US$5.99. The Krystal's Burger outlets are open seven days a week from 5 am until midnight.

Behind Tedi of Samoa, the unpleasantly flourescent *Pizza Time* (☎ 633 1199) sells pizzas (US$10 for a medium-sized pizza) and other fast foods. Call for deliveries. Keep an eye out for *Paisano's Pizzeria Deli*, which

is reportedly to reopen next to the Samoa News building in Fagatogo.

Evie's Cantina, adjoining the Motu-o-Fiafiaga Hotel at the south-western end of the bay, specialises in Mexican food. Dishes start at around US$5 and go up to US$15 for steaks. It's open daily for lunch and dinner. It also has karaoke nightly, and on Sunday night a latest release movie is shown with dinner.

The *Coffee Shop* at the Rainmaker Hotel, open from 6 am to 10 pm seven days a week, serves the usual range of American Samoan fare. A cooked breakfast here costs around US$6, sandwiches from US$4, fish and chips US$5.75, and steaks US$9.

The *Pago Pago Yacht Club* in Utulei serves lunch from 11.30 am Monday to Friday. For about US$4 you'll get a burger or hot dog, chips and coleslaw. On Friday nights during happy hour (5 to 7 pm), it serves similar fare.

The *Deluxe Cafe* (☎ 699 4000), out of town next to the Nu'uuli Cinemas, is a very pleasant, air-conditioned US-diner-style place open for breakfast, lunch and dinner seven days a week. Lunch and dinner specialities include fresh local fish, salads and imported steaks. The extensive breakfast menu includes (as do those at most places) a bottomless cup of real coffee. Other places in the Nu'uuli/Tafuna area include *A & A Pizza Mac's Drive-Thru* which serves everything from pizza and teriyaki sandwiches to burgers; *Chicken Out*, near the hospital, with (you guessed it) chicken-in-a-basket; the *Powerhouse Bar & Grill*, which is mostly for the benefit of lunch customers from the Tafuna Industrial Park; and the popular *Subway Sandwich Shop*, just west of the airport. There are a also couple of fast-food places in the new Laufou Shopping Center.

Oriental Restaurants American Samoa has plenty of Chinese restaurants as well as a few Korean restaurants and even one Filipino-style place. Most of the Chinese restaurants offer reasonably priced lunchtime buffets. For very good, inexpensive Filipino-style meals featuring lots of vegetables, try *Pinoys*

AMERICAN SAMOA

in the Samoa Sports building between Fagatogo and Utulei. In Pago Park at the head of the harbour you'll find a cluster of bargain-basement food stalls selling all sorts of Korean, Chinese and pseudo-Samoan dishes. US$3 will buy you a plateful of food big enough for a Samoan football player (in fact, quite a few do take a break here from practice in the park). The kiosks normally run out of food around 2.30 or 3 pm.

The most popular Chinese restaurant in town is the *Hong Kong Restaurant* (☎ 699 1055), in Nu'uuli, which offers an extensive menu featuring carefully prepared Chinese favourites. A full meal with rice costs around US$12, but you can order a very good vegetable deluxe for as little as US$5.95. The hot sour soup is excellent. The restaurant is open for lunch and dinner seven days a week. A new Hong Kong Restaurant is planned for the Pago Plaza.

Also good value is *Taima's Garden*, 100m west of the airport turn-off on the mountain side of the road, which serves Oriental and Samoan food, including great fish dishes, plantains, taro, curry and the like. The restaurant has a bar and a pleasant terrace. The Chinese menu at the *Pago Pago Bay Restaurant* is also very good, though a bit more expensive than the others. The *Pacific Restaurant*, just beyond the tuna canneries, serves some of the best Korean food in the territory.

More Expensive Restaurants

At the cheaper end of this category is *Rubble's Tavern* (☎ 699 4403) at the Nu'uuli Shopping Center. It's very popular with locals and expats alike and is a good option for a relaxed lunch or supper washed down with a cold beer. The lunch menu features very US-style items such as broiled jerk chicken, homemade meat loaf and New York steak (US$13.95). The dinner menu includes fresh fish (US$15) as well as featuring pasta dishes (US$13). Rubble's is open from 11 am to midnight seven days a week, with happy hour from 4.30 to 6 pm.

The *Country Club* at the 'Ili'ili Golf Course is another pleasant, upmarket option

with a similar range of dishes and prices. It's open daily for breakfast, lunch and dinner. The adjoining sports bar offers pool and darts and there's live music every Thursday, Friday and Saturday night.

With its period decor and atmosphere, *Sadie's Resaurant* (☎ 633 5981) is the most elegant and expensive restaurant in the territory. It's very popular with expats, yachties and business people but travellers and tourists will appreciate the option, too. The menu features lots of seafood, including scallops, lobster tails and enormous portions of sashimi. Most main courses hover at around US$18, going up to US$26 for lobster tails. The wine list features a good selection of Californian and Australian wines starting at around US$20 per bottle (US$3.25 by the glass). Sadie's is open Monday to Saturday for lunch and dinner.

The *Pago Pago Bay Restaurant*, a favourite with yachties, overlooks the water at the south-west end of the harbour. The menu (cheaper than Sadie's) features American, Chinese and Samoan dishes. The dining room at the *Rainmaker Hotel*, which is open from 6 am to 10 pm Monday to Saturday and for dinner on Sunday, offers burgers and steaks (from US$9 up to US$23), seafood, Chinese dishes and Samoan specialities. On Friday evening, a buffet dinner accompanies the Rainmaker's own *fiafia*, or 'Polynesian Floor Show'. *Sadie Thompson's Lounge*, the bar at the Rainmaker, often has live music, and happy hour from 4.30 to 6.30 pm Monday to Friday.

Self-Catering

If you want locally grown fresh fruit and vegetables, the central market in Fagatogo is the place to go. It is open Monday to Saturday, but if you want the best produce go late on Friday night (about 11 pm) or very early Saturday morning (around 5 am). Fresh fish is available at the *Star of the Sea* fish market, near the shore behind the main market. You'll find plenty of supermarkets and small Korean-run stores on Tutuila that sell more or less the same fare available on the mainland for only slightly higher prices.

Fly inc. in Nu'uuli sells a good range of groceries for reasonable prices. For the best bread on the island (olive bread, cheese bread, rye and foccacio plus NZ-style cream buns and steak pies) go to the bakery beside the Transpac Store at the Nu'uuli Shopping Center. Other favourites for provisions are *Kruse* at Leone village and *Haleck's* at Pavai'ia'i.

For local shoppers, *Tom Ho Ching*, near the hospital in Faga'alu, is popular due to its convenient opening hours: 7 am to 11 pm Monday to Saturday. There's a store open 24 hours a day – *Pila Patu's Store* – opposite the service station towards the south-western end of the harbour. The enormous *Cost-U-Less Store* near the airport sells imported groceries and household goods.

Entertainment

Bars & Nightclubs Rated by some as one of the best bars in the world, *Tisa's Barefoot Bar* (☎ 622 7447) is a characterful fale bar on Alega Beach, about 10km east of Pago Pago (50 cents by bus). It's open from 10 am until midnight seven days a week, and there's always something happening at Tisa's: jazz nights, kava nights, full moon parties, you name it. The beach itself is one of the best on the island; you can swim and snorkel here but there are strong currents so check with locals regarding the safest spots.

Sadie's Restaurant has an elegant bar which occasionally has live music. This is not to be confused with *The Sadie Thompson Lounge* in the Rainmaker Hotel. The lounge, open Monday to Friday from 11.30 am to midnight, features live music from the Why Why Band. Happy hour is between 4.30 and 6.30 pm. The *Dining Room* at the Rainmaker (☎ 633 4241) has a regular Friday evening buffet and 'Polynesian Floor Show'.

Rubble's Tavern, in Nu'uuli, is a pleasant place for a cold beer (and good food). The *Country Club* at the golf course has a big US-style sports bar with pool, darts and TV sport. Near the tennis courts on Ottoville Rd is the *Player's Sports Club*, with a bar, pool tables, dart boards and giant-screen video.

Adjoining the Motu-o-Fiafiaga Hotel in Pago Pago is *Evalani's Cabaret* which is open Monday to Saturday nights. There's karaoke until 10 pm followed by dancing to Rockamerica and ZTV Music videos on a big screen. The general age range is mid-20s to 30s. Evalani's also serves food and on Sunday nights latest release movies are shown with dinner.

Silver Bros, a popular nightclub near the turn-off to the airport, features live Polynesian-style rock and roll most nights. Nightclubs close at 2 pm. You can expect to pay around US$3 for a drink.

If you're hoping to crew on a yacht or would just like to meet and associate with yachties, the best time and place to do so would be during the Friday night happy hour from 5 to 7 pm at the *Pago Pago Yacht Club* in Utulei. During the cruising season, it's usually packed. Light meals are available. Free hot showers are also available, but plan on long queues, especially on Friday nights. Also on Fridays, locals hold rowing practice in the *fautasi* (longboats) stored in sheds outside. The yacht club is generally open from 11.30 am to 9 pm Monday to Saturday.

The seamy side of Pago Pago is to be found on the northern side of the harbour, where a rag-tag collection of Chinese and Korean-run bars, pool halls and 'nightclubs' with tell-tale names such as the *Red Door* are gathered above the tuna canneries.

Cinemas The new multiscreen cinema complex on the main road in Nu'uuli, just east of the Deluxe Cafe, screens latest-release commercial movies.

Around the Island

As soon as you leave the Pago Pago Harbor area, you'll feel as if you've entered a different world. In rural Tutuila, everything moves at more of a Polynesian pace than in the capital. Around the island there is quite a lot to see and do – nice walks, white beaches, archaeological and historical sites, waterfalls and the like. Because the island is so small

AMERICAN SAMOA

and the public transport so frequent, everything is fairly near at hand.

EASTERN DISTRICT

The eastern district of Tutuila includes the harbour area and everything east. Less populated and more rugged than the western half of the island, it is also less congested with traffic and commerce.

National Park of American Samoa

The Tutuila section of the national park is in the north-central part of the island between the villages of Fagasa to the west and Afona to the east. Bounded by the Maugaloa Ridge to the south, this section of the park covers 1000 hectares of land (most of which is covered in lowland and montane rainforest) as well as 480 hectares of offshore waters.

The national park was officially established in 1993 when a 50 year lease was signed; even though the National Park Service (NPS) manages the land, it belongs to traditional Samoan landowners who continue to grow subsistence crops around the villages of Vatia and Afono and in the Amalau Valley.

At the time of writing, the 5km trail from Fagasa Pass to Mt Alava (see Mt Alava in the previous section) was the only official hiking trail in this section of the park. The NPS, however, plans to extend the Mt Alava trail another 3km along the crest of the Maugaloa Ridge to Afona Pass on the road between Aua and Vatia. The NPS also proposes to rehabilitate the steep 2km trail which leads from the ridge down to the village of Vatia. At the time of writing, this trail was impassable. Anyone wanting to explore the national park should contact the superintendent by phone or email (see Information in the earlier Pago Pago section).

Amalau Valley

From the village of Aua on the north coast of the harbour, a surfaced road switchbacks steeply up to Rainmaker Pass and continues equally steeply down to Afono and beautiful Vatia. The views from the pass down to either side of the island are spectacular. Between Afona and Vatia is the secluded Amalau Valley which is home to many forest bird species and to Samoas two rare species of flying fox or fruit bat. Look for flying foxes early in the morning or late in the afternoon. The NPS plans to build a parking area and observation platform a short distance from the road here.

Vatia Situated on the edge of a wide, coral-fringed bay, Vatia is a charming and friendly village which seems a million miles away from the big smoke over the ridge. From Vatia you can view The Pola, a tiny uninhabited island just offshore whose magnificent sheer cliffs rise more than 120m straight out of the ocean. The craggy cliffs are home to numerous sea birds including frigate birds, boobies, white terns, tropicbirds and noddy terns. To get there, go to the end of the road through the village and then walk 300m along the coral rubble beach. The NPS plans to build a trail here for easier access as well as a scenic lookout across to The Pola along the road at Sauma Ridge about 3km outside Vatia.

Vatia offers basic accommodation for visitors who would like to sample village life. Ramona Tuiasosopo has inexpensive rooms in her village home and Rory West has a rustic cabin on his plantation above the village. (For details see Out of Town under Places to Stay in the Pago Pago section.) Rory also offers boat and fishing tours around the northern side of the island. Aiga buses go to Vatia (US$1.50) several times a day.

Rainmaker Mountain

Also known as Mt Pioa, this 523m mountain is the culprit that traps rain clouds and gives Pago Pago Harbor more than its fair share of wet weather. It is Tutuila's best example of a volcanic plug associated with the major fissure zone that created the island. Although it appears as one peak from below, the summit is actually three-pronged. The separate peaks are known locally as North Pioa, South Pioa and Sinapioa. Rainmaker Mountain and its base area are designated a national landmark site due to the pristine

Winged Guardians of the Forest

Flying foxes are an important part of Samoa's culture and are the source of many traditional stories, myths and legends. In Samoan legends, flying foxes are regarded as guardians of the forest and rescuers of people in distress.

There are two species of flying foxes in Samoa, *Pteropus tonganus*, called *pe'a fanua* in Samoan, and *Pteropus samoensis*, known as *pe'a vao*. The former translates as 'fruit bat of settled lands' and the latter as 'fruit bat of the forest'.

The *P. samoensis* roosts alone or in small groups in the canopy of ridge-top trees. This species is unique since it is active during the day, with two feeding peaks, one in the morning and the other in the late afternoon.

The *P. tonganus* often roosts in groups of up to several hundred. Although found in the primary forest, it also exists in secondary forest growth, sometimes close to villages.

Flying foxes play an essential role as pollinators and seed dispersers of a significant portion of the tropical forest plants. They are considered to be key species because their presence helps to maintain the ecological balance and community structure of the forest.

Adult members of both species have a wingspan of just under 1m and weigh about 500g. The *P. samoensis* has a distinct light-coloured face and a brown body sprinkled with greyish-white and broad wings. The *P. tonganus* has a black face and a seal-brown body with a mantle that varies from buff to pale cream, and narrower wings.

During the 1980s, there was a massive decline in the Pacific flying fox populations due to deforestation and commercial hunting. The major market for Pacific flying foxes is Guam, a US territory, where they are considered a delicacy. Both Samoas have now banned commercial export of all flying fox species. The National Park of American Samoa and the rainforest preserves at Falealupo and Tafua on Savai'i in Independent Samoa provide vital habitats for flying foxes. ■

AMERICAN SAMOA

nature of the tropical vegetation on the slopes.

Fagasa

Fagasa (meaning 'sacred bay'), the village over the pass from Pago Pago, has an interesting legend associated with it. A group of three men and three women sailed from the western end of Tutuila in search of better fishing grounds and a place to start a new village. At dusk, they passed the mouth of a strange bay and in it saw a circle of mysterious lights. They panicked, believing that the *aitu* (spirits) had thrown down stars from the sky to prevent them from entering the bay because it was a sacred and forbidden place. As the lights approached, it became apparent that they were the eyes of dolphins, sent by the voyagers' ancestors to light their way and lead them into this ideal spot. Today, the people of the village revere dolphins which shelter there on their annual migrations. The people believe that Tuiatua, the spirit of the elements, guards their bay and protects the dolphins.

Alega Beach

One of Tutuila's finest beaches, Alega

Star Mounds of Ancient Power

More than 140 distinctive earthen, and sometimes stone, mounds, dating back to late prehistoric times, have been found scattered across the Samoan archipelago. Dubbed star mounds, the structures range from 6 to 30m in length, are up to 3m high and have from one to 11 ray-like projections radiating from their base.

It is highly probable that these mounds were used for pigeon-catching, which isn't as pedestrian as it may sound. An extremely important sport of chiefs, it had a five month season, from June until the end of September, and involved nearly the entire population of the islands. The people would follow their *matai* (chiefs) into the forest to observe and support competitions.

In 1887, William B Churchward, the British Consul in Samoa, wrote:

Pigeon-snaring is the oldest and most cherished sport in all Samoa, and until lately, partook much more of the nature of a fixed ceremony than a mere amusement. It was made the occasion for feasting and junketing in a high degree, and whilst it lasted all sorts of irregularities could be indulged in without comment.

American archaeologists David Herdrich and Jeffrey Clark believe there is very strong evidence to suggest that though the structures were used primarily for pigeon-catching, they also served a much more complex function in Samoan society. There is evidence that they were used as sites for ritual activity related to marriage, healing and warfare. They also believe the star mounds came to reflect the position of the matai and the field in which personal ability and *mana* (supernatural power) could be expressed. Star mounds therefore would have become places of power in their own right.

In an interview with an American PhD student, C Forsyth, in 1983, a Samoan *ali'i* (high chief) commented:

Do you know the star mounds? Well, they had to do with the *taulasea* (traditional healer) and energy and with special powers. The ancient Samoans did not build those just to catch pigeons. No Sir! They were part of our ancient religion, and so were the taulasea and the *taulaitu* (spirit medium). Look into the archaeology data on the mounds. The energy is still so strong on those mounds that it raises the hair on your body to visit them. ■

Beach, is just 10km east of Pago Pago (50 cents by aiga bus). It's not only a great place to swim and snorkel (check currents and conditions with locals first) but with Tisa's Barefoot Bar (see Entertainment in the earlier Pago Pago section) right on the beach (where you'll find everything from full moon parties to Nude Fridays), it's the perfect spot for a cold beer or three. There's a small charge to use the beach.

Masefau & Sa'ilele

Near the village of Faga'itua, another cross-island road goes over to the north coast. At the pass, this one splits. The left fork leads down to the beautiful bay and village of Masefau. The right fork goes to the tiny settlement of Masa'usi and then through dense forest to Sa'ilele, which has one of the loveliest beaches on the entire island. The sandy area below the large rock outcrop at the western end provides an excellent place

for a barbecue or picnic. Ask permission in the village first, of course. On a track east of the village of Sa'ilele is a burial ground of reasonable interest where some *ali'i* (high chiefs) are buried.

Au'asi Falls

Above the village of Au'asi is a pleasant waterfall, a nice place to cool off on a hot day. It can be reached by walking up the stream for about half an hour. If it's been raining, the falls will be especially impressive. The ferry to Aunu'u Island leaves from Au'asi.

Aoa

Although the road between Amouli and Aoa is scenically rather uninteresting, more than 40 ancient star mounds have been discovered, but not yet excavated, in the bush near the spine of the island. In addition to the star mounds, Polynesian plainware (a type of undecorated pottery) has been found in the Aoa area. Some estimates date the potshards found here from as early as 1000 BC, but the figure currently accepted by the scientific community is 500 BC. The Samoan elders of today have no recollection or knowledge of the historical use of pottery by the culture, nor are there any legends pertaining to it.

Tula

Tula, the easternmost village on Tutuila, is a quiet and laid-back place with a pleasant white beach. It is the end of the bus line east, but if you have a reliable vehicle or feel like a nice walk, you can continue around the end of the island to Cape Mata'ula and Onenoa, a beautiful area of high cliffs, small plantations and forested slopes. As in all villages, it's a good idea not to wander into the more traditional area of Onenoa on Sunday, but the area between the villages has plenty of places to picnic, especially above the cliffs. There are apparently good right and left reef breaks at Tula – for more information on surfing see Activities in the American Samoa Facts for the Visitor chapter.

WESTERN DISTRICT

Although the western end of Tutuila sees much more activity than the area to the east of the harbour – primarily due to the placement of the airport, shopping areas and the Tafuna Industrial Complex – it still has numerous points of interest and secluded beaches and walks. If you have a vehicle, allow at least two days to explore this end of the island. Those relying on public transport should plan on at least twice that.

Virgin Falls

A 1km walk past the LBJ Tropical Medical Center in Faga'alu leads to a small rock quarry. From there, a rough trail climbs past a series of waterfalls. Some of the pools beneath the falls are suitable for bathing. The surrounding vegetation is beautifully lush so you may have to make your own trail in some sections. Watch for sudden rock slides, as the ravine is quite steep in areas. Allow a couple

of hours for the return walk if you plan to climb all the way to the top fall.

Matafao Peak

At 653m, Matafao Peak is the highest point on Tutuila. The peak itself, like Rainmaker Mountain across the harbour, is a remnant of the great volcanic plug and more evidence of the origins of Tutuila Island. Above the 350m level, the peak area is designated a national landmark site.

Nu'uuli

Nu'uuli is primarily a loosely defined shopping area along the main road between Coconut Point and the airport turn-offs. There are quite a few restaurants along here, including the recommended Hong Kong Restaurant, the Deluxe Cafe and Rubble's Tavern (see Places to Eat in the earlier Pago Pago section), as well as the Nu'uuli Shopping Center, the Laufou Shopping Center and the Nu'uuli Cinema complex.

American Samoa Community College

American Samoa Community College is the territory's only tertiary-education institution. The main campus at Mapusaga runs a variety of courses including business, prelaw and marine biology. Masters and PhD programs are available, too. Also associated

Fire and Forgiveness

When fire swept through the village of Vaitogi 100 years ago, the villagers knew that god was punishing them for their evil ways (it is said that the entire village made its living from stealing). Vaitogi and neighbouring 'Ili'ili were side-by-side, but the fire burned only the houses and lands of Vaitogi – 'Ili'ili remained untouched. As the fire raged, the people of Vaitogi crowded into their church to pray for forgiveness. When it began to rain, they knew their prayers had been answered.

On the anniversary of the fire, some time in late September, the main road into Vaitogi is closed and for 24 hours everyone in the village goes into the church to pray and give thanks for the salvation of their village. ∎

with the college are a nursing school at the hospital and vocational facilities in the Tafuna Industrial Complex. The college library has an extensive collection of South Pacific titles.

Tia Seu Lupe

The American Samoa Historic Preservation Office maintains a particularly well-preserved ancient Polynesian star mound, *tia seu lupe* (literally 'earthern mound to catch pigeons'), near the Catholic cathedral at Tafuna. The mound has a unique connecting platform and intriguing views across to Matafao Peak, the tallest point on the island. Call the Historic Preservation Office (☎ 633 2384) for an excellent personalised tour of the site. Adjoining the site is a small rainforest reserve. The nearby cathedral contains some beautiful woodcarving and a fabulous photo-realist painting of a traditional Samoan family by Duffy Sheridan.

Turtle & Shark Site

In the picturesque village of Vaitogi, along a scenic stretch of black lava coast, the most famous of Tutuila's legends is set. Unfortunately, there are so many versions of it that it's difficult to choose one that relates here. The two that follow are the ones that most often surface, but I suspect that you could ask five Samoans to relate the legend and get five completely different tales!

According to one explanation, a young husband on Upolu was selected as the 'guest of honour' at a cannibalistic feast to be given by King Malietoa Faiga. He chose, understandably, to decline the invitation. The man and his wife set out in a canoe, but while attempting to escape there was a storm and they were blown to Tutuila where they were put up by Letuli, the pulenu'u of 'Ili'ili.

When the practice of cannibalism fell into disfavour, Letuli offered them a free trip home, but they refused. Instead, as repayment for his kindness, they jumped into the sea. The husband became a shark and his wife a turtle. The husband told the chief that any time a gathering of children sang from

The legendary green turtle – listen for children singing

the shore at Vaitogi, a turtle and a shark would appear to greet them.

Another version relates that the turtle and shark are an old blind lady and her grand-daughter who jumped into the sea after being turned out of their village on Savai'i. It was during a time of famine and the two were incapable of providing for themselves. When their family learned what they'd done, they went to the shore, guilt-ridden, and called the pair by name. When the turtle and shark appeared, they knew that their family members were all right.

If you visit the site on a tour, you'll have the opportunity to watch a group of children singing to call the turtle and the shark. According to local sources, the shark will always turn up if given sufficient time. The turtle, unfortunately, isn't quite so reliable.

Even if the turtle and shark have taken the day off, you'll enjoy the solitude of the place, with its black lava cliffs, heavy surf, tide pools, blowholes and sandy beach. The walk up the road west to Sail Rock Point, through pandanus and coconut groves, is also nice.

Fagatele Bay National Marine Sanctuary

Fagatele Bay is a submerged volcanic crater

surrounded by steep cliffs. The area contains the last remaining stretch of coastal rainforest on the island. In 1986 the fringing coral reef in the bay was designated a national marine sanctuary.

Nearly 200 species of coral are recovering from a devastating crown-of-thorns starfish attack in the late 1970s which destroyed more than 90% of the corals. Scientists remain undecided as to whether the boom-and-bust cycle of the crown-of-thorns is natural or the outcome of human activity. It may be the result of increased erosion which provides an unnaturally high volume of nutrients that nourish the plankton that in turn support the young starfish. The coral is slowly recovering, however, and the fish population remains vibrant.

The sanctuary is also home to several marine mammal species. Southern humpback whales winter here from August to November, several varieties of porpoise occasionally visit and sperm whales have been seen. Threatened and endangered species of marine turtles such as hawksbill and green sea turtles also use the bay. Other less frequent visitors include the leatherback, the loggerhead and the olive Ridley sea turtle.

The rocky cliffs surrounding the bay are home to numerous seabirds. All but traditional fishing methods are prohibited in the inner bay, the taking of invertebrates is prohibited and historical artefacts found in the bay are protected. It is possible to dive, snorkel and swim in the bay, but access is difficult. Contact the Marine and Wildlife Resources Office (☎ 633 7354; fax 633 7355), down by the market in Fagatogo, to arrange transport.

Sliding Rock

The sliding rock, near Leone on the side road between Taputimu and Vailoa, is on an interesting coast of black, table-flat volcanic terraces. The tilted one farthest from the road is the sliding rock. It's nondescript when dry, but when it's wet, local children use it as a slippery slide.

Leone

The village of Leone is the second-largest settlement on Tutuila and served as the Polynesian capital of the island. It was also the landing site of the first missionary, John Williams, who arrived on 18 October 1832 after spending two years in Western Samoa. One product of his work is the imposing church in Leone, which was the first church in American Samoa.

There is a monument to Williams' efforts in front of the building. It is well maintained, and if it's open, the interior is worth a look – it has nice stained-glass windows and beautiful woodwork on the ceiling.

Also, if heading west from Leone, look for the tiny rocky islet across the bay which supports just a single coconut tree – the stuff of desert island cartoons! Leone village also has a post office, and a bakery that is a nice place to stop for something gooey. Aiga buses direct to leave every couple of minutes from the main terminal in Fagatogo, but

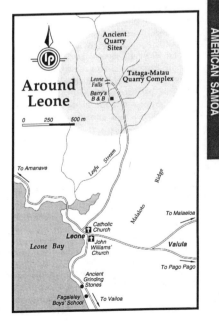

Leone is the turnaround point. If you'd like to travel beyond there on the main road, you'll have to wait in front of the church for a westbound bus.

Leone Falls & Ancient Quarry

The small waterfall and ancient stone quarry complex behind Leone village is close to Barry's B&B and, if you're staying there, Barry will be happy to point you in the right direction. Otherwise, to get to the waterfall go up the road past the white Catholic church near the town centre to the end of the pavement, then follow the short walking track to the head of the valley, where a ribbon-like waterfall plunges into a moss-covered basin. An artificial catchment barrier creates a freshwater pool at the bottom. It's a cool and pleasant spot, but wear strong footwear for the brief walk as the track can be extremely muddy.

The light is best for taking photographs between noon and around 2 pm. It's a fine spot for a swim if there's enough water.

The basalt quarry, known as Tataga Matau (meaning 'hit the rock'), above Leone is one of the most important archaeological sites in the South Pacific. Surveys carried out during the past 10 years have identified 10 quarry sites on Tutuila and archaeologists believe the island was the centre of a large trade network that stretched across the South Pacific. Artefacts made of stone from the Tutuila quarries have turned up as far away as the Solomons.

Unlike the western islands of the archipelago, the rock on Tutuila is exposed and therefore accessible. In 1985, archaeologists Helen Leach and Dan Witter, with the help of some local villagers, set about investigating the Leone quarry. Near Leafu Stream, they found numerous finished basalt adzes and cutting tools as well as 'pre-form' tools. Pre-form tools are those that have been excavated, chipped and worked on a bit, and then discarded before they have actually been finished. The finishing process of the day involved grinding the tool on a whetstone to a fine point or edge. There's a large number of grinding stones on the shoreline near

Fagaleley Boys' School (see the entry below). There's also a star mound at the Leone quarry similar to those found at Aoa near the eastern end of Tutuila.

Fagaleley Boys' School

Just south of Leone Bay are the remains of Fagaleley Boys' School, built by the London Missionary Society (LMS) as the first secondary school on the island in around 1855. Boys trained here for entry into the society's seminary in Western Samoa. The school closed in 1926 and has gradually fallen into disrepair. About 4km up the coast, and visible from the boys' school, is the ruin of Atauloma Girls' School, which was built by the LMS in 1900. About 300m north-east of Fagaleley Boys' School, you'll find an extraordinary series of perfectly round hollows ground into the volcanic rocks on the shoreline. These are ancient whetstones, used for grinding stone tools and weapons. Tutuila, seems, was the centre of a Pacific-wide trade network (see the entry above). Ask local families for permission to wander down to the shoreline.

Massacre Bay

The hiking trail down to A'asuat Massacre Bay leaves from the village of A'oloaufou, high on the spine of Tutuila, above Pava'ia'i on the main road. Massacre Bay is the site where, on 11 December 1787, 12 men from the crew of La Pérouse's ships La Boussole and Astrolabe as well as 39 Samoans were killed in a skirmish. There is an obscure monument in A'asu commemorating the European crew members who died there.

To get to A'oloaufou, take a Leone-bound bus from the market in Fagatogo to Pava'ia'i (75 cents) and wait on the corner there for one headed up the hill.

Across from the large park in A'oloaufou is the colourful garden that began life as an attempt by the Department of Tourism to create sites of interest on Tutuila. The trail to A'asu takes off downhill just east of that garden and continues for about 4km to the beach.

The first kilometre of the track is a little

intimidating; it's a veritable mudhole, and you'll be slogging in slippery, shoe-grabbing, ankle-deep ooze, so lace up your shoes tightly or remove them altogether. In the dry season, you can relax because you can be sure the trail will improve further on and will remain that way until just before the beach. Even so, most of the way down, the trail base is volcanic clay that turns waxy and treacherous when wet, which it is most of the time, and due caution should be exercised.

There is only one family living in the old deserted village of A'asu. On arrival, it's best to introduce yourself and ask for permission to use their beach. The worn-out admonition not to go on Sundays again holds. For this or any other hike in Samoa, wear long trousers since weeds grow close to the trail and thorns and sharp grasses can slice unprotected shins to ribbons.

For this trip, strong hikers should plan on an hour to walk down and half again as long for the climb back up. Take plenty of water, hat, sunscreen, insect repellent and a picnic lunch. There is no road outlet from Aasu. Also from A'oloaufou (which means 'new A'oloau') you will find a trail to the abandoned village of A'oloautuai (meaning 'old A'oloau') and another down the ridge to Fagamalo, where there are infrequent buses back to town. Most of the time both these trails are muddy and badly overgrown, so if they become particularly difficult it's probably best to turn back rather than press on in the hope that things will improve.

If you really enjoy walking, though, don't allow yourself to become discouraged by locals. Most of them have lived beside the tracks all their lives and never set foot on any of them. Most Samoans won't be able to fathom why anyone would want to do such a thing without some very good reason, and even if you can provide a good reason, they'll normally recommend you do it 'tomorrow'.

Cape Taputapu

The village of Amanave lies at the end of the beaten path. A short distance beyond the village on Loa inlet is a lovely white-sand beach, generally known as Palagi Beach. It's just east of Cape Taputapu, which is Tutuila's westernmost point and a national natural landmark site.

If you're in a rental vehicle, leave it by the bush store in Amanave and ask for permission to use the beach. You can walk to the beach via the track above the shoreline, or walk/wade along the reef at low tide. Be sure to check the tide times and don't go out alone. Allow about 10 or 15 minutes to get to the beach. You can paddle and snorkel in the small pool by the offshore island but be mindful of strong currents and a nearby *ava*.

Sea birds nest on the offshore island. The word *taputapu* means 'forbidden' (taboo-taboo), and the cape was so named because it was the only source of paper mulberry trees on the island. The discoverers wanted to keep the bark for themselves so they could sell it to folks on other parts of the island. No doubt they related fearful tales and a taboo was placed on it.

Beyond Amanave, the road climbs steeply and winds up and down through valleys and over ridges to the small villages of Poloa, Fagali'i, Maloata and Fagamalo, where the road ends. There are some spectacular views of the wild and trackless north coast of Tutuila.

Aunu'u Island

Tiny Aunu'u Island, only 3sq km in area, lies off the south-eastern end of Tutuila. It is a treasure house of natural phenomena and serves as a tranquil and pristine place to spend a day, if not longer. The waters around the island are clear and blue and the one village is spacious and unspoilt. What's more, with no vehicles on the island and the traffic-choked south coast of Tutuila far away, you'll appreciate the silence and solitude. Since it's only a couple of kilometres from end to end, the island can be quickly and easily explored on foot in a day, with plenty of time left over for a picnic at churn-

AMERICAN SAMOA

ing Ma'ama'a Cove, looking for shells on the beach and a swim in the harbour.

As usual in Samoa, Sundays in Aunu'u are only for sleeping, eating, visiting and attending one of the three churches serving the village of 500 people. Outsiders are not welcome on Sunday and the villagers will let such trespassers know it. However disagreeable that may seem, it's a fact of life in the Samoas, and visitors may as well learn to deal with it. At other times, however, they're a friendly lot, and most enjoy the diversion provided by the presence of visitors.

Pala Lake

Heading north from the village, you will arrive at Pala Lake after walking about 700m. This beautiful and deadly-looking expanse is a sea of fiery red quicksand, and it's a safe bet to say you'll never have seen anything like it before. During the rainy season, the sand thins out and is inhabited by Grey Ducks. All birds and bats are now protected in American Samoa, but once upon a time locals would shoot the ducks and then swim out to retrieve the carcasses. To avoid being sucked down into sandy doom, swim-

mers had to remain horizontal at all times and propel themselves only using their arms.

Red Lake

Red Lake lies in the middle of Fa'imulivai Marsh, which, in turn, lies in the middle of Aunu'u's pronounced volcanic crater. It is filled with eels and tilapia fish. They are sometimes caught with a hook, but thanks to the lake's frequent level changes, there is an easier method. When the water is high, the eels move out to the lake's margins in search of food in the newly flooded areas. When the water drains, it does so quickly, leaving the eels stranded around the edges. The people consider them good eating, and at this point all they have to do is gather them up.

The water of Red Lake really is reddish – the colour of weak tea. If you want to get a look at it and the eels, you can walk out to the edge on the sedges that surround the marsh. To get there, follow the track past Pala Lake and up the hill to the crater. There is a well-groomed track around the crater, but access to the lake is a little tricky, since it will necessitate a bit of bushwhacking on the approach. The best place to have a go at it is

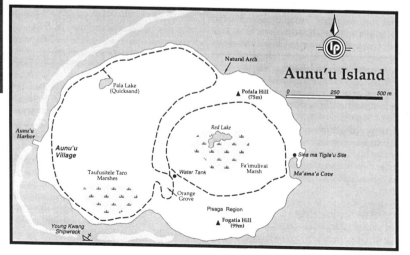

Aunu'u Island

Natural Arch

Pala Lake (Quicksand)

▲ Pofala Hill (75m)

0   250   500 m

Aunu'u Harbor

Red Lake

Aunu'u Village

Sina ma Tigila'u Site

Taufusitele Taro Marshes

Water Tank

Fa'imulivai Marsh

Ma'ama'a Cove

Orange Grove

Pisaga Region

▲ Fogatia Hill (99m)

Young Kwang Shipwreck

from the western side of the crater north of the intersection of the village trails. If you'd like a local guide to come with you, ask around in the village.

Ma'ama'a Cove

The word 'cove' may normally conjure up visions of a peaceful inlet, but this place is not what its name implies. This bowl in the rocks is actually more a cauldron of surf that boils, pounds and sprays dramatically over, through and around the rocks. The wave action here seems to be completely random and is good for hours of entertainment, but don't venture too close to the edge. Stray and completely unexpected waves appear out of nowhere and will wash away forever anything in their path.

Legends say that this is the site of Sina ma Tigila'u (Sina and Tigila'u), two lovers who were shipwrecked here. You can make out bits of crossed 'rope' and broken 'planks' embedded in the rocks around the cove. There is also a powerful blowhole not far from the edge. There is never any water blown out of it but sand thrown into it will be blown back out.

Pisaga

The Pisaga is a region just inside the crater, below Fogatia Hill. Here people are forbidden to call out or make loud noises lest they disturb the aitu that inhabit this place. The Samoans believe that those who make noise may be answered by an irritable spirit. When Gavin Bell, author of *In Search of Tusitala – Travels in the Pacific after Robert Louis Stevenson*, visited he felt that all he needed was 'a bit of swirling mist to imagine that around the next corner I would find a wicked witch in a gingerbread house, with a soul as black as her cooking pot'. For a superb view over Red Lake, as well as Aunu'u village, climb up past the water tank on the slopes of Fogatia Hill.

Other Attractions

The western slope of the crater is planted with an orange grove, a new crop diversification project in American Samoa. Below that, along the trail, are the Taufusitele Taro Marshes, which are planted Hawaiian-style with swamp taro, a rarity in this part of Polynesia. On the reef just south of town is the wreck of the Korean tuna boat *Young Kwang* (interestingly enough, a ship of the same name lies on the reef off Niuatoputapu Island in Tonga). It was empty when it became lodged here while on a test-run in the early 1980s. The harbour in the village is safe, calm and great for a refreshing swim. There is also a nice bit of coral nearby and excellent underwater visibility making for good snorkelling.

Places to Stay & Eat

There is no formal accommodation available on Aunu'u. If you'd like to stay with a family, you'll need to have a Tutuila connection beforehand – a 'sponsor' if you will – who can ensure that your activities on the island won't be disruptive. There is a bush store in the village where you can buy soft drinks and basic supplies.

Getting There & Away

Getting to Aunu'u is fairly straightforward. Take the bus to the harbour at Au'asi (fare US$1 from Pago Pago). From here, a ferry travels frequently to and from Aunu'u Harbor for US$2 per person. If you can't be bothered waiting for the ferry, you can charter a boat in the bush store at Au'asi for US$10 each way for as many people as will fit. The trip takes about 15 minutes, harbour to harbour, and can get a bit hairy through the strait, especially if the wind is blowing.

Swains Island

Swains Island is not geologically part of the ridge that forms the other Samoan islands. Situated about 350km north-north-west of Tutuila, it consists only of a 3.25 sq km ring of land surrounding a brackish lagoon to which there is no entrance from the sea. Both culturally and geographically it belongs to the Tokelau Islands.

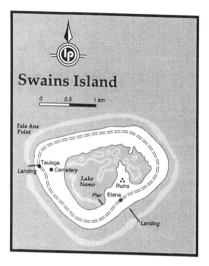

Swains Island was 'discovered' in 1841 by an American, WL Hudson, who learned of its existence from a whaler by the name of Swain. It was soon colonised by some Tokelauans, who had long known it as Olohega, and some French entrepreneurs who saw its potential as a copra plantation (and incidentally impressed the Tokelauans into service there).

The operation was taken over by Eli Jennings, an American and his Samoan wife in 1856 and has been private property of the Jennings family ever since. When Britain formed the colony of the Gilbert and Ellice Islands in 1916, Swains was included in the Union Group (later to be known as Tokelau).

In 1925, however, Tokelau was transferred to the New Zealand administration. Pressure from the Jennings family, who wanted to see their island under US jurisdiction, persuaded the USA to annex the island as part of American Samoa. US control really wasn't much of an issue, though, until 1953, when labour disputes between the Tokelauan workers and the Jennings family brought a US government representative to oversee the political affairs there and maintain 'law and order'.

In 1983 the USA and Tokelau signed the Treaty of Tokehega, which gave sovereignty over the island to the USA in exchange for US recognition of Tokelauan fishing rights. Culturally, however, the island remains Tokelauan. Renewed disputes in the mid-80s caused the Department of Public Works to discuss the building of an airport on the island. This would not only provide easy access to the island but would also ensure continued US sovereignty there. The problem would be that an airport would cover a good percentage of the land and would severely cut into the island's plantation land.

In the early 1990s, the Treaty of Tokohega was again challenged when Tokelau's Director of Agriculture & Fisheries, Foua Toloa, said that the treaty had been unfairly explained to the Tokelauan leadership and that he'd take the issue to the United Nations. He warned that the Tokelauan people were prepared to 'declare war on the US' and launch a canoe invasion of Swains Island. As yet, the USA hasn't budged and nothing has come of the threat.

Getting There & Away

It is not possible to visit Swains Island without permission from the Jennings family. Transport is also infrequent and difficult to arrange. If you're interested in trying, however, contact the Marine and Wildlife Resources Office (☎ 633 7354; fax 633 7355), down by the market in Fagatogo.

The Manu'a Islands

The three small islands of the Manu'a group (Ofu, Olosega and Ta'u) lie only 100km east of Tutuila, but in many ways, they are also 100 years away. As you arrive at Ofu, prepare for a jolt from both the time warp and the sensory overload you're certain to experience. Offering what is unquestionably the most stunning scenery in either Samoa (sparkling white beaches, soaring sea cliffs, crystal lagoons and wild mountain peaks), they are unspoilt by the outside influences that have so altered Tutuila and much of Upolu.

Geologically, the Manu'a Islands are, of course, of volcanic origin. Ofu and Olosega, just a few metres apart, are a complex of volcanic cones that have been buried by lava from two merging shield flows. During a long period of dormancy, deep valleys were carved out, leaving very high, sheer cliffs around the islands. The bight along the south coast of the islands was caused by the collapse of one wall of the caldera. The fringing coral reef here, part of the American Samoa National Park, is one of the best preserved reefs in the Samoas and offers excellent snorkelling.

Remote Ta'u Island is a hulking shield volcano, half of which has fallen away in the south, leaving an island that really looks like half an island. On the dramatic south coast, sea cliffs which are some of the highest in the world, rise 900m to Mt Latu. More than 2000 hectares of Ta'u, which is covered in dense rainforest and dotted with inactive cones and craters, is national park.

History

Many Samoans believe that Manu'a was the first creation – the first land to emerge at the hands of the god Tagaloa. With the islands so favoured by Tagaloa, the Tu'i Manu'a – the paramount chief of these islands – would certainly have been held in high esteem by the Samoans, and indeed, many supernatural powers have been ascribed to holders of the

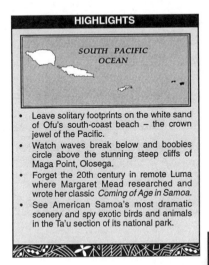

HIGHLIGHTS

SOUTH PACIFIC OCEAN

- Leave solitary footprints on the white sand of Ofu's south-coast beach – the crown jewel of the Pacific.
- Watch waves break below and boobies circle above the stunning steep cliffs of Maga Point, Olosega.
- Forget the 20th century in remote Luma where Margaret Mead researched and wrote her classic *Coming of Age in Samoa*.
- See American Samoa's most dramatic scenery and spy exotic birds and animals in the Ta'u section of its national park.

title down through history. Certain *tu'is* were credited with the ability to fly and to become invisible. All, of course, had exceptional prowess at war. Many believe that, directly and indirectly, the Tu'i Manu'a was revered as the sovereign of all Polynesia. Although wars and fragmentations split the islands, he was still a proud and powerful figure at the time of cession to the USA.

The last Tu'i Manu'a ceded the islands in

AMERICAN SAMOA

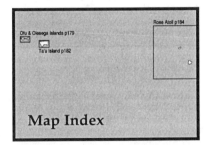

Rose Atoll p184

Ofu & Olosega Islands p179

Ta'u Island p182

Map Index

177

Coral Reef Conservation

- Avoid touching or breaking coral branches, whether or not they appear to be dead.
- Don't go sailboarding or boating in shallow lagoons where coral is present.
- Leave shells, starfish, sea urchins and other creatures where you find them.
- If at all possible, avoid walking on coral beds; swim or stick to the sandy bottoms.
- Don't fish in reef areas; hooks, harpoons, nets, anchors and other fishing apparatus are deadly to coral.
- Don't throw rubbish into the sea either from the shore or from boats. It fouls reefs and beaches.
- Resist buying shells, coral jewellery and other marine products, regardless of their origin. By avoiding this largely illegal trade, you're preserving the reefs in other parts of the world. ■

1904, but in his will he stipulated that his title would die with him. By allowing themselves to come under the jurisdiction of a foreign power, the islanders at the centre of the Polynesian world lost much of the respect they had once been accorded and the revered chief apparently decided that such a title would thereafter be superfluous. He died on 2 April 1909. Many American Samoans, however, whether they live on Tutuila or abroad (even those who have never set foot in the Manu'a Islands), give their official address as Manu'a out of respect for the place that Tagaloa created before all others.

In January 1987, Manu'a was hit by Cyclone Tusi, one of the worst storms in its recorded history. Ofu and Olosega suffered badly and many buildings were destroyed, but Ta'u was the hardest hit. All three villages on the island were reduced to heaps of rubble, coconut trees were decapitated and crops ruined.

Thanks to a shortage of supplies, proper equipment and reliable transport, as well as political disputes, contract squabbles and bureaucracy, reconstruction wasn't completed for at least three years. To compound

matters, in early 1990 and late 1991, Cyclones Ofa and Val also ploughed through the Manu'a Islands. Though there is little obvious evidence of the cyclone damage today, vegetation, coral reefs, and bird and bat populations are still recovering. In 1993, the Ofu and Ta'u sections of the National Park of American Samoa were officially established after the signing of a 50 year lease with traditional owners.

Orientation & Information
If at all possible, don't miss Manu'a, which is worth two days or two weeks, depending upon your interests and available time. If you want to see the sights quickly and move on, a couple of days will be sufficient. The islands aren't full of 'must-see' items; in fact, the only thing that qualifies for must-see status is the beach on Ofu's south coast.

Although the lack of transport will slow you down considerably, that's just what the Manu'a Islands do best. If you're not pressed for time, Manu'a can absorb a lot of it. You can sit for hours relaxing or reading on a 4km-long deserted white beach, go snorkelling over the reefs, gaze at sea birds riding thermals over sheer cliffs, climb rainforested peaks and meet the people in the tiny, still-traditional villages. Manu'a is American Samoa at its best, and it promises to remain that way for a long time to come. Bring your own snorkelling equipment, reading material and any particular foods you may need for your stay. There are no banks or restaurants on the islands. Ofu village has a basic medical clinic.

Getting There & Around
Air Ofu airport is a lovely 500m surfaced strip at Va'oto on the south coast of the island. Fortunately for travellers heading for Ta'u, the old 400m nightmare airstrip – which had a cliff on one end, a mountain at the other and lots of quirky air currents in between – has been decommissioned and replaced by a flash new facility in a more suitable location at Fiti'uta, 7km east.

Samoa Air flies twice a day between Tutuila and the Manu'a Islands. The planes

AMERICAN SAMOA

stop at both Ta'u and Ofu whenever there are passengers to be picked up or dropped off. The schedule (ie which island the plane stops at first) changes all the time, however, so make prior arrangements if you want to fly between Ofu and Ta'u or vice versa on a particular day. Between Pago Pago and either Manu'a airstrip, the fare is US$44 each way or US$86 return. Phone and make a reservation (☎ 699 9106 in Pago Pago; ☎ 655 1103 in Ofu; ☎ 677 3569 in Ta'u) then reconfirm the return flight upon arrival. The trip between Ofu and Ta'u is US$22 each way.

Sea Water transport to the Manu'a Islands is at present limited to private yachts, which very infrequently call in at Faleasao on Ta'u and at Ofu village. Cruising yachts arriving from the east must check into Pago Pago before they'll be permitted to land at Manu'a, and once they've arrived in Pago Pago, they're facing a fierce beat into the wind to get back to Manu'a. Few people bother with it. The harbours of both Ofu and Ta'u are marginal, and can prove disastrous in the event of any carelessness. The cargo boat that services the

Manu'a Islands (12 hours by sea from Pago Pago) doesn't accept passengers.

Hitching Much of your getting around on the Manu'a Islands will involve hoofing it. There are some vehicles on the islands, however, and few drivers will pass a walker without offering a lift.

OFU ISLAND

Ofu is the most dramatic and beautiful of the Manu'a Islands, and it is the place most often seen by outsiders. It is also the easiest to visit, with a superb airstrip on Va'oto Marsh, the only available bit of flat land, and a good, reasonably priced hotel adjoining it.

The Beach

Ofu's crown jewel is the beach along the south coast. It is surely one of the finest in the South Pacific – 4km of shining, palm-fringed white sand, and the only footprints to be seen other than your own are those of birds and crabs. This is the sort of place visitors to Waikiki and Surfers Paradise are actually dreaming of. Once you've seen it, you'll want to settle in for a few days and

AMERICAN SAMOA

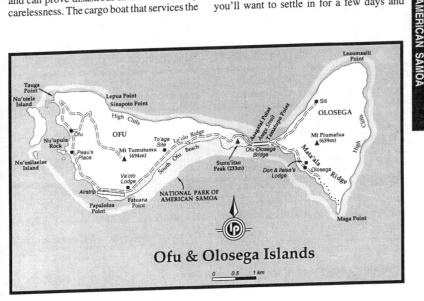

Ofu & Olosega Islands

savour the good fortune of turning up in such a lovely spot.

The strip of beach stretching from Va'oto Lodge to the beginning of the Ofu-Olosega bridge plus 140 hectares of offshore waters comprise the Ofu section of the National Park of American Samoa. With your own snorkelling equipment, parts of the stretch offshore are deep enough for some excellent viewing of coral and tropical fish. Although the reef has suffered cyclone damage, attacks by crown-of-thorns starfish and coral bleaching, it is considered to be one of the few healthy, intact reefs in all of the Samoan islands. Almost 300 species of fish have been identified and the reef is believed to contain about 150 species of coral. Go out at low tide (at high tide waves break over the reef and wash into the lagoon) and watch out for stinging flame coral.

On both Ofu and Ta'u, plants are still collected for medicinal purposes and the narrow strip of land that comprises the Ofu unit of the national park has been found to be an extremely important source of medicinal plants for the villages of Ofu and Olosega.

To'aga Site

About 1km north-east of Va'oto Lodge, behind Ofu Beach, is the To'aga site, where in 1987 archaeologists found an unprecedented array of artefacts, ranging from the earliest times of Samoan prehistory to modern times. Pottery unearthed here has been dated to 1000 BC. The site also has legendary and spiritual significance for Samoans. In fact, the entire area of bush between the road and Ofu Beach is strongly believed to be infested with devilish *aitu*. Wander down here alone in the dark and you're very likely to agree. Archaeologists reckon that virtually all the coastal flatlands and broad upland slopes of the Manu'a Islands are intensively covered in archaeological sites and features. Tito Malae of

Reef but Meaningful Relationships

A number of reef species engage in interesting symbiotic relationships, where two unrelated species get together in some activity for their mutual good.

The best recorded and, to the casual onlooker, most visible of these relationships is probably that

Clown fish with anemone

of the anemone fish and the anemone. The brightly coloured anemone fish is a type of damselfish which has become acclimatised to living amongst the stinging tentacles of anemones. The bright orange clown anemone fish, with its white vertical stripes edged with black, is one of the most instantly recognisable fish on the reef. A typical group of anemone fish will consist of several males and one larger female fish. They spend their entire lives around the anemone, emerging briefly to feed, then diving back into the protective tentacles at the first sign of danger. Anemone fish are not naturally immune to the anemone's sting; it is thought they gradually acquire immunity by repeatedly brushing themselves against the tentacles. Possibly they coat themselves with a layer of the anemone's mucus. The anemone does not sting the fish and its tentacles avoid stinging one another.

The relationship between anemone fish and the anemone is probably somewhat one-sided. While the anemone fish may attract other fish within the anemone's grasp, an anemone can survive without the anemone fish; however, anemone fish are never seen without a protective anemone nearby.

Even coral itself is involved in a symbiotic relationship. Within the cells of coral polyps are tiny, single-cell plants known as *Zoocanthellae*. Like other plants, they utilise sunlight to create energy; they also consume carbon dioxide produced by the coral. Their presence enables coral to grow much faster. ∎

Va'oto Lodge can take interested visitors to some of the major sites on Manu'a.

Ofu Village

Just 2km north of the airstrip is Ofu village, which was completely rebuilt after being devastated by Cyclone Tusi. Along the shore is a calm lagoon for swimming (ask permission), but avoid the pass between Ofu and Nu'utele Island just offshore as the currents are powerful and dangerous. In 1994, a new cyclone-proof wharf was built near Tauga Point. You can swim here, too, but again, don't venture out too far and don't swim alone. It is possible to walk along the shoreline beyond Tauga Point to the wild north coast but the going is over huge volcanic boulders and it's a very rough proposition.

Mt Tumutumu

The road to the summit of Mt Tumutumu (494m) leaves from near the wharf and twists and climbs up to the TV relay tower atop the mountain. (The original tower, which was built to withstand winds in excess of 200km per hour, was destroyed in the cyclone of January 1987). The road can be negotiated in a sturdy 4WD vehicle. Most of the time, however, the trip to the top involves a hot and sweaty 5.5km climb but the vegetation and views make it well worthwhile. If it's hot, allow a full day and don't forget to carry all the food and water you'll need as nothing is available anywhere above the village.

Places to Stay & Eat

The only hotel on Ofu is the friendly *Va'oto Lodge* (☎ 655 1120), conveniently located beside the airstrip and a few steps from the beach. It is run by a friendly couple from Tutuila, Tito and Marjorie Malae. The 10 rooms, all with electric fan, hot shower and toilet, are clean and quiet. You'll find cold beer, books and TV as well in the large dining/common room. If you're not on the strictest of budgets, it's a perfect place to relax for a few days. Single/double rooms cost US$35/40, with discounts for longer stays. Dinner costs US$8 per person, lunch is US$2 and a cooked brekkie costs US$5.

In Ofu village itself, *Peau's Place* (☎ 655 1110) has five rooms with private shower (cold) for US$35/40 plus US$15 for three meals. Transport from the airstrip can be arranged, though it only takes 15 or 20 minutes to walk.

OLOSEGA ISLAND

Olosega, only 3 sq km, is Ofu's twin island, and when viewed from the sea the two appear to be almost mirror images of each other. Olosega lies only 137m or so from Ofu and is joined to it by a cyclone-proof bridge. Strong winds and water currents are funnelled through this pass by steep cliffs on both islands. They are both encircled by the same reef. Olosega has a very nice beach along its south-west coast between the pass and the village. Ask permission if you'd like to swim or snorkel here. There's another small settlement at Sili on the north-western side of the island.

Maga Point

The short walk (about 1km) along the coral rubble beach from just beyond Olosega village to Maga Point on the southern tip of the island is well worthwhile. Nothing vaguely human disturbs the view of steep cliffs, blue ocean, hovering sea birds and scuttling crabs. The weathered cliffs of the point are magnificent and you could sit for hours watching the waves below and the boobies perching high up on the rocky ridges. Go early in the morning or late in the afternoon. Take water, and binoculars if you have them.

Places to Stay & Eat

Don & Ilaisa's Lodge (☎ 655 1212) in Olosega village is slightly less expensive than Va'oto Lodge on Ofu and is recommended for anyone looking for an even more remote setting than the 'airport hotel' can offer. No-one is able to say who Don and Ilaisa are or were, but that was the original name of the place and it has stuck. Pleasant rooms cost US$20 per person, less for a family. Meals are available if ordered in advance and there's a kitchen that guests can

AMERICAN SAMOA

use. Three of the five rooms have private shower (hot) and toilet. Transport from the airstrip can be arranged. Basic, albeit expensive, supplies – soft drinks and tinned foods – are available at the store in Olosega village.

Getting There & Away
Since there is no harbour or airstrip, access to Olosega is on foot or by vehicle from Ofu. To walk from Ofu village to Olosega village will take about two hours.

TA'U ISLAND
Mt Lata, the sacred mountain of Ta'u, is 966m high, the highest point in American Samoa. Although a better case is made for Savai'i in Western Samoa, some people believe that Ta'u is the ancient Hawaiki frequently referred to in Polynesian legend – the place from which the Maoris say they sailed to Aotearoa (New Zealand). Manu'a was the spiritual 'capital' of Polynesia, and Ta'u was the capital of Manu'a, and it was from here that the Tu'i Manu'a reigned. The last Tu'i Manu'a is buried in Luma, the northern section of Ta'u village on the west coast.

Also in Luma, the young Margaret Mead researched and wrote her classic anthropological work *Coming of Age in Samoa* in 1925. Ta'u and the island's other two villages, Fiti'uta and Faleasao, were rebuilt after being flattened by Cyclone Tusi in 1987.

Quite different from all the other Samoan islands, Ta'u feels seriously remote. Which is all the more odd when you keep meeting people who went to school in LA. There is little in the way of limpid lagoons on Ta'u. The coastline is extremely wild and rugged and so untouched in parts that it's not difficult to imagine you've just been dropped off by a whaling boat.

The island sees few visitors and isn't really set up for tourists; if you'd like to spend a couple of days exploring (bearing in mind that much of the island is inaccessible) bring food supplies with you. It's fairly easy to hitch a ride between the eastern and western ends of the island. Although traffic is sparse, if someone is going your way, they're sure to offer a lift.

Fiti'uta Village
At the north-eastern corner of Ta'u is the tiny, sleepy village of Fiti'uta. The airstrip is here,

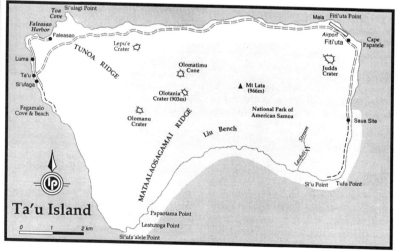

along with the only official place to stay, a small video shop and a store selling basic supplies.

National Park of American Samoa
The Ta'u unit of the national park occupies 2160 hectares of land, comprising most of the uninhabited southern half of Ta'u, and 400 hectares of offshore waters. As would be expected, the protected area takes in some of American Samoa's most dramatic scenery. Ta'u is a shield volcano that has undergone dramatic changes. The apocalyptic collapse of half its caldera left a spectacular escarpment along the southern side and cliffs as high as 900m along the coast. On the northern slope, numerous craters and cones remained active after the big event and continued to build that side of the island.

Ta'u's protected lowland and montane rainforest provide excellent habitat for flying foxes and many native birds. Species include black noddies, white terns, white-tailed tropicbirds, Tahiti petrels, Audubon's shearwater, the Fiji shrikebill, the friendly ground dove, the multi-coloured fruit dove, the spotless crake and the most important bird in Samoan culture, the Pacific pigeon, or *lupe*. Other native wildlife includes the Pacific boa, which lives only on Ta'u and in very small numbers; 13 species of amphibians and reptiles, most of which are geckos and skinks; and 20 species of land snail. It is believed that endangered sea turtles nest along the remote shorelines of Ta'u. The NPS plans to build an elevated canopy walkway in the rainforest of Ta'u similar to the one which has been built in the Falealupo Rainforest Preserve on Savai'i. Check with the National Park Visitor Information Center in Pago Pago for the latest news.

Saua Site Halfway down the east coast of the island (about 2.5km from Fiti'uta) is the important Samoan legendary site of Saua. This is where the god Tagaloa is said to have created the first humans and sent them out to Polynesia. Here also he crowned the first Tu'i Manu'a. Only volcanic boulders, wild surf and a windswept beach mark this very

sacred place. Archaeologists have located the remains of an ancient village near Saua as well as numerous grave sites between Saua and Si'u Point. More intensive surveys are yet to be carried out. During calm seas (usually from October to March) the offshore waters near Saua are used by Fiti'uta residents for fishing and reef foraging. Coral reefs are only found along the eastern shoreline of Ta'u.

Laufuti Stream A rough plantation track follows the east coast as far as Tufu Point, and from here it's possible to hike 2km along the shoreline (slow going over volcanic boulders) to Laufuti Stream where there's a waterfall and a nearby spring. The NPS plans to build a trail for easy access to Laufuti. The southern coastline of Ta'u is so wild and pristine that it's worth a look even if you don't want to walk all the way to the stream. You may be able to find local transport from Fiti'uta to Tufu Point. It's recommended that anyone going beyond Si'u Point take a guide. If you intend to do any hiking in the Manu'a Islands, contact the National Park Visitor Information Center in Pago Pago before heading out.

Mt Lata & Judds Crater The NPS plans to build a new trail into the cloud forest on Mt Lata as well as trails to Judds Crater and other significant geological features. Basic campsites will also be established. Both walks are possible with a local guide, but must be organised through the National Park Visitor Information Center in Pago Pago. Judds Crater, above Fiti'uta, is a three hour climb; Mt Lata (966m) is an overnight expedition requiring sleeping bag, tent and warm clothing.

Ta'u Village
The main settlement on Ta'u consists of the twin villages of Luma and Si'ufaga at the north-western corner of the island. In Luma are the tombs of the last Tu'i Manu'a and several other early politicians.

There are basic stores scattered around the villages. Around the point at Faleasao is

AMERICAN SAMOA

the new harbour where once a month (or once every two months in the winter) a barge from Pago Pago brings basic supplies for the islanders. The waters off the north-west coast are treacherous. Three ancient star mounds have recently been discovered high on the ridges above Faleasao.

Fagamalo Cove

From Ta'u village, the walk south to the sandy beach at secluded Fagamalo Cove is a pleasant way to pass a couple of hours. The track along the west coast can be muddy at times but it offers some nice views of the cliffs above and pounding surf below. Mosquitoes, even at midday, are voracious, so don't forget some sort of repellent or you'll be miserable. The best time to go is in the cool of the morning, before the brilliant afternoon sun turns the white sand into a furnace of reflected heat.

Places to Stay & Eat

The main place to stay is the *Fiti'uta Lodge* (☎ 677 3155/3501), a slightly run-down, western-style house near the airport in the village of Fiti'uta. Basic rooms with shared bathroom (hot water) cost US$25 per person. Meals are not available, but there is a kitchen in the house. Next door is a shop that sells basic supplies. There is another hotel in Ta'u village, but it is mainly used to house workers temporarily staying on the island. There are no restaurants on the island. Bring any food or supplies you'll be needing from Tutuila.

ROSE ATOLL

Rose Atoll, 100km east of the Manu'a Islands, is composed of two tiny specks of land and the surrounding reef. Rose Islet, only 3m above sea level at its highest point,

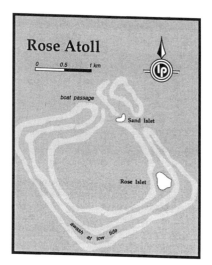

has an area of five hectares. Sand Islet, soaring to an evalation of 5m, is only 2.5 hectares in area. The atoll is probably a shield volcano (like Manu'a), but one that has been completely eroded away since the Pleistocene era. Coral reefs have built up on the remnants making the island visible today. Rose Atoll is designated a US national wildlife refuge and permission to visit, which is very difficult to obtain, must be secured from the controlling agency in Hawaii. The refuge exists primarily to protect the green turtle, which lays its eggs in the sand here, as well as the extremely rare and endangered hawksbill turtle. Numerous species of sea birds nest on the atoll, including the sooty tern (whose numbers on Rose Atoll represents 85% of the total sea bird population of American Samoa), and a variety of other terns, tropicbirds, noddies and boobies.

Glossary

aiga – family, descent group

aitu – spirit, ghost

ali'i – one of two orders of high chief (*matai*)

aualuma – society of unmarried women, one of four untitled groups within a traditional village. The other three are aumaga, faletua mu tausi and tamaiti

aumaga – society of untitled men in a village

ava – passage through reef

'ava – traditional, mildly intoxicating drink (also called kava) produced from the root of the *piper methysticum* or pepper plant

esi – papaya, pawpaw

fa'afafine – effeminate man

fa'afetai – thank you

fa'alavelave – occasion, such as a wedding or funeral, when family assistance should be given

fa'a Samoa – according to Samoan customs and tradition

fagogo – story, usually told in the night, with a moral to it; oral history

fale – Samoan house with thatched roof and open sides

fale talimalo – traditional Samoan guesthouse or hotel

faletua/tausi – wives who came from outside the village

fai – banana

fautasi – Samoan longboat, made from the *fau* tree

fiafia – time of celebration, dance performance

foaga – grinding stone

fono – governing council of a village made up of its *matai*; the national parliament

ie faitaga – man's undecorated formal lavalava

ie toga – finely woven mat made from pandanus fibres

ifilele – large tree used for timber and kava bowls

kava – see *'ava*

kirikiti – Samoan cricket

laumei – sea turtle

lavalava – wraparound sarong

lotu – religious observance

malae – village green, sacred site in pre-Christian times

mana – supernatural power

matai – political representative of an *aiga*

mo'o – gecko

oka – Samoan dish of marinated raw fish

palagi – white man, literally, 'those who came from the sky'

paopao – traditional outrigger canoe

pili – skink

pisupo – corned beef

pola – coconut leaf blinds

popo – mature coconut

puaa – pig

pulenu'u – village mayor

puletasi – long skirt and tunic worn by Samoan women

sa – sacred, forbidden

siapo – bark cloth made from the paper mulberry tree

ta'amu – large edible tuber, 'big taro'

tamaiti – children

taulaitu – spirit medium

taulasea – traditional healer

taupou – title of office bestowed by high-ranking *ali'i* upon a young (virgin) woman of his *aiga*

to'ona'i – Sunday lunch

tulafale – an orator chief, one of two orders of *matai*

u'a – inside bark of the mulberry tree, used for making *siapo*

umu – stone oven in the ground

vai Samoa – traditional medicines

Index

MAPS

TEXT

Map references are in **bold** type.

LONELY PLANET

ON THE ROAD

Travel Guides explore cities, regions and countries, and supply information on transport, restaurants and accommodation, covering all budgets. They come with reliable, easy-to-use maps, practical advice, cultural and historical facts and a rundown on attractions both on and off the beaten track. There are over 200 titles in this classic series, covering nearly every country in the world.

Lonely Planet Upgrades extend the shelf life of existing travel guides by detailing any changes that may affect travel in a region since a book has been published. Upgrades can be downloaded for free from **www.lonelyplanet.com/upgrades**

For travellers with more time than money, **Shoestring** guides offer dependable, first-hand information with hundreds of detailed maps, plus insider tips for stretching money as far as possible. Covering entire continents in most cases, the six-volume shoestring guides are known around the world as 'backpackers bibles'.

For the discerning short-term visitor, **Condensed** guides highlight the best a destination has to offer in a full-colour, pocket-sized format designed for quick access. They include everything from top sights and walking tours to opinionated reviews of where to eat, stay, shop and have fun.

CitySync lets travellers use their Palm™ or Visor™ hand-held computers to guide them through a city with handy tips on transport, history, cultural life, major sights, and shopping and entertainment options. It can also quickly search and sort hundreds of reviews of hotels, restaurants and attractions, and pinpoint their location on scrollable street maps. CitySync can be downloaded from **www.citysync.com**

MAPS & ATLASES

Lonely Planet's **City Maps** feature downtown and metropolitan maps, as well as transit routes and walking tours. The maps come complete with an index of streets, a listing of sights and a plastic coat for extra durability.

Road Atlases are an essential navigation tool for serious travellers. Cross-referenced with the guidebooks, they also feature distance and climate charts and a complete site index.

LONELY PLANET

ESSENTIALS

Read This First books help new travellers to hit the road with confidence. These invaluable predeparture guides give step-by-step advice on preparing for a trip, budgeting, arranging a visa, planning an itinerary and staying safe while still getting off the beaten track.

Healthy Travel pocket guides offer a regional rundown on disease hot spots and practical advice on predeparture health measures, staying well on the road and what to do in emergencies. The guides come with a user-friendly design and helpful diagrams and tables.

Lonely Planet's **Phrasebooks** cover the essential words and phrases travellers need when they're strangers in a strange land. They come in a pocket-sized format with colour tabs for quick reference, extensive vocabulary lists, easy-to-follow pronunciation keys and two-way dictionaries.

Miffed by blurry photos of the Taj Mahal? Tired of the classic 'top of the head cut off' shot? **Travel Photography: A Guide to Taking Better Pictures** will help you turn ordinary holiday snaps into striking images and give you the know-how to capture every scene, from frenetic festivals to peaceful beach sunrises.

Lonely Planet's **Travel Journal** is a lightweight but sturdy travel diary for jotting down all those on-the-road observations and significant travel moments. It comes with a handy time-zone wheel, a world map and useful travel information.

Lonely Planet's eKno is an all-in-one communication service developed especially for travellers. It offers low-cost international calls and free email and voicemail so that you can keep in touch while on the road. Check it out on **www.ekno.lonelyplanet.com**

FOOD & RESTAURANT GUIDES

Lonely Planet's **Out to Eat** guides recommend the brightest and best places to eat and drink in top international cities. These gourmet companions are arranged by neighbourhood, packed with dependable maps, garnished with scene-setting photos and served with quirky features.

For people who live to eat, drink and travel, **World Food** guides explore the culinary culture of each country. Entertaining and adventurous, each guide is packed with detail on staples and specialities, regional cuisine and local markets, as well as sumptuous recipes, comprehensive culinary dictionaries and lavish photos good enough to eat.

OUTDOOR GUIDES

For those who believe the best way to see the world is on foot, Lonely Planet's **Walking Guides** detail everything from family strolls to difficult treks, with 'when to go and how to do it' advice supplemented by reliable maps and essential travel information.

Cycling Guides map a destination's best bike tours, long and short, in day-by-day detail. They contain all the information a cyclist needs, including advice on bike maintenance, places to eat and stay, innovative maps with detailed cues to the rides, and elevation charts.

The **Watching Wildlife** series is perfect for travellers who want authoritative information but don't want to tote a heavy field guide. Packed with advice on where, when and how to view a region's wildlife, each title features photos of over 300 species and contains engaging comments on the local flora and fauna.

With underwater colour photos throughout, **Pisces Books** explore the world's best diving and snorkelling areas. Each book contains listings of diving services and dive resorts, detailed information on depth, visibility and difficulty of dives, and a roundup of the marine life you're likely to see through your mask.

OFF THE ROAD

Journeys, the travel literature series written by renowned travel authors, capture the spirit of a place or illuminate a culture with a journalist's attention to detail and a novelist's flair for words. These are tales to soak up while you're actually on the road or dip into as an at-home armchair indulgence.

The range of lavishly illustrated **Pictorial** books is just the ticket for both travellers and dreamers. Off-beat tales and vivid photographs bring the adventure of travel to your doorstep long before the journey begins and long after it is over.

Lonely Planet **Videos** encourage the same independent, tough-minded approach as the guidebooks. Currently airing throughout the world, this award-winning series features innovative footage and an original soundtrack.

Yes, we know, work is tough, so do a little bit of deskside dreaming with the spiral-bound Lonely Planet **Diary** or a Lonely Planet **Wall Calendar**, filled with great photos from around the world.

TRAVELLERS NETWORK

Lonely Planet Online. Lonely Planet's award-winning Web site has insider information on hundreds of destinations, from Amsterdam to Zimbabwe, complete with interactive maps and relevant links. The site also offers the latest travel news, recent reports from travellers on the road, guidebook upgrades, a travel links site, an online book-buying option and a lively travellers bulletin board. It can be viewed at **www.lonelyplanet.com** or AOL keyword: lp.

Planet Talk is a quarterly print newsletter, full of gossip, advice, anecdotes and author articles. It provides an antidote to the being-at-home blues and lets you plan and dream for the next trip. Contact the nearest Lonely Planet office for your free copy.

Comet, the free Lonely Planet newsletter, comes via email once a month. It's loaded with travel news, advice, dispatches from authors, travel competitions and letters from readers. To subscribe, click on the Comet subscription link on the front page of the Web site.

Lonely Planet Guides by Region

Lonely Planet is known worldwide for publishing practical, reliable and no-nonsense travel information in our guides and on our Web site. The Lonely Planet list covers just about every accessible part of the world. Currently there are 16 series: Travel guides, Shoestring guides, Condensed guides, Phrasebooks, Read This First, Healthy Travel, Walking guides, Cycling guides, Watching Wildlife guides, Pisces Diving & Snorkeling guides, City Maps, Road Atlases, Out to Eat, World Food, Journeys travel literature and Pictorials.

AFRICA Africa on a shoestring • Botswana • Cairo • Cairo City Map • Cape Town • Cape Town City Map • East Africa • Egypt • Egyptian Arabic phrasebook • Ethiopia, Eritrea & Djibouti • Ethiopian Amharic phrasebook • The Gambia & Senegal • Healthy Travel Africa • Kenya • Malawi • Morocco • Moroccan Arabic phrasebook • Mozambique • Namibia • Read This First: Africa • South Africa, Lesotho & Swaziland • Southern Africa • Southern Africa Road Atlas • Swahili phrasebook • Tanzania, Zanzibar & Pemba • Trekking in East Africa • Tunisia • Watching Wildlife East Africa • Watching Wildlife Southern Africa • West Africa • World Food Morocco • Zambia • Zimbabwe, Botswana & Namibia
Travel Literature: Mali Blues: Traveling to an African Beat • The Rainbird: A Central African Journey • Songs to an African Sunset: A Zimbabwean Story

AUSTRALIA & THE PACIFIC Aboriginal Australia & the Torres Strait Islands •Auckland • Australia • Australian phrasebook • Australia Road Atlas • Cycling Australia • Cycling New Zealand • Fiji • Fijian phrasebook • Healthy Travel Australia, NZ & the Pacific • Islands of Australia's Great Barrier Reef • Melbourne • Melbourne City Map • Micronesia • New Caledonia • New South Wales • New Zealand • Northern Territory • Outback Australia • Out to Eat – Melbourne • Out to Eat – Sydney • Papua New Guinea • Pidgin phrasebook • Queensland • Rarotonga & the Cook Islands • Samoa • Solomon Islands • South Australia • South Pacific • South Pacific phrasebook • Sydney • Sydney City Map • Sydney Condensed • Tahiti & French Polynesia • Tasmania • Tonga • Tramping in New Zealand • Vanuatu • Victoria • Walking in Australia • Watching Wildlife Australia • Western Australia
Travel Literature: Islands in the Clouds: Travels in the Highlands of New Guinea • Kiwi Tracks: A New Zealand Journey • Sean & David's Long Drive

CENTRAL AMERICA & THE CARIBBEAN Bahamas, Turks & Caicos • Baja California • Belize, Guatemala & Yucatán • Bermuda • Central America on a shoestring • Costa Rica • Costa Rica Spanish phrasebook • Cuba • Cycling Cuba • Dominican Republic & Haiti • Eastern Caribbean • Guatemala • Havana • Healthy Travel Central & South America • Jamaica • Mexico • Mexico City • Panama • Puerto Rico • Read This First: Central & South America • Virgin Islands • World Food Caribbean • World Food Mexico • Yucatán
Travel Literature: Green Dreams: Travels in Central America

EUROPE Amsterdam • Amsterdam City Map • Amsterdam Condensed • Andalucía • Athens • Austria • Baltic States phrasebook • Barcelona • Barcelona City Map • Belgium & Luxembourg • Berlin • Berlin City Map • Britain • British phrasebook • Brussels, Bruges & Antwerp • Brussels City Map • Budapest • Budapest City Map • Canary Islands • Catalunya & the Costa Brava • Central Europe • Central Europe phrasebook • Copenhagen • Corfu & the Ionians • Corsica • Crete • Crete Condensed • Croatia • Cycling Britain • Cycling France • Cyprus • Czech & Slovak Republics • Czech phrasebook • Denmark • Dublin • Dublin City Map • Dublin Condensed • Eastern Europe • Eastern Europe phrasebook • Edinburgh • Edinburgh City Map • England • Estonia, Latvia & Lithuania • Europe on a shoestring • Europe phrasebook • Finland • Florence • Florence City Map • France • Frankfurt City Map • Frankfurt Condensed • French phrasebook • Georgia, Armenia & Azerbaijan • Germany • German phrasebook • Greece • Greek Islands • Greek phrasebook • Hungary • Iceland, Greenland & the Faroe Islands • Ireland • Italian phrasebook • Italy • Kraków • Lisbon • The Loire • London • London City Map • London Condensed • Madrid • Madrid City Map • Malta • Mediterranean Europe • Milan, Turin & Genoa • Moscow • Munich • Netherlands • Normandy • Norway • Out to Eat – London • Out to Eat – Paris • Paris • Paris City Map • Paris Condensed • Poland • Polish phrasebook • Portugal • Portuguese phrasebook • Prague • Prague City Map • Provence & the Côte d'Azur • Read This First: Europe • Rhodes & the Dodecanese • Romania & Moldova • Rome • Rome City Map • Rome Condensed • Russia, Ukraine & Belarus • Russian phrasebook • Scandinavian & Baltic Europe • Scandinavian phrasebook • Scotland • Sicily • Slovenia • South-West France • Spain • Spanish phrasebook • Stockholm • St Petersburg • St Petersburg City Map • Sweden • Switzerland • Tuscany • Ukrainian phrasebook • Venice • Vienna • Wales • Walking in Britain • Walking in France • Walking in Ireland • Walking in Italy • Walking in Scotland • Walking in Spain • Walking in Switzerland • Western Europe • World Food France • World Food Greece • World Food Ireland • World Food Italy • World Food Spain **Travel Literature:** After Yugoslavia • Love and War in the Apennines • The Olive Grove: Travels in Greece • On the Shores of the Mediterranean • Round Ireland in Low Gear • A Small Place in Italy

The Lonely Planet Story

Lonely Planet published its first book in 1973 in response to the numerous 'How did you do it?' questions Maureen and Tony Wheeler were asked after driving, bussing, hitching, sailing and railing their way from England to Australia.

Written at a kitchen table and hand collated, trimmed and stapled, *Across Asia on the Cheap* became an instant local bestseller, inspiring thoughts of another book.

Eighteen months in South-East Asia resulted in their second guide, *South-East Asia on a shoestring*, which they put together in a backstreet Chinese hotel in Singapore in 1975. The 'yellow bible', as it quickly became known to backpackers around the world, soon became *the* guide to the region. It has sold well over half a million copies and is now in its 9th edition, still retaining its familiar yellow cover.

Today there are over 350 titles, including travel guides, walking guides, language kits & phrasebooks, travel atlases, diving guides and travel literature. The company is the largest independent travel publisher in the world. Although Lonely Planet initially specialised in guides to Asia, today there are few corners of the globe that have not been covered.

The emphasis continues to be on travel for independent travellers. Tony and Maureen still travel for several months of each year and play an active part in the writing, updating and quality control of Lonely Planet's guides.

They have been joined by over 120 authors and 280 staff at our offices in Melbourne (Australia), Oakland (USA), London (UK) and Paris (France). Travellers themselves also make a valuable contribution to the guides through the feedback we receive in thousands of letters each year and on our web site.

The people at Lonely Planet strongly believe that travellers can make a positive contribution to the countries they visit, both through their appreciation of the countries' culture, wildlife and natural features, and through the money they spend. In addition, the company makes a direct contribution to the countries and regions it covers. Since 1986 a percentage of the income from each book has been donated to ventures such as famine relief in Africa; aid projects in India; agricultural projects in Central America; Greenpeace's efforts to halt French nuclear testing in the Pacific; and Amnesty International.

LONELY PLANET OFFICES

Australia
Locked Bag 1, Footscray, Victoria 3011
☎ 03 8379 8000 fax 03 8379 8111
email: talk2us@lonelyplanet.com.au

UK
10a Spring Place, London NW5 3BH
☎ 020 7428 4800 fax 020 7428 4828
email: go@lonelyplanet.co.uk

USA
150 Linden St, Oakland, CA 94607
☎ 510 893 8555 TOLL FREE: 800 275 8555
fax 510 893 8572
email: info@lonelyplanet.com

France
1 rue du Dahomey, 75011 Paris
☎ 01 55 25 33 00 fax 01 55 25 33 01
email: bip@lonelyplanet.fr
www.lonelyplanet.fr

World Wide Web: www.lonelyplanet.com *or* AOL keyword: lp
Lonely Planet Images: lpi@lonelyplanet.com.au

Lonely Planet Mail Order

Lonely Planet products are distributed worldwide. They are also available by mail order from Lonely Planet, so if you have difficulty finding a title please write to us. North and South American residents should write to 150 Linden St, Oakland, CA 94607, USA; European and African residents should write to 10a Spring Place, London NW5 3BH, UK; and residents of other countries to Locked Bag 1, Footscray, Victoria 3011, Australia.

INDIAN SUBCONTINENT & THE INDIAN OCEAN Bangladesh • Bengali phrasebook • Bhutan • Delhi • Goa • Healthy Travel Asia & India • Hindi & Urdu phrasebook • India • India & Bangladesh City Map • Indian Himalaya • Karakoram Highway • Kathmandu City Map • Kerala • Madagascar • Maldives • Mauritius, Réunion & Seychelles • Mumbai (Bombay) • Nepal • Nepali phrasebook • North India • Pakistan • Rajasthan • Read This First: Asia & India • South India • Sri Lanka • Sri Lanka phrasebook • Tibet • Tibetan phrasebook • Trekking in the Indian Himalaya • Trekking in the Karakoram & Hindukush • Trekking in the Nepal Himalaya • World Food India **Travel Literature:** The Age of Kali: Indian Travels and Encounters • Hello Goodnight: A Life of Goa • In Rajasthan • Maverick in Madagascar • A Season in Heaven: True Tales from the Road to Kathmandu • Shopping for Buddhas • A Short Walk in the Hindu Kush • Slowly Down the Ganges

MIDDLE EAST & CENTRAL ASIA Bahrain, Kuwait & Qatar • Central Asia • Central Asia phrasebook • Dubai • Farsi (Persian) phrasebook • Hebrew phrasebook • Iran • Israel & the Palestinian Territories • Istanbul • Istanbul City Map • Istanbul to Cairo • Istanbul to Kathmandu • Jerusalem • Jerusalem City Map • Jordan • Lebanon • Middle East • Oman & the United Arab Emirates • Syria • Turkey • Turkish phrasebook • World Food Turkey • Yemen **Travel Literature:** Black on Black: Iran Revisited • Breaking Ranks: Turbulent Travels in the Promised Land • The Gates of Damascus • Kingdom of the Film Stars: Journey into Jordan

NORTH AMERICA Alaska • Boston • Boston City Map • Boston Condensed • British Columbia • California & Nevada • California Condensed • Canada • Chicago • Chicago City Map • Chicago Condensed • Florida • Georgia & the Carolinas • Great Lakes • Hawaii • Hiking in Alaska • Hiking in the USA • Honolulu & Oahu City Map • Las Vegas • Los Angeles • Los Angeles City Map • Louisiana & the Deep South • Miami • Miami City Map • Montreal • New England • New Orleans • New Orleans City Map • New York City • New York City City Map • New York City Condensed • New York, New Jersey & Pennsylvania • Oahu • Out to Eat – San Francisco • Pacific Northwest • Rocky Mountains • San Diego & Tijuana • San Francisco • San Francisco City Map • Seattle • Seattle City Map • Southwest • Texas • Toronto • USA • USA phrasebook • Vancouver • Vancouver City Map • Virginia & the Capital Region • Washington, DC • Washington, DC City Map • World Food New Orleans **Travel Literature:** Caught Inside: A Surfer's Year on the California Coast • Drive Thru America

NORTH-EAST ASIA Beijing • Beijing City Map • Cantonese phrasebook • China • Hiking in Japan • Hong Kong & Macau • Hong Kong City Map • Hong Kong Condensed • Japan • Japanese phrasebook • Korea • Korean phrasebook • Kyoto • Mandarin phrasebook • Mongolia • Mongolian phrasebook • Seoul • Shanghai • South-West China • Taiwan • Tokyo • Tokyo Condensed • World Food Hong Kong • World Food Japan **Travel Literature:** In Xanadu: A Quest • Lost Japan

SOUTH AMERICA Argentina, Uruguay & Paraguay • Bolivia • Brazil • Brazilian phrasebook • Buenos Aires • Buenos Aires City Map • Chile & Easter Island • Colombia • Ecuador & the Galapagos Islands • Healthy Travel Central & South America • Latin American Spanish phrasebook • Peru • Quechua phrasebook • Read This First: Central & South America • Rio de Janeiro • Rio de Janeiro City Map • Santiago de Chile • South America on a shoestring • Trekking in the Patagonian Andes • Venezuela **Travel Literature:** Full Circle: A South American Journey

SOUTH-EAST ASIA Bali & Lombok • Bangkok • Bangkok City Map • Burmese phrasebook • Cambodia • Cycling Vietnam, Laos & Cambodia • East Timor phrasebook • Hanoi • Healthy Travel Asia & India • Hill Tribes phrasebook • Ho Chi Minh City (Saigon) • Indonesia • Indonesian phrasebook • Indonesia's Eastern Islands • Java • Lao phrasebook • Laos • Malay phrasebook • Malaysia, Singapore & Brunei • Myanmar (Burma) • Philippines • Pilipino (Tagalog) phrasebook • Read This First: Asia & India • Singapore • Singapore City Map • South-East Asia on a shoestring • South-East Asia phrasebook • Thailand • Thailand's Islands & Beaches • Thailand, Vietnam, Laos & Cambodia Road Atlas • Thai phrasebook • Vietnam • Vietnamese phrasebook • World Food Indonesia • World Food Thailand • World Food Vietnam

ALSO AVAILABLE: Antarctica • The Arctic • The Blue Man: Tales of Travel, Love and Coffee • Brief Encounters: Stories of Love, Sex & Travel • Buddhist Stupas in Asia: The Shape of Perfection • Chasing Rickshaws • The Last Grain Race • Lonely Planet ... On the Edge: Adventurous Escapades from Around the World • Lonely Planet Unpacked • Lonely Planet Unpacked Again • Not the Only Planet: Science Fiction Travel Stories • Ports of Call: A Journey by Sea • Sacred India • Travel Photography: A Guide to Taking Better Pictures • Travel with Children • Tuvalu: Portrait of an Island Nation